A War to the Knife

A WAR

to the

KNIFE

England vs West Indies in the 1930s.

Richard Bentley

Matador
9 Priory Business Park,
Wistow Road, Kibworth Beauchamp,
Leicestershire. LE8 0RX
Tel: 0116 279 2299
Email: books@troubador.co.uk
Web: www.troubador.co.uk/matador
Twitter: @matadorbooks

ISBN 978 1789017 496

British Library Cataloguing in Publication Data.
A catalogue record for this book is available from the British Library.

Printed and bound by CPI Group (UK) Ltd, Croydon, CR0 4YY
Typeset in 11pt Adobe Garamond Pro by Troubador Publishing Ltd, Leicester, UK

Matador is an imprint of Troubador Publishing Ltd

To Dad
my first reader
with love.

Contents

Chapter 1

LORD'S OF LONDON

There has been a Lord's cricket ground in St John's Wood, London, for 203 years. Tucked away behind high walls, we are inured to what an odd place it is. The playing area, a circle of the greenest grass in a grey city, is as incongruous as an Aztec temple in the rainforest. Its empty acres surrounded by some of the most expensive real estate in the world are an affront to the priorities of a commercial capital.

The history of Lord's, its manicured grass and pristine white stands, summons up a folk memory of a cricketing golden age when the sport was supreme and the social waters it sailed in undisturbed. But a cricket ground is a place where two teams come together to play a game and that coming together has always involved the releasing and leashing of social forces. And cricket, like all spectator sports, was never insulated from the requirements of cold, hard cash. As cricket developed as an international sport, nationalism was dragged into the vacant spaces of the cricket field.

This book is about two test match series: the West Indian tour to England and Wales in 1933 and England's visit to the West Indies in 1935. It is a story filled with great players, glorious achievements and grave defeats. But I have also tried to look at the two series against the background of the 1930s. Because cricket writers of the time did not believe they were living through a golden age, for them the golden era of cricket had ended on 4th August 1914. They lived in a world of economic dislocation, political extremism and fretted that cricket, as they knew it, might not survive. There were cricketing controversies in the 1930s so severe as to threaten the end of test matches between England and Australia and these issues were re-run in the two series against the West Indies.

And it wasn't only cricketing disputes that had to be mediated. The West Indian team was a racially mixed side from the British Empire's scattered Caribbean colonies playing a game, cricket, regarded as epitomising English virtues. The series of 1933 and 1935 were about countries and societies, empires and nationalism, as well as cricket and I have tried to show that in the chapters which follow.

Chapter 2

TWO CRICKET MATCHES AND AN ASSASSINATION ATTEMPT

The crowd unfurls in the May sunshine, taking their first look at the West Indian cricket tourists of 1933. They have seen George Headley, score a hundred in his first innings at Lord's and the MCC bowlers take advantage of a hard and fast pitch to restrict the West Indians to 309 all out. Now it is the West Indies' turn to bowl. In the cooling of the day, the drowsy hum of chatter subsides and the spectators shift to the edges of their seats. The West Indies have two proper fast bowlers in Learie Constantine and Emmanuel (Manny) Martindale, preparing to bowl in the fading light.

The first over is a succession of near misses. The batsmen prod uncertainly in the direction of the ball as it thuds into the wicketkeeper's gloves. But they hang on, stay in, things get a little easier and the ball begins to hit the bat. The bowlers respond. The length of delivery shortens, the ball rears, threatening fingers and weeks off without match fees. The MCC and Middlesex opener Joe Hulme is struck in the ribs. He reels from the wicket "rubbing furiously". West Indian captain George (Jack) Grant jogs in from cover point to ask if Hulme is all right. Not all observers are so sympathetic; the "best cricket correspondent in England" considers: "The English batsmen childishly helpless against fast bowling."[1] Of course, the best cricket correspondent in England is writing from the safety of the stands.

MCC opening batsman, Joe Hulme, also looks like he wants to be somewhere else. He is a professional footballer as well as cricketer, a member of Arsenal's 1932-1933 title winning side. If it wasn't for the cricket, he might have played in the May international against Italy in Rome's Stadio del Partito Nazionale Fascita. But for Hulme cricket comes first, it pays better than football and its maximum wage.

The other opener, John Hearne, is caught by West Indian wicketkeeper Ivan Barrow off the bowling of Constantine for 12.

The MCC side has plenty of good batsmen, including England captains Douglas Jardine and Percy Chapman. But with ten minutes left and in fading light it is William Franklin who comes out to bat as night watchman. Franklin

---

1   From *Chances of the West Indies in the First Test* by CLR James, published in the Port of Spain Gazette and republished in: *A Majestic Innings: writings on cricket* by CLR James. I think the best cricket correspondent in England is James' then boss, Neville Cardus.

is the weakest player in the MCC team, has never played county cricket, but is still sent in to face two quick, international standard bowlers ahead of players better able to defend themselves. Hulme defends a ball onto the leg side and sets off for a single and the safety of the non-strikers' end. Franklin sums up his situation, he raises his hand like a policeman and in a voice that rolls across the ground shouts, "Go back, I know where I'm well off."[2]

Franklin can't stay off strike forever and not surprisingly is clean bowled by Martindale for five in the last over of the day. Hulme, who has got through twenty awkward and painful minutes, scuttles back to the dressing room. The spectators go home well entertained, in a day with over 300 runs scored and twelve wickets lost.

With a gate of almost 20,000, the MCC treasurer would also have been satisfied. The attendance was, in large part, due to Learie Constantine playing for the West Indians. On the 15th May *The Times* included a short article on the hours of play and admission fees for MCC vs West Indies at Lord's. One column across and at exactly the same height was a notification that Learie Constantine would be playing in the game. This wasn't a coincidence. There were many famous cricketers in the 1930s: Bradman, Larwood, Hammond and O'Reilly. But the game could be static, rates of scoring

---

2   From David Frith, *Bodyline Autopsy,* page 361, attributed to Wally Hammond Cricketers' school.

slow, the fielding ponderous. Whether batting, bowling or fielding, Learie Constantine was a cricketer in motion. *The Morning Post* believed he was blessed with "A vivid sense of the improvisatory and far from formal energy which is the essence of Jazz."

The reference to jazz, the art form of black America, is telling and Constantine's ethnicity is stressed later in the piece, "He reaches the extreme limit of human energy – like the coloured sprinters who have put up world records."

One emerging black sprinter, Jesse Owens, was only nineteen years old in May 1933 but, running in the USA interscholastic championships, had matched the world record for the 100 yards. Owens was just one example of a black American who was internationally famous. Eddie Tolan and Ralph Metcalfe had been successful in the 1932 Olympics, popular music was dominated by black performers: Billie Holiday, Louis Armstrong and Count Basie. As far as the *Morning Chronicle* columnist was concerned, Constantine and the eight other non-white players in 1933 were part of a movement of black excellence in music and sport now revitalising cricket.

But although the crowds for the MCC game and enthusiasm in the press were encouraging, West Indies cricket remained an experiment. The West Indies were admitted to the Imperial Cricket Conference ("ICC") in 1926, along with India and New Zealand, joining the three original members: England, Australia and South Africa. Although all six ICC members had test match status, cricket between the six teams was not established by 1933 and there were concerns over whether the new cricketing "nations" were of a sufficiently high standard to provide engaging contests. After the West Indies' first test series in 1928, *Wisden* commented:

"So far from improving upon the form of their predecessors, the team of 1928 fell so much below it that everybody was compelled to realise that the playing of Test matches between England and West Indies was a mistake."

Subsequently, the West Indies had lost a series in Australia 4:1, which was bedevilled by flat pitches, small crowds and financial losses. The West Indies had to play well enough in 1933 to convince other test-playing countries they were worthy opponents and that West Indies tours would be financially viable.

The charismatic Constantine might be central to a successful tour but, although he was playing in this game against the MCC, he did not have a contract with the West Indies Cricket Board of Control ("WICBC"). Constantine's contract was with Nelson in the Lancashire League and it wasn't clear if he would be available for the three test matches against England. This posed a threat to the tour, future West Indies tours and to the comparatively recent idea of test match cricket. Perhaps the successful model for cricket's future would be big-paying club teams who could scour the world for available cricketing talent. After all, such club-based entrepreneurialism had been the dominant format in the rise of cricket in the early and mid-nineteenth centuries.

As well as posing questions about cricket's future, the West Indies multi ethnic touring party was built upon the fault lines where race and sport connected. It was made up of six black players[3], six white players[4] and three[5] who did not fit easily into a black vs white schemata. The squad stood out in an age when cricket in South Africa was already segregated and black American baseball players were not allowed to play in the major leagues. Up to a point, the West Indies team was a sign of thirty years of increasing integration in Caribbean cricket.

But the black players in 1933 were playing in a structure where the most important jobs were not open to them. None had a realistic prospect of being appointed captain by the WICBC. Captain was a job for a white man. Similarly, the West Indies selection committee, which picked the touring party and the selection panel that picked the team for each game were made up entirely of white men.

Cricket characterised by black participation but on white terms was in advance of West Indian politics and society. Although the West Indies were an independent cricketing nation, politically the scattered islands of the Caribbean were possessions of the British crown. Electorates were limited by property qualifications and true political power rested with the British governor. Discrimination extended into the world of work; although a handful of non-white men had progressed as lawyers and doctors, for most black people the reality was a perfunctory education followed by a career of manual labour.

---

3   Herman Griffith, George Headley, Manny Martindale, Clifford Roach, Ben Sealey and Vincent Valentine.
4   Jack Grant, Teddy Hoad, Oscar Da Costa, Freddie Martin, Cyril Merry and Archie Wiles.
5   Ellis Achong, Cyril Christiani and Ivan Barrow.

Not surprisingly, some West Indians believed that it was necessary for the West Indies to be independent of British rule. The desire for independence was widespread in the British Empire of the 1930s and the demands for independence were loud and, on occasion, violent.

The 6th February 1932, Stanley Jackson, British politician and governor of Bengal, is addressing the convocation of the state university in Calcutta. A young woman, Bina Das, who is graduating from the university, leaves her seat and walks towards the dais. Perhaps she intends to say something but whatever it is she changes her mind and sits down. Jackson continues. Bina Das rises again; this time as she approaches the stage she brings out a revolver from underneath her gown. The hall is filled with noise and smoke. Vice Chancellor Hassan Shurawardy leaps from the stage and onto Das. They grapple for control of the gun. A further four shots are fired before she is disarmed. The governor is untouched.

Bina Das, the would-be assassin, is a former pupil of St John's Diocesan Girls' School and member of the Chhatri Sangha, an all-female nationalist group prepared to use violence to force the British to quit India. Witnesses see her hand shake as she prepared to shoot.

After Das is bustled away, and with the hall still filled with gun smoke, the governor carries on with his speech.

Governor Jackson was used to appearing in front of a crowd. Prior to the First World War, he was one of the World's best all round cricketers and captain of England in the ashes victory of 1905. When Jackson was appointed governor of Bengal in 1927, some British newspapers hoped his achievements as a cricketer would provide a point of contact with the Indian public; it was Jackson as captain of Cambridge who selected the Indian batsman Ranjitsinhji for the university side. Such hopes proved to be naïve when met with reality. On becoming governor, the Conservative Jackson embarked on a program of repression tantamount to martial law and sufficient to alienate moderate nationalist opinion without noticeably reducing the incidence of revolutionary violence.

The increasingly febrile situation in Bengal was one instance of the British Empire being challenged by the growth and assertiveness of non-European nationalist movements. In the West Indies, discontent with British rule was generally expressed through strikes and other forms of labour unrest rather than demands for political change and democracy. But by 1933 there were nascent nationalist movements in the larger Caribbean islands and one of the most prominent of the Caribbean nationalists was Cyril "CLR" James, a Trinidadian cricket writer for the Manchester Guardian and (non-paying) lodger of Learie and Norma Constantine in Nelson. The bond between Constantine and the impecunious James was just one of the many sometimes ambiguous links between West Indies cricket and the democratisation of West Indian politics and society.

West Indian cricket was one cautious step ahead of West Indian society, but in Great Britain the situation was reversed. Universal suffrage was introduced in 1928[6], but in cricket the distinction between amateur and professional continued. Professionals were paid and amateurs were not, but a better representation of the gulf between an amateur and a professional was the styling of amateurs as gentlemen and professionals as players. An amateur cricketer might be employed as a cricket club secretary or treasurer but remained a gentleman and would have his initials before his name on the scorecard, change in the amateurs' dressing room and, unlike his professional colleagues, could captain the team. This was the British class system reimagined as caste.

Nor was the administration of the English game democratic. The members of the Marylebone Cricket Club ("MCC"), owners of Lord's cricket ground and the hosts of the 1933 fixture against the West Indies, remained in charge of cricket in the United Kingdom[7]. The MCC were also at the apex of cricketing administration throughout the British Empire where they held a dual role. When England teams toured abroad they did so not as England but as the MCC[8] and the MCC would organise the tour and select the squad. But at the same time, the committee of the MCC was the ultimate arbiter of the "laws" of cricket. For ordinary people, players both playing the game and making the rules might have been a conflict of interest, but the gentlemen

6   https://en.wikipedia.org/wiki/Universal_suffrage#Dates_by_country

7   The first class game was run by the MCC in conjunction with the Advisory County Cricket Committee (ACCC), but this body met at Lord's and its membership was near identical to the MCC committee.

8   Although they were styled as England when they played overseas test matches arranged by the MCC.

of the MCC were confident they could be trusted to act in everybody's best interests.

The MCC's governance implied responsibilities beyond maintaining the written rules of cricket; the spirit of the game also had to be considered. All games have a code of conduct, guides to action where the rules don't apply (or are ignored by the participants), but in cricket this code, this spirit, was held to be particularly important. In 1933 you could say "it's just not cricket" with a fair chance of being understood from Calcutta to Melbourne, London to St Lucia. Cricket was fair play, team spirit and the stiff upper lip. These were the ostensible values of the English public school system and had been propagated throughout the British Empire.

But by May of 1933, the MCC's role as arbiters of fair play and guardians of the laws of cricket was contested. To understand why and how, we have to move away from Lord's in 1933, back five months in time and half a world in distance, to where MCC were playing Australia in the third test match at Adelaide.

There are 50,000 people crammed into the Adelaide Oval and a generalised resentment in the hot Australian air. The spectators queued up for over an hour to get into the ground and watch England grind to 341 all out in 146 overs. Most of those are bowled by Australia's spinners: Bill (Tiger) O'Reilly, fellow leg spinner Clarrie Grimmet and fifty-year-old slow left-armer, Bert Ironmonger. Now it is Australia's turn to bat, but against a very different attack. England have three quick bowlers: Harold Larwood, George (Gubby) Allen and Bill Voce backed up by Hedley Verity's left arm spin and the medium fast of Wally Hammond. Of the pace bowlers Voce with his height and left arm delivery is fast enough, Allen is a genuinely quick bowler. And Larwood? Larwood is just too quick. Captained by the remorseless Douglas Jardine they are a fast bowling attack. An attack which, the dissenting Allen aside, uses bodyline: fast, short-pitched bowling aimed at the body; backed up by a gaggle of short legs poised for a catch. Even if a batsman can stay in against bodyline, scoring runs is difficult and the possibility of physical injury high. The method seems to most Australians, and one or two English players to boot, to have nothing to do with the spirit of cricket.

With England having won the first test match and Australia the second, a remarkably ill-tempered series is in the balance. The resentment in the crowd echoed in disputes between the two sides. The England batsman Maurice Leyland accuses Ironmonger of using resin to tamper with the ball, Ironmonger turns out his pockets in the middle of the pitch. Jardine takes issue with Australian fielders moving whilst the bowler is running in[9].

Australia's first innings starts poorly, when Fingleton is caught Ames bowled Allen. Don Bradman comes in to bat. Bradman only made his test debut in 1928 but is acknowledged as the finest batsman in the world, a title he will hold until his retirement in 1948. The twenty-four-

---

9   The *Argus Melbourne* 16th January 1933 http://trove.nla.gov.au

year-old Bradman's success is a welcome distraction from the depression of the 1930s, which has punched holes in the Australian economy. Bradman averaged 139 in the 1930 test series against England and is a hero to Australians, but the "little bastard" is an affront to Jardine who develops bodyline as a tactic designed with Bradman in mind, aiming to bring about his psychological disintegration. Jardine believes his tactics have started to work when Bradman misses the first test of the series suffering from exhaustion.

In his second over, Larwood runs in to bowl to Woodfull. Twelve long rhythmical strides, fast but controlled, as he approaches the wicket the umpire turns; when Larwood was fired up he ran in on his toes and so sweetly that umpires couldn't hear him coming. Larwood's delivery is a leap and pivot bringing him to the fast bowler's textbook sideways-on position with his left arm for an instant pointing straight up to the blue sky. The right arm and side comes through in a massive sweep transferring the energy of that run in to the released ball too quick for the eye to follow. By the time we see Woodfull, he's been hit, he throws his bat away, reels from the stumps and falls to the ground. The fielders rush towards him. Most come from the off side of the wicket. At this stage the bodyline field has not been set, but it makes no difference to the crowd who go wild, boo and holler for three minutes.[10]. "Well bowled, Harold," says Jardine.

Woodfull manages to carry on. The next over is bowled by Allen, but when Larwood comes to bowl his third over, Jardine makes the signal for the field to switch from the off

---

10   *Harold Larwood* Duncan Hamilton.

to the leg. Now Larwood, dangerous enough when bowling conventionally, will be aiming the ball at the batsman with a field set for the purpose. The atmosphere changes from tense to violent, the abuse thrown at the England players constant. Bradman does not last long, caught in the leg trap by Allen fending off a ball from Larwood, just as Jardine had planned. McCabe goes the same way before Allen bowls Woodfull for a painful twenty-two runs from sixty-six balls.

It is time for a son of the West Indies to enter the action. By 1933, the fifty-nine-year-old Pelham Warner is well on the way to being the grand old man of English cricket. He captained the England team that regained the ashes in 1903-1904, toured the world playing cricket and now manages to be simultaneously an important figure in the MCC, chairman of selectors, a cricketing journalist and the proprietor of *The Cricketer* magazine. He is also co-manager of the 1932-1933 bodyline tour. But this typical representative of the English establishment was born in Port of Spain Trinidad, to a family well established in the islands' planter aristocracy. He played both for and against West Indian teams and his brother, Aucher Warner, was captain of the West Indies first tour to England in 1900.

Hearing that Woodfull has been hurt and aware of the attitude at the ground and throughout Australia towards bodyline, Warner decides to visit the injured Australian captain and apply a little diplomacy. What happens next passes into cricket's history. The Australian captain says to Warner, "I don't want to see you, Mr Warner. There are two teams out there. One is trying to play cricket and the other is not." Woodfull, a schoolteacher, believes he knows all about playing the game the right way.

Initially this is merely one more spat in a spiteful series, although bad enough for a shaken Warner to burst into tears. But what is said in the Australian dressing room doesn't stay there; how it escaped has never been established, but Woodfull's comments are carried in Monday's newspapers. The Australian captain, like many of his fellow Australians, believes England are traducing the spirit of cricket. To say such a thing is shocking, to have it reported in the newspapers, doubly so. Warner attempts to make things better by announcing Woodfull subsequently apologised for his comments; Woodfall, via the Australian Cricket Board of Control (ACBC), denies any apology. Once again, Plum Warner has made things worse.

On the Monday, Larwood, bowling with the second new ball, sends down a bouncer at Australian wicketkeeper Oldfield. As with the ball that hit Woodfull, Larwood is bowling to conventional fields, but Oldfield, trying to hook, edges the ball onto his forehead and falls to the ground. Larwood fears he has killed him, although a partially stunned Oldfield manages to say, "It wasn't your fault, Harold." The crowd has a different opinion and their mood worsens as captain Woodfull, dressed in street clothes, runs onto the ground and takes his player back to the pavilion and from there to the home of a local doctor. Oldfield is eventually diagnosed as having a fractured skull. The England players gather in the centre of the pitch and discuss what to do if the crowd comes over the picket fence. Police guard the boundary's edge and mounted units are in reserve; there isn't a riot but the animosity between the two teams since the start of the tour has spread to the Australian press, public and now the ACBC who send a telegram to the MCC.

"Bodyline bowling has assumed such proportions as to menace the best interests of the game, making protection of the body by the batsmen the main consideration. This is causing intensely bitter feeling between the players, as well as injury. In our opinion it is unsportsmanlike. Unless stopped at once, it is likely to upset the friendly relations existing between Australia and England."

They can't be any clearer, the game that England are playing simply isn't cricket. The ACBC have explicitly sided with Woodfull, the spirit of cricket is now a matter on which anybody can have an opinion.

The MCC responds.

"We the Marylebone Cricket Club, deplore your cable. We deprecate your opinion that there has been unsportsmanlike play."

The MCC's message is equally clear: the colonials are a bunch of sore losers.

For a time, it seemed as if the tour might end with two tests un-played. Eventually, the ACBC after protracted negotiations dropped the accusation of unsportsmanlike behaviour and the tour continued with England winning the last two tests and the series 4:1.

It's been said that England's 1932-1933 tour of Australia threatened Australia's place in the Commonwealth. This is probably an exaggeration, the politicians involved in the dispute seem to have acted informally for a negotiated settlement between the two cricket boards. But bodyline did lead to an agitated debate in Australia and England and there were doubts about the continuation of test matches between the two countries.

One factor in the 1932-1933 tour being completed was a split in the ACBC between the States who had already seen a test match and those who hadn't. Massive crowds watched the series providing a financial bonanza for the hosting grounds and associations. But once the tour was completed the financial pressure was on the MCC. The MCC cash book for 1933 includes a receipt of £24,709 pounds seven shillings and five pence from the Union Bank of Australia; MCC's profits from the 1932-1933 bodyline tour, with a modern day value of approximately £1.5 million. This money was distributed throughout English cricket with each first class county receiving a payment. These distributions were vital, especially for smaller counties struggling to survive financially. Australia were due to tour England in 1934, but if that tour was cancelled it would be hard times for English cricket.

The ACBC had begun to lobby for a change in the rules and in April 1933 sent the MCC a draft amendment that would prevent "direct attack bowling". This was exactly what the MCC had feared; once its moral authority had been questioned the next step was a challenge to its role as the rule setting body for the global game. Warner always had doubts about the bodyline tactic and now other MCC administrators could see continued support for Jardine would have serious consequences.

What did the English public think about bodyline? Was it a legitimate tactic in the eyes of English cricket watchers? Had they been against it from the start? Were they like the MCC beginning to feel uneasy about its implications? Letters sent to Pelham Warner's *Cricketer* magazine in early 1933 were evenly split between those who wanted some action taken to curtail bodyline and those who regarded Australian protests as bad sportsmanship. But *The Cricketer*'s readers came from a particular subset of cricket watchers, what did a wider cricketing public think about bodyline? It is always difficult to know what a large group of people think about any complicated issue and with bodyline there is a gap of eighty-five years to contend with. But we do have newspapers from the 1930s and these can provide some insight into what was going on in the minds of the reading public. And the MCC vs West Indies match gave the Lord's crowd an opportunity to express their opinions on England's bodyline captain, Douglas Jardine.

Chapter 3

BACK PAGES: THE PRESS AND THE 1933 TOUR

The British cricketing public could experience the West Indies 1933 tour in one of three ways. Firstly, they could go and see a game; there were plenty to choose from, the West Indies played forty-four games in 1933 playing all seventeen first class counties (Lancashire and Glamorgan twice), Oxford and Cambridge and a variety of minor counties and scratch sides. However, they couldn't play everywhere and at no stage did they play outside of England and Wales. For many of the county games, crowds were not particularly large. RH Mallett kept a record of West Indian receipts[11] from the 1933 tour, these totalled £9,017, but of this £4,837 (54%) came from the top four grossing matches, which were

---

11   Now in the MCC archives.

the three test matches and the MCC game at Lord's. Precise attendance figures are not available but, at a rough estimate, paying spectators for the tour would have been in the region of 250,000.[12]

An alternative to attending a game was listening to radio reports and updates. But radio coverage of cricket in 1933 was not expansive and there was no broadcast ball by ball commentary until the 1934 ashes series[13].

Most people followed sport via a third route, a daily newspaper. The circulation of the national press in 1930 was approximately 8.5 million copies per day out of a population of forty – six million[14]. As institutions from West End clubs to pubs provided newspapers for free, actual readership would have been higher.

There was a symbiotic relationship between newspapers and sport; newspapers provided sport with publicity and helped to establish leading sportsmen as national figures. And, from the early nineteenth century, sport provided copy for the press. For commercial newspapers, sport is a particularly valuable resource in a time of economic depression such as the 1930s. Depression is dull, by definition it constitutes the same economic facts repeating themselves over a protracted period; there are none of the sudden changes that appeal to

---

12 The Lord's attendance for all three days is confirmed as 46,449 and generated net receipts of 1,937 for WI being 21% of total net receipts for the tour. This scales up to about 220,000 spectators and I have rounded up to 250,000 to allow for lower prices at grounds other than Lord's.

13 http://www.espncricinfo.com/ci/content/story/214571.html

14 https://en.wikipedia.org/wiki/List_of_newspapers_in_the_United_Kingdom_by_circulation#Before_1950

the reading public. By contrast, sport always has new stories to tell; the game remains unchanged, but there's always the possibility of something new. The champion can be knocked out, the 250:1 outsider wins the race.

Newspapers in the 1930s devoted a considerable amount of coverage to sport, the *Daily Express*, which was fourteen to sixteen pages long, always carried two full pages of sport and sometimes included sporting news on other pages. The *Manchester Guardian* would have sport on two to three pages out of a twenty-page newspaper. Both papers covered cricket in detail; there would be a full report on the previous day's play in a test match often accompanied by a picture and coverage of games in the County Championship. The trade union *Daily Herald* had two pages of sports coverage in a twenty-page newspaper, three pages on a Monday during the football season. It too had a good deal of cricket coverage and a specialist cricket reporter, but did not feature cricket as much as the *Manchester Guardian*, football and horse racing were the favourite sports of the *Herald* and, presumably, its working-class readership.

Newspapers are an important resource for the cricket historian, sport before television was ephemeral and newspapers provide the first and, often, the only draft of history. Those of us interested in the 1933 series are fortunate as it was covered by two celebrated cricket writers: Neville Cardus and CLR James, both of whom were working for the *Manchester Guardian* in 1933. Although the two men are often seen as contrasting writers, it was Cardus who recruited James to the *Guardian* and, in his enthusiasm for the cricket of the pre-World War One era, James, at the cricket, was a Cardusian with Marxist leanings.

Although James and Cardus stand above the other cricketing journalists of the 1930s, their work had a relatively small circulation, the *Guardian* sold approximately 50,000 copies a day in the 1930s compared to the million plus circulations of the three largest selling newspapers. But across newspapers as disparate as *The Guardian*, *The Daily Herald* and *The Daily Mail* there were consistent attitudes towards the West Indian team of 1933.

Principally, there was a widespread belief that the West Indies could not hope to defeat England. This opinion was supported by the relative playing strength of the two teams but was perhaps reinforced by an assumption of an innate British superiority.

Sometimes the English press was dismissive of West Indian success. When Ivan Barrow became the first West Indian to score a hundred in a test match in England the headline in the *Daily Express* was "Test Player who did not bat well enough to get out". Barrow had been dropped on three or perhaps four occasions in his innings but, by focusing on Barrow's luck, the *Express* was downplaying his durability. It was also overlooking George Headley who scored a chanceless hundred on the same day (there was a reference to Headley's innings in a sub headline). As well as underplaying West Indian achievement, the press in general and cricket's document of record, *Wisden*, in particular, would sometimes jump on West Indian failures as proof that the expansion of test match cricket was a mistake. The West Indians were subject to a double jeopardy, their successes were characterised as down to luck or poor play by England, but their losses to a very strong England side demonstrated their unsuitability for test cricket.

Another feature of the British sporting press of the 1930s was a lack of curiosity about political and race issues. Post the sporting boycott of South Africa in the 1970s and 1980s it is natural to view playing sport as an activity with political implications. But this wasn't the case in the British press of the 1930s. It is difficult to find any comment on the fact that Jack Grant was captain of the West Indies, whilst other players in the party who would have been more suitable for the role were excluded by the colour of their skin. This applies just as much to Cardus writing for the *Guardian* as sportswriters on the fascist supporting *Daily Mail*. Not surprisingly, CLR James was an exception to this blindness (or was it dumbness), but he was a junior journalist at the *Guardian* in 1933 and confined his comments on the captaincy to reports home in the *Port of Spain Gazette*.

Another tendency in the UK newspapers was to attribute to the West Indian side an excess of sentiment, which meant they were formidable when things were going well but could fall into despair when luck was against them. Such views were often expressed by commentators who were generally well disposed to the West Indians, Neville Cardus certainly believed racial differences were important in cricket and the *Daily Herald* in its preview of the second test match described the West Indian team having "A boyish exuberance of spirits." Learie Constantine regarded this emphasis of racial differences as patronising and inconsistent with his experiences of playing with white cricketers.

However, it would not be true to describe British press coverage of the West Indian tour as explicitly racist. Neville Cardus was keenly interested in the subject of race but was in this, as in many other respects, an outlier amongst journalists. Most make very little if any reference to the colour of a player's skin and it would be possible to read a press report from the 1930s without realising there were both black and white players on the field of play.

And throughout the British newspapers there was a recognition that Constantine, Headley and Martindale were the best players in the West Indian team, a genuine enjoyment of their successes and an appreciation of the entertainment they gave to the British sporting public. This was the generous side of the sporting personality and in general it won out over its sour, nationalist alter-ego.

Although it is possible to talk about attitudes as characteristic of the British sports press, there were times when sharp differences of opinion between newspapers became apparent. One such rift came during the ashes tour of Australia in 1924-1925. England, captained by Arthur Gilligan, lost the series 4-1. Gilligan was, hopefully, unique amongst English test match captains in being a member of the British fascists and, like many an England captain, he had a terrible tour of Australia as a player, averaging fifty-two as a bowler and ten as a batsman. Some commentators, most notably professional cricketer Cecil Parkin writing in the *Weekly Dispatch*, suggested Gilligan be dropped and replaced as captain by the professional, Jack Hobbs. The controversy simmered for some months and a division appeared in the British press between the establishment newspapers, who ignored the controversy over the captaincy and emphasised the fine diplomatic work Gilligan was doing, and the popular press who wanted to win and were prepared to support a professional captain if that was what it took.

That controversy died down when amateur captain Percy Chapman led England to their first post-World War 1 ashes series victory in 1929. But by May of 1933, there were signs that the distinction between playing to win and cricket as an instrument of empire was again dividing newspapers.

The British press had initially gloried in Jardine's success in the 1932-1933 ashes series and dismissed Australian complaints about the strategy used to achieve it. But Warner had always been uneasy about bodyline and now, back on British soil, was opposed to it. Warner was a central figure in English cricket and influenced an establishment press that was just beginning to hedge their bets on the appropriateness of bodyline as a tactic. But in the popular press there were no such doubts – Jardine had done what he had been tasked to do. The *Daily Herald*, the paper of the working man, might have been expected to side with the Australian players against the ruthless upper-class Jardine, but they continued to argue the Australians were bad losers and fears about bodyline ridiculous.

The MCC match against the West Indies marked Jardine's return to cricket and gave the cricketing public at Lord's their first opportunity to express their opinions over the bodyline series.

The 22nd May 1933, Empire Day bank holiday, and another large crowd is gathered at Lord's. More fast bowling is expected with Martindale and Constantine resuming their attack. Constantine soon takes the wicket of Hulme, caught behind by West Indian keeper Barrow.

Next man in is a gaunt figure, with a beak of a nose and wearing a striped Harlequins cap. Stalking to the wicket, he is Douglas Jardine. The crowd begins to clap, one or two cheers ring across the outfield. The clapping increases in intensity as Jardine reaches the wicket. Some people stand to show their appreciation, from the pavilion to the cheap seats the Lord's public makes its feelings plain: Jardine is a hero.

Walking to the wicket is the best part of Jardine's day. Constantine and Martindale are still bowling with real pace and although they have most of their fielders on the off side there is always a short leg in place for the short-pitched ball aimed at the body and fended away. Constantine takes the wickets of both Jardine and Patsy Hendren using this tactic. Jardine is dismissed by a pale imitation of the bodyline he had used so effectively in Australia, and the MCC are 70 for 5, still 239 runs behind the West Indies' first innings score.

A second England captain comes to the crease. Although Percy Chapman shared his public-school background with Douglas Jardine, he is his antithesis as a man and a cricketer. Jardine is dour and introverted, Chapman a cordial socialite. Jardine, despite his athletic physique is a stiff, poor ground fielder[15], Chapman fields brilliantly. The right-handed Jardine bats carefully, the left-handed Chapman always takes risks. Chapman was popular with the Australian public who so detested Jardine. The two men do, however,

---

15   But a fine catcher.

share a liking for extravagant head gear, Chapman is batting in a Quidnuncs[16] cap.

Neville Cardus once described Chapman as "the schoolboy's dream of the perfect captain of an England cricket eleven."[17] His career has had great days and Chapman was captain of the MCC side that won the 1928-1929 ashes series 4-1. By 1933, the schoolboy's dream is a little ragged. Chapman has put on weight and his drinking goes beyond the merely social. There are whispers he was drunk on the field when captaining England in the 1930 series against Australia. But the 22nd May is one last glorious day in the sun for Percy Chapman. He mixes solid defence with bold counterattacking shots. Short balls he pulls to the boundary; any bowler pitching the ball up is hit back over his head. Chapman and Valentine bat on into the afternoon, the Lord's crowd, relaxing in the May sun emits a happy beehive hum. But Chapman going for another lofted drive is caught by George Headley off the bowling of Learie Constantine – agonisingly out for ninety-seven. With Martindale hustling through the tail the MCC are all out for 246, sixty-three runs behind the West Indies and, with plenty of time left in the second day, any result is possible.

Bill Bowes opens the bowling for the MCC and dismisses Clifford Roach, bringing George Headley to the crease. Bowes bowls a bouncer. The ball rises sharply, striking Headley who, "fell on the earth rather convulsively. Probably he fainted.[18]" It takes Headley five minutes to

---

16 Worn by members of the Cambridge University cricket team
17 https://en.wikipedia.org/wiki/Percy_Chapman
18 *Manchester Guardian.*

regain consciousness[19] and, although he bats on, he is out to Allom for twenty and is to miss three first class games recovering from his injury. The ball is beginning to turn and, without Headley, the West Indies show the susceptibility to spin bowling that is to be a feature of the summer. At 95/5 they are just 158 ahead and have lost their grip on the match as Learie Constantine comes in to bat.

As a batsman, Constantine responds to all situations by declaring war on the ball. Playing himself in with a period of cautious defence really isn't his game. At various times in his career this has attracted criticism. In the first innings of this game he was out for eleven trying to thump the leg spinner Brown out of the ground. Cardus in *The Guardian* commented: "It will be a pity if Constantine allows the crowd to endow him with the irresponsibility of a jazz coon cricketer."

Constantine didn't pay any attention. His first ball from the England seam bowler Maurice Allom is straight driven to the Nursery End for four. The second pulled to the Grand Stand boundary – four more. Having played himself in, Constantine is moving down the pitch as Allom runs in to bowl his third ball. Constantine is so far down the wicket that Allom attempts to float a slow full toss over his head and onto Constantine's stumps. "Accordingly, he pivoted on his heel and delivered a prodigious blow that sent the ball past the startled wicketkeeper's ear and high over the flag by the player's dressing room."[20]

---

19   Per Learie Constantine in *Cricket in the Sun.*
20   Report in *The Daily Telegraph.*

Constantine is on fourteen from three balls faced, including a flip over the wicketkeeper's head for six. Jardine sends his fielders to the boundary.

In the next over, Constantine plays two delicate late cuts to send the ball speeding to the boundary fine of third man. The helpless Allom is then hit for three more fours in an over.

Jardine calls Bill Bowes back into the attack. Twice he bounces Constantine, twice he goes for four. In Bowe's autobiography[21] he describes one of the shots as follows: "Learie put his left leg right down the wicket and sank to his right knee. As the ball came up on the bounce he hit upwards at it and it went over his left shoulder to very fine leg for six[22]." Eventually Bowes has his revenge; he bowls Constantine with "An off-stump half volley that Constantine was trying to hit over square leg.[23]" Constantine has scored fifty-one runs in twenty-six minutes at the crease; forty-two in boundaries.

On the 25th May Neville Cardus, who had been so critical of Constantine's first innings performance, has a piece in the *Manchester Guardian* with the headline "Genius in Cricket: Constantine". Other reports on the match refer to West Indians in the crowd singing spirituals. They have something to sing about – 403 runs and fifteen wickets in a day's play.

---

21 *Express Deliveries*
22 None of the newspaper reports has Constantine hitting Bowes for six, so maybe Bowes' memory is adding a little something.
23 *The Guardian* match report

But *The Cricketer* in its coverage of the match writes: "It is to be regretted that some of their too enthusiastic supporters in the Mound stand on Monday should have been allowed to behave in the manner they did. We want nothing of that nature on our cricket fields."

The third day is a less extravagant affair but, as the cricket becomes more sober, it gains in intensity. First an innings of forty-seven from Cyril Merry takes the West Indies' second innings to 268, a lead of 331. When the MCC bats for the second time, Martindale takes the wicket of Hearne, who shows little enthusiasm for facing the West Indies pace attack. The popular Patsy Hendren comes in to bat. Like Jardine and Chapman, he is wearing an unorthodox cap. However, as Hendren is a professional, his cap is for protection and not for show. Hendren's wife has added two extra rubberised peaks, lifted up and secured at the crown, described in the press as a, "Sort of balaclava helmet".[24] Hendren wears the cap for Constantine but takes it off when Martindale is bowling.

Wearing this protective cap seems a sensible precaution on Hendren's part. He knows it is a quick pitch, he has seen one of the world's best batsmen knocked unconscious and Hendren himself had been seriously injured by Harold Larwood earlier in his career. However, the reaction in the press to the cap is a mixture of amusement and derision.

---

24 *Morning Post.*

"The crowd were either too polite or too startled to laugh but surely there is a limit to the hysteria about fast bowling[25]."

By the third day, the wicket is a little slower than on the first two, but it is taking an increasing amount of turn and the left-arm spinner Ellis Achong dismisses first Hulme and then Valentine to leave the MCC at a perilous 64/3. Douglas Jardine returns.

Deciding victory is beyond them, Jardine and Hendren begin the type of backs to the wall defensive effort where English cricketers are often at their best. Jardine plays the part of patrician officer, Hendren the cockney NCO. The two bat securely and sedately against the spinning ball and the MCC reach tea with no further loss. At a quarter to five with just over an hour's play left, the game has drifted to a near certain draw with the MCC on 140 for three. But Jardine is out to the bowling of Da Costa, caught by Barrow for forty-four. A pitch that had gone dead springs back to life as Achong and Da Costa get the ball to turn and bounce. The scores for the second half of the MCC batting order are: nine, nought, nought , thirteen (not out), one and nought. Hendren battles on for sixty-one, but when he is clean bowled by Achong the MCC are done for. In just thirty-five minutes of play, they have lost seven wickets for thirty-nine runs and the game by the spanking margin of 152 runs.

The West Indies have beaten the MCC, the aristocratic guardians of the game, and they have defeated a team, eight

---

25   The Morning Post, *The Guardian* described it as absurd.

of whom have played test cricket for England[26]. Perhaps they have a chance in the test series; especially if Learie Constantine is available.

MCC vs the West Indies in 1933 shows how cricket has changed in the last eighty years. There were amateurs and professionals, Jardine and Chapman swanning around in their university caps, a West Indian team captained by a white man and Hulme who played cricket in preference to football. But it also contained incidents that pre-empted modern cricket: fast bowling, protective headgear, outrageous scoop shots and loyalties split between club and international sides. As the West Indies and England selected their teams for the first test match of the summer of 1933, they would have to resolve the contradictions of the old and the new cricket.

In modern day cricket nothing attracts discussion and controversy like the selection of a test match team. This is not surprising. Cricket watchers have, generally, accepted they will never play test cricket, but think we'd make an excellent chairman of selectors. And modern-day selectors in England and the West Indies have a straightforward, if difficult, job. Twenty-first century cricket has, become commoditised, and playing success is the unit of value for all selections[27].

26　Hulme, Valentine and Franklin hadn't played for England at this point, although Valentine was to play a test in India in the 1933-1934 series. Franklin hadn't played county cricket at all.

27　But maybe not in South Africa where there is still the issue of racially balanced sides.

But in the 1930s the selectors were not only concerned with picking eleven men who could win a match, the team picked also had to reflect the values of the established society it represented. As we shall see, neither the West Indies nor England picked the strongest team available to them to play in the first test match at Lord's because winning wasn't the only criteria for selection.

Chapter 4

AMATEUR AFFAIR

The snap and crackle of ordnance marks the start of the Marlborough rebellion. Fireworks are banned at the school, but it is bonfire night and the truculent pupils decide to have their fun. Most of the boys are sons of the Anglican clergy but survival of the fittest is the school's creed. Marlborough was founded in 1844 and now in 1851 it has over 500 pupils and is the second largest public school in the country. The rapid expansion has strained the school's finances and, in an attempt to make ends meet, the boys are given little to eat. They respond with a series of depredations on the surrounding countryside, young boys are habitués of local pubs and poaching deer a popular schoolboy hobby. The school tries to confine pupils to school premises. But conditions inside the school are bad, fights common, bullying systematic and grotesque and, with a shortage of teachers, a semblance of discipline is only maintained by beating and birching. Now discipline is shot into the

Wiltshire night along with "eighty dozen squibs and crackers and a variety of larger fireworks.[28]" The firing goes on all night, accompanied by general lawlessness, and the school is to smell of cordite for the remainder of the rebellion.

By daylight the authorities are able to exert sufficient authority to expel one boy judged to be the ring leader. But this only sets off a new cycle of insubordination and affray, the boys break through the school gates following the expelled pupil down High Street and knock a local resident off his pony. Returning to the school, the headmaster's residence is stoned, the gatekeeper beaten up and the racquets court set on fire. "Windows were smashed, desks were broken and anarchy reigned everywhere throughout the week." The riot is only brought to an end by the surrender of the school authorities; boys are given the freedom to leave the school premises.

A more permanent solution was required, and GEL Cotton was appointed as headmaster. It was a shrewd appointment, Cotton had taught at Rugby school and had seen the transformation produced by its headmaster, Thomas Arnold, who had changed Rugby from "a system of anarchy tempered by despotism" to "a place of really Christian education."[29]

Arnold's aims at Rugby school were revolutionary, but his methods were moderate. He continued the liberal use of

---

28 https://archive.org/stream/ahistorymarlbor00baingoog/
    ahistorymarlbor00baingoog_djvu.txt

29 From Eminent Victorians, Lytton Strachey.

corporal punishment and left the day to day running of the school in the hands of the senior pupils. Arnold devoted his energies to influencing those senior boys.

Arnold realised sport was one way pupils could be influenced. It channelled the natural energy of boys and young men into a delineated space at specific times and in accordance with a set of rules. Cotton was quick to follow Arnold's example; playing fields were marked out in the Marlborough school grounds and the house system with its emphasis on sporting competition introduced to the school. Cotton's reforms brought Marlborough into line with what was becoming general practice in British public schools.

Cotton, like Arnold, was a Christian academic who had little interest in sport of itself, but teachers he recruited, who had been educated either at Marlborough or Rugby, believed sport could be a moral influence as well as a diversion. Sport encouraged cooperation and sublimation of the self to the needs of the team, it inculcated respect for the rules of the game and helped develop the healthy body without which there could be no healthy mind. Muscular Christianity was born.

Games increasingly dominated English public schools in the late nineteenth century with most schoolboys engaging in some physical activity six days a week[30]. Sport remained central in British attitudes to education well into the

---

30 Although the way this program was administered differed between schools and there was often a range of sports that boys could choose. When Pelham Warner arrived at Rugby it was decided that he was too small and delicate for the school's eponymous sport, so instead he spent winter afternoons walking in the Warwickshire countryside.

twentieth century, although the emphasis shifted somewhat from Christian morality to character more generally and the skills needed for leadership in particular.

In 1943, another one-time headmaster of Marlborough school, Cyril Norwood, delivered his report on the school curriculum. The first area of the curriculum considered is Physical Education and this initial chapter begins with a statement of the benefits of sport that could have been written at any time in the previous 100 years.

"On healthy growth and vigour of body largely depends his intellectual development, and right discipline of the body can contribute powerfully to moral strength."[31]

Victorians and Edwardians expected their sports to carry a heavy load: provide the healthy body essential for a healthy mind, teach rough boys the gentle Christian virtues and provide an empire with leaders of courage and decisiveness. Muscular Christianity was an amalgam of two different value systems, the martial requirements of empire and Christianity, where life is something more than a never-ending struggle for dominance. Perhaps this split personality is one reason for the range of sports that were formalised in the second half of the nineteenth century: football, rugby and tennis.

Cricket was particularly well suited to the development of young gentlemen. It is a game that poses a variety of challenges, the player, physically and intellectually, has to win his own battles, but needs to play as part of a team. The captain has to manage the range of talents available to him

---

31   The Norwood report

to produce a whole greater than the sum of their parts. And cricket straddles the two sides of muscular Christianity, the game has an essential toughness, it's played with a hard ball and if the bowler hits the batsman on the head with the hard ball, everybody claps. But cricket is not a sport where physical contact is a consistent feature of the game as it is in rugby or football[32].

Cricket also allowed sport to access an English pastoralism valued in the increasingly urban England of the late nineteenth and early twentieth centuries. Cricket is the most beautiful of games and an English cricket season mirrors nature: dying in the autumn, reborn in the spring. And, unlike football and rugby, cricket's existence as a formalised sport preceded the industrial revolution. The MCC first published the "laws" of cricket in 1795[33], but the earliest references to cricket go back to the seventeenth century and the game was well established by the eighteenth century. As Britain and the world beyond became increasingly industrial, the link between cricket and an idealised, pre-industrialised England became more important. This pastoralism perhaps reached its height in AG Macdonnel's cricket match in *England Their England*, first published in February 1933[34], three months before the arrival of the West Indies touring party[35]

For all these reasons, cricket was first amongst equals of the sports that were codified and developed in the English

---

32 The way the English play football.
33 Rules were codified for football in 1848 and rugby in 1845.
34 See *Cricket pastoral and Englishness* by Anthony Bateman in *The Cambridge Companion to Cricket.*
35 *England Their England* By AG Macdonnel

public schools of the mid-nineteenth century. The great Victorian public school novel, *Tom Brown's Schooldays*, ends with a cricket match, even though it is set at Rugby school.

The development of organised sport in the English public school produced the sporting ethos of amateurism. At its simplest, amateurism in sport prevents professional sportsmen from competing in certain events, but at heart it is the association of sport with the complex of values that made up muscular Christianity. Some of those values, such as teamwork, complemented the competition, which is an essential part of sport, but "fair play", another aspect of the amateur ideal, contradicted the idea that winning was all that mattered. Additionally, in cricket, amateurism required the taking up of an aesthetic burden; the amateur batsman should bat in a manner that would improve the game as a spectacle and trigger in the properly attuned spectator an image of a different, rural England. But batting as an art was not always conducive to winning matches.

In contrast to the virtues of amateurism were the vices, real and imagined, of professional sport. Professional sportsmen would play to earn and would use any tactic to win the game. This also resulted in dull cricket where runs were churned out on a utilitarian basis with no thought for aesthetics.

There was some merit in amateurism: in its licentious infancy, cricket had a close association with gambling and was undermined by suspicions the result was determined off the field rather than on it. Removing money as a factor in the game might eliminate corruption, and indeed cricket in the first half of the twentieth century seemed largely free of gambling scandals. It was also natural for an aristocratic cricket establishment to regard cricket as a property held in common, to be propagated and passed on. Modern administrators, from business backgrounds, see cricket as a commodity to be replicated and sold with no thought to the long term.

But, more importantly, amateurism undermined the meritocracy, which is sport's main and perhaps only virtue. Life is a tricky business, success and failure hard to judge. In sport everybody knows what the result is at the end of the game. On the field it doesn't matter whether you are the Lord of the Manor or the under butler, success and failure is apparent and dependent on the individual.[36] Amateurism took that away, it put the underperforming Lord of the Manor back in charge of the butler on the cricket field: sport's Saturnalia was replaced with business as usual. The belief that the amateur was superior to the cricketer who played for money was appealing to those educated at public school who were already encouraged to see themselves as leaders of men and contributed to the endemic snobbery of the British Empire.

In England, amateur administrators dominated cricket. English teams toured as the MCC and, although they played as "England" in home matches, selection, both home and away, was carried out by a handful of the great and the good, most of whom had been notable amateur players in their time; men like Pelham Warner, Lord Hawke and Stanley

---

36 Although I'm not trying to argue that sporting success is entirely separate from off-field considerations.

Jackson. There seemed to be an unwritten rule each should put in a stint as a selector before stepping down and giving someone else a turn. After his exertions as selector and manager of the bodyline tour, Pelham Warner made way for his mentor, Lord Hawke for the summer of 1933.

For men like and Hawke and Warner, the captain of the national side had to be an amateur. The hallowed custom of amateurism didn't, in reality, stretch back that far; professional cricketers had captained England in the late nineteenth century. It was sometimes a tough job for a selection committee to find a suitable amateur captain for the England side who wouldn't be out of place in test cricket and had the savvy to run the team. However, Douglas Jardine, a fine tactician and a test level cricketer fitted the bill nicely. With the ethics of bodyline becoming a matter for debate there were already some doubts over whether Jardine would be the right man for the 1934 ashes series, but he was safe for the moment.

The selectors didn't only have to select a captain who was an amateur, they also had to fill a de facto amateur quota. Between the start of the 1932-1933 ashes series and the end of the 1934-1935 West Indies series, England played twenty-two test matches[37]. In this period the lowest number of amateurs selected was two; this happened in the final test match on the MCC tour of India and the fourth test match of the 1934 ashes series[38]. In total, amateurs

---

37 See http://sideoncricket.blogspot.co.uk/ for details.
38 Both these occasions were cricketing crises: in India illness had taken a toll of the squad and anyone who could stand up played, in 1934 the series vs Australia was poised at one all.

made up seventy-three of the 242 selections, 30% of the players selected. This is roughly in line with the percentage of first class cricketers who were amateurs; a review of *The Cricketer* for 1933 shows that just less than a third of those who played regularly were amateurs.

However, when amateur participation is filtered for playing standards a different picture emerges. In 1933 and 1934 amateurs made up only18%[39] of the English qualified players in the top ten of the batting and bowling averages. Whilst Yorkshire, who were by far the strongest first-class county prior to the Second World War, invariably fielded a team of ten professionals captained by a lone amateur. By contrast, amateurs were particularly prevalent in some of the poorest sides. Somerset were little more than a country house side made up of amateurs, most of whom would only play a handful of games a season. It would seem that amateurs were over represented in English cricket sides of the 1930s and the selections of 1933 provide further circumstantial evidence of bias.

It was the third day of the fourth test match of the 1933-1934 ashes series. Australia had made 340 in the first innings, a decent if not remarkable score on a good Brisbane pitch, but England had suffered a mid-innings collapse and were 216 for six. Effectively seven wickets down as England's Eddie Paynter has an acute bout of tonsillitis, a serious matter

---

39   Source Cricket archive: seven amateurs out of forty positions.

in the pre-antibiotics era, and has gone to hospital with a temperature of 102 degrees.[40] The Australian players must have felt they had a good chance of winning the game and squaring the series. What the Australians didn't know was that Douglas Jardine had already been to visit Paynter, not so much to comfort him but to suggest he might still be able to bat. As England wickets begin to fall, Paynter pulls on his dressing gown, discharges himself from hospital and gets into a taxi headed for the "Gabba". Now he is coming out to bat, having replaced the dressing gown with cricket whites, panama hat and a handkerchief knotted around his neck.

Woodfull, the Australian captain, generously offers Paynter a runner, but Paynter refuses. Batting: he is too weak to play any attacking shots but, defending doggedly, he reaches the close with England at 271 – 8, Paynter changes and returns to hospital. He is back at the ground the next day and plays something like his normal game making the majority of the runs in a partnership of ninety-two with Hedley Verity giving England a small but vital first innings lead.

Paynter isn't done for the day; he refuses to give way to a twelfth man and fields in the Brisbane heat. Australia are bowled out for just 175 and on the sixth day (timeless tests, remember) Paynter hits a six to win the game and seal the series victory.

---

40 *The Ashes Strangest Moments* By Mark Baldwin

It was a performance that met the amateur ideal. Paynter had sacrificed himself to meet his captain's and his country's call. But his refusal to use a runner or a twelfth man to field in his place had shown a commitment to the spirit of the game. And the six off the final ball of the match was a typically amateur flourish. But Paynter wasn't an amateur, born in Oswaldtwistle, Lancashire, but growing up in Enfield, his first job on leaving school was to work as an operative in a cotton factory where he lost the top two joints of a finger in an accident. His route to first class cricket had been years in the Lancashire seconds not an appearance in the varsity match.

And now on returning home the hero was dropped for the first test. Two amateur players, Cyril Walters of Worcestershire and Maurice Turnbull of Glamorgan, were brought into the side. Turnbull, who took Paynter's place batting at five, averaged less than thirty across his first-class career. It was four years until Paynter returned to the test side, and when he did he was, again, strikingly successful. His final batting average in test match cricket was over fifty-nine, the second highest batting average for an England player who played twenty or more tests[41]. Paynter tended to succeed when England were in trouble, was a good fielder and bowled a few tidy overs; and should have been a fixture in the test side from 1933 onwards. But the England selectors were always on the lookout for decent amateur players who could preserve the social balance of the side and might one

41   Paynter played bang on twenty (https://en.wikipedia.org/wiki/Eddie_Paynter).

day be England captain. Paynter just had to make way. His mood probably wasn't helped by the fact that both Walters and Turnbull were (paid) secretaries for their counties. In Walters' case, his appointment to the position came at the same time as a Worcestershire member was appointed honorary (i.e. unpaid) secretary. The implication was clear: Walters wouldn't have to spend much time on his secretarial duties – and, like Paynter, was being paid to play cricket.

In selecting a test side, the England selectors weren't only concerned with having a requisite number of amateurs in the team. They also had to consider the ructions of the bodyline series of the previous English winter. The next chapter looks at one of the bowlers who was left out of the team for the way he bowled and examines the bonds and the tension between the amateur cricket of the South and the professional game played in the North of England.

Chapter 5

PREJUDICIAL TO THE BEST INTERESTS OF THE GAME

Just two weeks before the first test match of the summer of 1933, the MCC had cabled the ACBC rejecting the ACBC's proposal that the rules of cricket should be changed to allow umpires to stop bodyline bowling. The MCC suggested the barracking of Australian crowds was a bigger concern than so-called bodyline. However, there was one slight softening of tone when the MCC undertook to "watch carefully during the present season for anything which might be regarded as unfair or prejudicial to the best interests of the game." The West Indies had shown against the MCC that they had the fast bowlers to bowl bodyline. What would happen to the interests of the game if there was a season where both sides used the tactic?

The 1933 spring edition of *The Cricketer* commented: "It is satisfactory to find that in spite of adverse rumours first from one county and again from another, the prospect of a share in the surplus for the Australian tour during the winter coupled with 1934 in view, makes the financial position very much easier than it was." But this assumed Australia would tour in 1934. If the repercussion of bodyline was the cancellation of the 1934 ashes, one or more counties would move closer to bankruptcy.

Hawke and his fellow selectors, including Captain Douglas Jardine, picked a side with four changes from the team that had played the final test of the bodyline series against Australia. As we have seen, batsman Eddie Paynter was dropped, along with Bob Wyatt, and replaced by Cyril Walters and Maurice Turnbull. In the bowling, Nottinghamshire's Harold Larwood and Bill Voce were replaced by spin bowlers Walter Robins and George Macaulay.

The changes shifted the balance of the side. In the fifth test of the Australian summer, the England attack had been based on pace, with three fast bowlers in Voce, Allen and Larwood. For the first test of 1933, there was no danger of Douglas Jardine persisting with a prolonged bodyline attack because his only quick bowler was Gubby Allen, who had refused to use the tactic in Australia.

Harold Larwood was injured for pretty much the whole of the 1933 season, relieving the selectors of the conundrum of whether to pick the controversial fast bowler. Bill Voce was available, but was left out of the team. As was another bodyline tourist: Bill Bowes. Bowes had led the attack for the Yorkshire team that had won all their 1933 games prior to the first test, taking his wickets at an average of less than sixteen. But originally Gubby Allen and Nobby Clark were selected as the pace bowlers for the Lord's test.

Bowes must have been a little disappointed he hadn't been picked to replace Larwood and when Clark pulled out with injury[42] he surely felt his chance had come. But the selectors instead selected his county colleague, the medium-paced spinner George Macaulay. Macaulay had started the 1933 season in great form, but if the selectors had wanted to play Macaulay then shouldn't the amateur Walter Robbins have been left out?

There were three potential reasons for the failure to select Bowes. Firstly, a cricketing one: Bowes was an awful fielder and, possibly, an even worse batsman, taking more first-class wickets than he scored runs in his career. Robins averaged twenty-seven with the bat in test cricket. Although a concern with how well a bowler bats is regarded as a modern development, runs down the order were always a feature of teams captained by Douglas Jardine.

Secondly, Robins was an amateur cricketer. Lord Hawke chairman of selectors was, even by the standards of the cricketing establishment, a great believer in amateurism; he is now best known for his comment, "Pray God no professional shall ever captain England." The team picked to play against the West Indies contained five amateurs, the most of any side picked between the 1932/1933 bodyline series and England's 1935 tour of the West Indies and was Hawkes's attempt to reinvigorate the amateur cause.

---

42   http://www.espncricinfo.com/ *Wisden*almanack/content/ story/151775.html

Finally, Bowes had form for bowling in a hostile and controversial manner. In the 1932 season, playing against Surrey at the Oval, Bowes had bowled a succession of bouncers at forty-nine-year-old Jack Hobbs. Hobbs wasn't hit but, walked down the pitch and made an ostentatious job of patting down the short-pitched length the ball had landed on. The combustible and incendiary George Macaulay helpfully pointed this out to Bowes who responded with another short ball. This time Hobbs' walk down the pitch carried him all the way past the stumps at the bowler's end where he "remonstrated with some of the Yorkshire players".[43] Inevitably another bouncer was to follow.

Bowes' tactics were criticised both by the Oval crowd and in the press. Pelham Warner in the *Morning Post* wrote: "Bowes bowled with five men on the leg side and sent down several very short-pitched balls, which repeatedly bounced head high and more. Now, that is not bowling; indeed, it is not cricket and if all fast bowlers were to adopt his methods the MCC would be compelled to step in and penalise the bowler who bowled less than halfway up the pitch."

The contrast between Warner as a journalist in the summer of 1932 and his ineffectual role as manager of the bodyline tour of that winter is marked. The field Bowes set for Hobbs was not a true bodyline field, if there were five on the leg side, then allowing for bowler and wicketkeeper, there must have been four on the off; in the bodyline series there were sometimes just one or two fielders on the off side. But for Warner even five men on the leg side is worthy

---

43   From, *Jack Hobbs England's Greatest Cricketer* By Leo McKinstry

of mention, for it to be cricket it seems as if the fielding team should have a majority of fielders on the off side of the wicket. As the LBW law prior to 1935 meant a batsman could not be out to a ball that pitched outside of off stump (even if it hit the batsman on the line of off), the batsman would be able to move across his stumps and play the ball to the leg with little chance of being given out LBW and, if Warner had his way, without the fielding side having more than four fielders in place to stop him.

Warner's article didn't just condemn the field setting but the very act of bowling short – the MCC, of which Warner was a highly influential member, might have to ban it. In this Warner pre-empted the response of the Australian public and Don Bradman himself to bodyline; it wasn't just the bodyline field they objected to, but short-pitched bowling in general. For others, Douglas Jardine springs to mind – CLR James another – playing fast, short bowling was a measure of a batsman's technique and courage, batting was more than just eye allied to technique, the heart would have to be tested. These different perceptions of what was fair play in cricket continued past bodyline, at least to the 1980s and the era of West Indies cricketing dominance, and Warner is not unique in having his view on the legitimacy of short-pitched bowling shaped by who was on the receiving end.

Commentators seem to agree that Bill Bowes wasn't a truly fast bowler, and with his rather gawky appearance and circular, rimless, thick lensed glasses he didn't look like a terroriser of batsmen. His *Wisden* obituary included the line: "There has probably never been a great cricketer who looked less like one than Bowes." Certainly Bowes didn't come in off the fast bowlers traditional long run up, ten paces was enough for somebody who did a lot of bowling in county cricket and would take his hundred first-class wickets in a season on a regular basis. Len Hutton described him as a *"little bit of Bob Willis, and a lot of Richard Hadlee."*[44]

Although he didn't bowl with extreme pace, Bowes used his six feet three inches to great effect and seemed to have a real knack for hitting batsmen. As we have already seen, he had started 1933 by laying out George Headley in the MCC vs West Indies game. Against Glamorgan, in front of an angry crowd, he hit two batsmen and then in early June a bouncer from Bowes had knocked Lancashire's Frank Watson senseless[45]. With this record, the selectors probably believed keeping Bowes out of the side would help prevent the bodyline controversy from flaring up.

For all the batsmen he hit, Bill Bowes was no tearaway fast bowler, he was the product of a close-knit, tough Yorkshire dressing room that, like most successful cricket teams, valued hard work and the application of intelligence. A man coming from this environment didn't just get angry or excited and start bowling short; Bowes' line of attack was a considered response to a batsman who shuffled across his stumps with his bat raised, blocked balls outside of the off stump with his pads and turned straight deliveries to the leg side. The straight, short ball, would disturb this batsman-centric world and, although he didn't use a full

---

44 www.cricketweb.net/bill-bowes-the-elland-express/
45 *It's Not Cricket* By Simon Rae

bodyline field in 1932 or 1933, Bowes was moving towards something rather like bodyline at the same time as Douglas Jardine's equally meticulous preparation for the 1932-1933 ashes series.

As with many fast bowlers, Bowes argued that he never meant to hurt a batsman. This may well have been true, in that when he sent down a bouncer he did not envisage the batsman being hit, but if you are a good fast bowler and bowl at the batsman's head for long enough, you will hit the target eventually. Bowes first found the target bowling for the MCC, a ball from him hitting Indian batsman Wazir Ali in the face. Bowes saw a picture of the aftermath, with him included in a semicircle of MCC players surrounding the stricken Indian, looking concerned. Bowes decided he hadn't meant to cause the injury and therefore it was stupid to look worried. "From then onwards I put on an act. I never said "Sorry" to a batsman whom I had hit, never went to inquire how he was. I tried to keep my face expressionless at all times."[46] They played their cricket tough in Yorkshire.

So tough that it raises the issue of how universal was the amateur ethos of the MCC and the public schools? Bowes and his fellow professionals dominated the northern counties of Yorkshire, Lancashire and Nottinghamshire in contrast to Surrey, Middlesex, Kent and Sussex where there was a higher quotient of amateur cricketers. For men with livings to earn and careers to make, winning was never an optional extra. The difference didn't just apply to first-class cricket: Northern club cricket was characterised by vibrant

---

46 *Express Deliveries* By Bill Bowes

competitive leagues contrasting with the friendlies-only amateur cricket generally played further south.

And it wasn't just on the field of play where things were different up North. In 1933, *The Cricketer* included a description of what could be expected from the crowd at a Whitsun Roses match: "Occasionally partisanship causes discussion, often these discussions are settled in the old-fashioned English manner than which there is no better. It is not unusual to see four or five of these arguments going on at the same time round the ring." Having read a lot of contemporary accounts of 1930s cricket stressing the rural nature and visual delights of the game, this frank and rather approving report of violent affray comes as a shock. Second Slip[47] skilfully conflates chronic violence with old-fashioned English values and makes the whole thing sound rather jolly.

Amateur and professional cricketers had different attitudes and cricket in the North of England was different to cricket in the South. But North and South were not, generally, warring tribes. Like many a northern cricketer, Bowes started out playing in a Sunday school league. Participation in these leagues was dependent on at least spasmodic church attendance. It was probably the case that cricket was the game of the respectable church-attending, chapel-going population; the link to organised religion a counterpart to the importance of the public school, Oxford and Cambridge in amateur cricket.

Although professional cricketers never believed it's not the winning it's the taking part, they generally observed

---

47 The nom de plume of the person writing *The Cricketer* piece.

both the written rules of cricket and the spirit of the game. There is very little documentary evidence of an umpire's decision being disputed in club, league or first-class cricket.[48] Accepting the umpire's decision was more arduous for the professional cricketer than his amateur counterpart. A bad decision might mean being dropped and the loss of match fees and there is anecdotal evidence amateur captains, who filed reports on the umpire's performance, could expect more than the benefit of the doubt when it came to LBW decisions.

Similarly, there was a general acceptance of the unwritten rule that only amateurs could captain a side. Jack Hobbs, whose skill as a batsman and grace as a man made him an almost de facto amateur, was occasionally touted as a potential England captain, but always insisted the captaincy was a job for an amateur. Fellow professionals such as Patsy Hendren at Middlesex were similarly content in the senior pro role, serving under a succession of amateur captains. Harold Larwood didn't share the apparent placidity of Hobbs and Hendren, but although he had plenty of arguments with his county and international amateur captains, he believed, according to his biographer Duncan Hamilton, that "proper" gentlemen, like Douglas Jardine and Arthur Carr were the natural leaders of English cricketing teams.

And not all professional cricketers came from working class backgrounds. Jack Hobbs' father, for instance, worked as a groundsman for Cambridge University, so although

---

48   From Jack Williams *Cricket and England: A Cultural and Social History of Cricket in England Between the Wars (Sport in the Global Society)*

Hobbs wasn't from an upper or middle class background he wasn't really working class either. Bill Bowes was the son of a Goods Super-intendant on the Lancashire and Yorkshire railway and other professional cricketers such as Hedley Verity and Herbert Sutcliffe came from similar, working, but not working class, backgrounds. Cricket often emphasised the vertical links between classes, churchmen and industrialists were included on the Committees of northern league cricket teams[49] whilst at county level aristocrats were often to the fore, Lords Hawke and Harris at Yorkshire and Kent and the Calthorpe family at Warwickshire.

Self-interest was another factor in professional acquiescence to amateur rule. County cricket didn't pay badly; for the better cricketers at the better counties it paid distinctly well. A cricketer who kept his nose clean could hope to add to his earnings with a benefit year, a coaching job in the winter or a post-retirement job coaching in a private school. And in the 1930s, the long dole queue was a disincentive to any discontented cricketer who was thinking of letting rip and telling the Committee what he really thought.

Bill Bowes was a professional, northern cricketer who brought an element of toughness to the way he played cricket that paid homage to a working man's game. Although the MCC had benefitted from a combination of northern competitiveness and Douglas Jardine's disdain in Australia, it was now trying to, subtly, distance itself from

---

49   Jack Williams *Cricket and England: A Cultural and Social History of Cricket in England Between the Wars (Sport in the Global Society)*

bodyline. The team selected to meet the West Indies in the first test included five amateurs and copied the Australia side they had beaten so comfortably in 1932-1933 by picking a bowling attack with three spinners. It's telling that the 1934 edition of *Wisden* referred to the team for the first test being, "Picked, for the most part, on form".

What is remarkable is that even with Larwood and Clark injured, and Bowes and Paynter pushed to the side lines to make way for sound amateur chaps like Allen and Turnbull, the England selectors still assembled a notable side. Indeed using the very crude system of adding up the batting averages for all eleven players and subtracting from that aggregate, the average, average of the four best bowlers, multiplied by eleven, the team had hardly declined from the fifth test of the bodyline series.[50] This was a golden age for English cricket, top professional batsmen such as Hammond and Sutcliffe, fast bowlers in Larwood, Voce, Bowes and Clark; a phalanx of spinners headed by Hedley Verity, Les Ames, a wicketkeeper who averaged over forty when batting and amateurs such as Jardine and Allen who were of test standard.

The next chapter shows how the selection of a West Indian side for the first test of the 1933 series was also based on a combination of cricketing considerations and a desire to reflect West Indian society and its racial divisions. West Indian cricket was less well placed to overcome bias in selection than its English counterpart.

---

50 Averages used are test averages unless a player has fewer than ten tests, in which case first-class average. Comparative averages are England fifth test bodyline 103, England first test WI 100, England first test ashes whitewash 2013-2014 = 50.

Chapter 6

A WAR TO THE KNIFE

In English cricket, class, generally, trumped race. Members of the Indian aristocracy, the ragbag of Maharajahs, Nawabs and Nizams, who exercised nominal control of India's Princely states, were often educated at British public schools and some became cricketers of test match standard. The first and most notable of these was Ranjitsinhji who, in 1896 and after considerable controversy, was selected to play for England against Australia, becoming both a cricketing Englishman (not the last of those) and the first non-white person to play test cricket. Indian princes played for the gentlemen in the annual Gentlemen vs Players game and Ranjitsinhji's nephew Duleepsinhji had been captain of Sussex in 1931-1932. An English professional would have to call the black man sir, or perhaps in this case, your highness.

There were no native princes in the West Indies where the dividing lines of class and race were closely linked. But the amateur versus professional distinction was not used to distinguish between black and white players in the 1933 West Indian team. The scorecard for the first test of 1933 shows all eleven players as amateurs (i.e. initials before the first name), even though George Francis had been plucked from his job as a professional cricketer for Radcliffe in the Bolton league. Francis was classed as an amateur as, like all the other players in the squad, he wasn't paid to play[51].

Amateur status for all meant that West Indian cricketers, regardless of race, would enter the field of play by the same gate and share the same dressing room. But a degree of integration didn't mean equality. Whereas England had to have an amateur captain, the West Indies had to have a white man as captain, and it was Trinidadian Jack Grant who was in charge of the 1933 series, as he had been for the West Indies 1931 tour of Australia. Grant hadn't played for the West Indies when he was first made captain and there were only three players on that tour younger than him. And in 1931, Grant hadn't played a single first-class game of cricket in the West Indies. Grant said subsequently, "It could not be disputed that my white colour was a major factor in my being given this post."[52] As well as the colour of his skin, Grant had another considerable advantage when it came to being selected as captain: he was the brother of Fred Grant, president of the WICBC.

---

51 In 1939 the West Indies did contract three players, but all three continued to be treated as amateurs on English grounds. Similarly, the Australian touring party of 1938 were amateur cricketers, being paid £600 a man; not lavish, but decent money.

52 *Jack Grant's story* page 30

Racial discrimination in selection was not confined to the choice of captain. In the same way England selectors picked two amateurs, West Indian teams would generally include at least one "spare" white cricketer. In the 1933 tour there were six white players in the party, but Freddie Martin was forced out of the series by an injury sustained before the first test match. Of the remaining five, Grant, Teddy Hoad, Cyril Merry and Oscar Da Costa played in the first test; Grant, Hoad, Archie Wiles and Da Costa in the second and Grant, Merry and Da Costa in the third. All of these players were batsmen and their test career batting averages were: Grant twenty-six, Da Costa nineteen, Hoad twelve, Merry nine and Wiles one. By contrast, Ben Sealey, who was black, had to wait for the third test match of the tour to make an appearance. Sealey averaged over thirty-nine in first-class cricket that summer placing him second in the West Indian averages to George Headley and was also a handy bowler. The black player, Derek Sealy, was not selected for the tour, although he was to end his test career with a comparatively robust test batting average of twenty-eight.

Another player not included in the party for the 1933 tour was Jamaican fast bowler, Leslie Hylton. Hylton was twenty-seven years old when the West Indies commenced the 1933 tour of England, and in his bowling prime. He had performed well in the trial game prior to the tour taking 3/30 and 1/45. The West Indian selectors cannot be faulted for taking a chance on Manny Martindale in 1933 but, with Constantine and Francis playing league cricket in England and unavailable, Hylton seemed to be a logical choice as the third fast bowler. Instead, Vincent Valentine also of Jamaica was selected. Valentine's figures in the trial match didn't match those of Hylton and he was ineffectual in the test series taking 1 wicket for 104 runs. The reason for Hylton's non-selection seems to have been an incident in the trial match when the "fiery" Hylton had been so disgusted by an umpire's decision that he had thrown the ball down[53]. Unfortunately for Hylton, the umpire was yet another member of the Grant clan, Leslie, brother of both West Indian Captain Jack and Fred Grant, president of the WICBC.

Leslie Hylton had a different background to other West Indian cricket stars. Whereas Learie Constantine and George Headley had started or been considering careers in law and dentistry respectively before they became professional cricketers, Hylton had left school in his early teens. He had things tough; both his mother and the elder sister who assumed her place died when he was a young boy.[54] In 1933, he started to work in the Kingston docks, an unambiguously working-class occupation.

Leslie Hylton's exclusion could have been an example of how white webs of patronage magnified the minor transgressions of black cricketers and his working-class status may have exacerbated that double standard. After all, if bad behaviour was a bar to selection, Douglas Jardine wouldn't have got as far as the Winchester school first xi. Perhaps there was a fear Hylton would embarrass the West Indies on a tour that would include meeting the King,

---

53 Jeffrey Stollmeyer quoted at page 224 of *Jamaica at the Wicket* by Arnold Bertram

54 http://www.thesundayleader.lk/2012/02/12/the-hanging-cricketer/

and Pelham Warner. Vincent Valentine, also a black man, might have been a more socially acceptable cricketer than Leslie Hylton. Valentine worked as a teacher[55] and in team photos he is often wearing that symbol of the well to do, the cravat.

There were some mitigating factors for the seeming bias in selection: Hoad, despite his lousy test average, was a decent cricketer with a first-class average of over thirty-nine and outside of the test matches he had performed well on the 1928 tour of England, Merry had some success in first-class cricket in 1933. But there was little, if any, cricketing justification for the selection of Wiles for the second test or indeed the tour as a whole; he had an undistinguished first-class record and was over forty by the time the tour started. It is impossible to escape the conclusion that racial bias in West Indian selection did not stop at the captaincy.

That a West Indian team of the 1930s should have a white captain was, for many people, just a fact of life, even some black West Indians accepting it as unfortunate but unalterable. But both Learie Constantine and CLR James were acutely aware of the disparities in selection and determined for change. By the time the West Indian side had arrived in the UK, in April of 1933, James was leaving Nelson for London, a move that was accompanied by a cooling in his relationship with Learie Constantine. The two remained in touch but saw each other infrequently, if at all, before they were reunited in Trinidad in 1958. In his biography of Constantine, Peter Mason attributes this

---

55 The *Cricketer* 1933

to growing political differences between Constantine and James, who joined the Independent Labour Party. Mason also suggests James' "caddish extracurricular activities" might have contributed to the two men drifting apart. James had left his first wife in Trinidad and, by 1934, had commenced a long relationship with Louise Cripps.

However, James' year in Lancashire was an important period for both him and Constantine and had, as a tangible result, the publication in 1933 of Constantine's autobiography, *Cricket and I*. The book was based on a manuscript James brought to Britain from Trinidad and it addressed the issue of race and the selection of West Indian cricket teams.

And Constantine and James also hinted that the racial divisions in West Indian society and the insistence on a white captain were a brake on the development of West Indian cricket.

"Of all test match playing combinations the West Indies team alone is composed of men of different race. Test match cricket today is no sort of game. It is a battle. And to win you need not only the strenuous effort of individual players: the work of each player must be backed by a sense of solidarity, of all the others supporting him, not only actually but so to speak in the spirit. The lack of this is the chief weakness of the West Indian team in big cricket. We have not been able to get together in the sort of spirit which says look – look here, we are going out today against those fellows and it is a war to the knife."

This is a clear challenge to the amateur orthodoxy, the structure of West Indian cricket in the 1930s and the colonial society from which it developed. Firstly, Constantine's depiction of test cricket as a war to the knife, is in keeping with the tactics England used in the 1933 bodyline series, but very different from a view of cricket as a game characterised by fair play. Secondly, by starting the paragraph on the need for solidarity with a reference to the different races playing for the team, Constantine is drawing attention to the racial divisions he believed were hampering West Indian cricket. It is not a big leap to infer it is the white players in the team whom Constantine regards as lacking in solidarity: they have alongside their West Indian identities a second personality, as members of the British Empire. Finally there is a parallel between cricket and the way that West Indian society is run, the people at the top only see themselves as West Indian in a limited sense and cannot govern in the interests of the wider population.

Learie Constantine lived his life intertwined with cricket, a game which originated in England. That did not mean he accepted the superiority of the English amateur. Constantine played all of his professional cricket against white opponents and the fierce on-field competition of men such as Douglas Jardine gave Constantine a firm belief that fair play was certainly no more, and perhaps a little less, developed in the English amateur cricketer than his West Indian opponent.

For all the self-inflicted weaknesses of West Indian cricket, the squad made a decent fist of the matches leading up to the first test. They had played eleven first-class games: winning four, drawing five and losing two. The two defeats were in the first (first class) game on tour and a match against Worcester when both Headley and Martindale were injured. The results were notable given the limited playing resources. To cover a tour starting in April and which involved playing cricket five or six days a week until the middle of September, the West Indies had just fifteen players, a manager and a scorer, but no coach. The tour was so long that Ellis Achong had time to meet, court and marry during his stay in England[56].

The win against the MCC had shown that, despite their limited squad, the West Indies could be a decent side when inspired by the talent of Learie Constantine. The problem was that Constantine was paid £650 (plus various extras) by Lancashire League club Nelson, compared to the thirty shillings a week available to a West Indian tourist. By the standards of the 1930s, £650 for a summer's work was a good income. Simply scaling it up by the retail prices index gives a figure of just over £40,000[57] compared to a modern-day value of £4,800 playing for the West Indies. But this doesn't take into account that the standard of living was generally much lower in the 1930s than today. If a wage rather than a prices index is applied to Constantine's £650 the modern value is roughly £110,000 and, of course, Constantine could also expect to make money in the off season. The poor boy from Trinidad wasn't rich in the way Joe Root is rich, but he was certainly comfortably off. A

---

56   Obituary *The Cricketer* November 1986
57   Httos://measuringworth.com

regular English professional cricketer would probably make less than half of Constantine's earnings.[58]

As test matches started on a Saturday they clashed with Nelson's games. At the start of the season there was an expectation that Constantine would play in only one test match, probably the second at Lancashire's Old Trafford ground.

In March of 1933, William Findlay, secretary of the MCC, wrote to JE Scheult, the Honorary secretary of the WICBC. He was replying to an earlier letter from Scheult informing the MCC of the West Indian players selected for the 1933 tour. Unfortunately, Scheult's letter isn't in the MCC archives, but it was clearly a tale of woe. Findlay is sorry the test trials were not a financial success and disappointed to hear about the "Constantine situation." The overall tone of Findlay's response is rather bland sympathy. However, behind the scenes the MCC did take some measures to try and secure the release of Constantine for the Lord's test match. There is a letter in the MCC archives to JH Warburton, Secretary of the Nelson Club, applying moral pressure on the club to release Constantine: "The MCC Committee appreciate the difficulties which no doubt would confront the Nelson CC if they were to comply with this request, but they do feel that in the interests of cricket generally everything possible should be done to enable the West Indies to place their best side in the field."

---

58 In Alan Hill's book *Les Ames*, he states that a Kent cricketer of the 1930s was on £3 a week, plus an additional match payment of £8 for home games and £12 for away.

Findlay also suggests Kennedy of Hampshire might be a suitable replacement for Constantine. However, when Findlay writes to Freddie Martin on 16th June, commiserating with the West Indian on the injury that forced him out of the tour, he also mentions that Nelson have written to MCC, "and cannot see the way to release Constantine."

The MCC were the supreme body in world cricket in the 1930s. They decided on the rules of the game, and the Imperial Cricket Conference, in charge of test matches, was essentially the MCC under a different name. All this counted for nothing with the NCBC (Nelson Cricket and Bowling Club). They were similarly unmoved when the WICBC made a direct appeal for Constantine's release.

Although Constantine was not available for the first test, the MCC continued to work behind the scenes to secure his availability for the second. There is a letter in the MCC archives sent to Somerset noting Nelson had consented to the release of Constantine for the Old Trafford test and suggesting either Young or Wellard[59] of Somerset might play as a substitute professional in Nelson's match of the 22nd July.

Of course, MCC and the WICBC only used moral persuasion on Nelson. At heart this was a financial issue. Nelson paid Constantine good money and Constantine brought the crowds to the Lancashire League. If the WICBC really wanted Constantine to play in the first test they could have paid him and paid Nelson for the

---

59 Neither did play in the game against Burnley.

revenue they would lose without their star attraction. Prior to the West Indies tour of England in 1939, Martindale, Headley and Constantine were all released from their league contracts and instead signed to play for the West Indies for the summer. This reduced the wage bill of the clubs and gave them time to recruit replacements. In 1933 there was no such organisation and Nelson were being asked to pay the price for a lack of foresight on the part of the WICBC.

Constantine did, as we have seen, play for the West Indies in the game at Lord's against the MCC in May. This clashed with a home fixture for Nelson and Herman Griffith from the West Indies touring party was sent north to play for Nelson. It's not clear what made Nelson prepared to release Constantine for the MCC game and second test, but not the first test match. There might be a clue in the MCC archives where there is correspondence between the WICBC and their three star players, Learie Constantine, Manny Martindale and George Headley, about payments for the 1939 tour of England. Martindale and Headley wanted to secure equality with Constantine and stated they were determined, "To end the advantage in terms against themselves, Constantine had on occasions – which were mentioned – previously enjoyed." So it might have been that Constantine was paid to play in the 1933 MCC game.

As often happens, the bad planning of the WICBC was accompanied by bad luck. The injury to Freddie Martin deprived the West Indies of an experienced batsman for the rest of the tour. Although Martin's test average was only just over twenty-eight, this was better than a lot of the batsmen in the West Indies party and he had scored a test hundred in the 1930-1931 tour of Australia. Without Constantine and Martin, the West Indies team for the first test scored, on the methodology described above, minus fifty-seven, compared to plus one hundred for the England team[60]. Worse still, George Headley injured his ankle prior to the test. He still managed to play but wasn't completely fit. What lay in store for the weakened, patched-up West Indian team?

---

60 If Constantine were available the score would have improved to minus twenty-six.

Chapter 7

EMPIRE

The first day of the first test of the 1933 series, Saturday 24th June, was interrupted by rain. In the little play possible, England reached forty-three for nought and the most noteworthy event was the arrival of King George V who was introduced to the two teams. The Royal visit symbolised test cricket as a colonial game. The rules of the Imperial Cricket Conference restricted test match status to countries within the British Empire and its dominions. Teams competed on the field, but when play stopped, all test cricketers bowed to the king of the United Kingdom and the British Dominions, Emperor of India. The *Cricketer*, which enthusiastically expounded the imperialist philosophy of its proprietor, Pelham Warner, wrote: "The good that is done by these *(i.e. the king's)* visits is incalculable, not only to cricket, but also to the Empire."

The West Indies' bowling on the truncated Saturday was described as poor. Sunday was a day of rest in both the

Bible and 1930s first-class cricket and on Monday the West Indian bowling improved, with Manny Martindale leading the attack.

Martindale had suffered an ankle injury before the first Test but opened the bowling with George Francis and bowled with "good pace". The Lord's pitches of the 1930s were frequently generous to quick bowlers, particularly those bowling from the Pavilion End who could benefit from a ridge on the pitch that, if hit at the correct angle, would send the ball rearing up at the batsman. Martindale got one just right and had Herbert Sutcliffe caught in the gully by Jack Grant, Martindale's first test wicket and a good one to get. But Cyril Walters and Wally Hammond, batting carefully, moved England to the strong position of 103 – 1.

The modern team photograph is a well-choreographed event, both players and the photographer know what is expected of them. In the 1930s, things were more informal, somebody turned up with a camera and the players would line up, some in whites some in street clothes. A photo of the West Indies' 1928 side was taken on the field, presumably immediately before or after a session of play. It is the picture of a team having a hard time of it, some players have their hands in their pockets, others look past the camera as if there has been an incident on the far side of the ground and captain Karl Nunes looks weighed down by the burden of command and an infeasibly large pair of wicketkeeping gloves. One man stands apart, short but powerfully built he has his hands neatly clasped behind his back, his weight evenly balanced with his feet at a military forty-five degrees.

Where others are caught in the moment, he captures the camera in his steady gaze: Herman Griffith.

And now Herman Griffith, at the age of forty was bowling in a test match and troubling a batsman as good as Wally Hammond. Griffith had long ceased to rely on just pace, but was a wily swing bowler and worker-out of batsmen. CLR James, wrote about Griffith: "He was as strong as a horse, he always bowled well within himself, and he would wait for an opening."[61] His *Wisden* obituary described him as: "getting plenty of pace off the pitch and swinging away sharply, he relied greatly on catches in the slips."

And he still had those attributes of control, swing and patience, *The Times* judged him the best of the West Indian bowlers in England's first innings. First he tempted Wally Hammond to edge a catch to George Headley at slip and he quickly snaffled up Maurice Leyland, caught by wicketkeeper Ivan Barrow. Griffith and Martindale of the West Indies had reduced England to 105 – 3.

The West Indian fast bowlers playing in the first test: Martindale, Griffith and Francis, were all from Barbados, an island with a population of less than 200,000. And the two wicket takers, Martindale and Griffith, played for the Empire club based in Bridgetown, Barbados. Griffith didn't only play for Empire, he was a founder member of the club and central to it becoming a significant force in an island that had long had a distinctive and successful cricketing culture.

---

61   *Beyond a Boundary*

Cricket was introduced to Barbados by the white planter elite and the British military, but was quickly embraced by black Barbadians. Games between the all-white clubs, Wanderers and Pickwick, would draw crowds of black spectators and the unique place of cricket in the culture of Barbados was established by the end of the nineteenth century. Some estimates of crowds at a Pickwick Wanderers game are in the region of 8,000/10,000[62]. Even if the true figure was half of the estimate it is still remarkable for an island with a population of only 150,000.

In the first half of the twentieth century, Barbados was rigidly divided by race and class, but the Island's education system had a degree of integration with Harrison school admitting pupils from the black upper middle classes. For this group it was a relatively simple matter to transition from school cricket to club cricket with the largely black Spartan club taking part in the Barbados Cricket Challenge Cup and playing against white teams from the late nineteenth century onwards. But for poorer black cricketers there was no such opportunity. When in 1899 Spartan extended membership to the fast bowler Delmont Hinds (Fitz Lily) who had previously worked as a groundsman[63], players at other clubs refused to play them. After 1899 and the Hinds affair, the rules of the Barbados Cricket Challenge Cup banned professionals[64]. As no one in Barbados made any money from playing cricket, the

---

62   See Keith Sandiford *Cricket Nurseries of Colonial Barbados.*
63   Clem Seecharan in *Muscular Learning: Cricket and Education in the Making of the British West Indies at the End of the 19th Century* identifies him as an apprentice housepainter at the time he joined Spartan.
64   *Cricket Nurseries of Colonial Barbados.*

professional tag was a euphemism: it excluded from organised cricket anyone who had at any time worked as a groundsman at a cricket club and was regarded as too common, too black to play the game with gentlemen. The English class-based distinction between gentlemen and players had been reinvented in Barbados as a barrier to racial integration in cricket. Right up to the 1930s, professional (generally black) cricketers were banned from inter-island competition.

In 1913, Herman Griffith, whom we have seen twenty years later playing in the first test match of 1933, applied for membership of the Spartan club. Perhaps mindful of the reception afforded to the unfortunate Hinds, the club rejected him. The rejection of Griffith by the Spartan membership has been described as being based on skin colour, but colour was seemingly not the only, or even the main reason for his exclusion. The brochure produced for the seventy-fifth year anniversary of the Empire Club describes the Spartan club's recruitment policy as follows: "Spartan Club ... Admitted some men who were unmistakably black as opposed to those euphemistically described as coloured. In the main, however, the yardstick for measuring acceptability was the respectability of one's occupation and the care one took to the forthrightness which could be interpreted as disrespect." Although there is sadly no biography of Griffith, there seems to be little doubt that he did not lack forthrightness. In *Beyond a Boundary*, CLR James described him as follows: "Griffith had a secondary education, called nobody mister except the captain, and had the reputation of being ready to call anybody anything which seemed to him to apply." And although Griffith received a private education, he came from a less prosperous background than many of the Spartan club members. He was educated at Combermere, a second-grade school[65] more racially mixed than Harrison and went on to work as a hospital orderly and then as a sanitary engineer.

Whatever the reason, the decision to exclude Griffith was lacking in human sympathy and inevitably distressing to a section of the Spartan membership; they must have felt worse still when they considered the club was giving up on the chance to acquire a fast bowler who would take wickets and put the fear of God into the opposition. Griffiths and the other dissenters met on the 24th May 1914, Empire day, and founded their own club. From the start, Empire was a club run by and for its membership who were mostly from what could be loosely described as the black middle and lower-middle classes. The club's seventy-five-year anniversary brochure notes that John Beckles, contesting a seat on the St Michael's vestry, included in his manifesto the promise of funding for the Empire club. This call was taken up by his opponent for the seat. So, the shock of Empire's formation rippled into Barbadian politics. The club made swift progress: acquiring the land for a ground, hiring a groundsman and producing a pitch. By 1916, Empire was admitted to the Barbados Cricket Challenge Cup and lower-middle-class black men could, on the cricket field, participate in the wider life of the island – a contrast with the racial segregation of the social and business worlds.

---

65   See page 106 of *Cricket Nurseries of Colonial Barbados: The Elite Schools, 1865-1966*. Keith A. P. Sandiford.

It seems Griffith brought an abrasiveness to the sports field. In *50 Great West Indian Cricketers,* HM Dalrymple says Griffith would: "Barrack batsmen and fielders alike," which seems a long way from the amateur ideal, but not perhaps so different from the cricket played in the Lancashire leagues. As a founding member, captain and, on his retirement from playing, the club's second president, the Empire club was dominated by Griffith's fiercely competitive spirit and no game was more fiercely fought than matches between Empire and the Spartan club.

The rift between Spartan and Empire ran along social fault-lines; so strong was the animosity between the two clubs that one Empire player described the fixtures as a war[66]. Spartan not only refused Griffith membership, but had also attempted to smother Empire at birth, voting against Empire being admitted to the Barbados Cricket Challenge Cup. Spartan's no vote was supported by the Pickwick club and Empire's entry to the competition was only secured thanks to the vote of the establishment Wanderers club, Harrison school and the chairman's casting vote[67].

Spartan versus Empire wasn't only a big deal for the players of the two clubs; club cricket in Barbados was a spectator sport. Empire players, who lived and worked alongside their supporters, would often be stopped in the street prior to a Spartan game and told how important it was they should win. Thousands would crowd into Empire's compact Bankside ground to watch matches played on

---

66   Horace King interview.
67   Empire club seventy-five-year anniversary publication, as before.

consecutive Saturdays. Of course, playing standards were higher in a test match than in a Spartan versus Empire game, but cricketers like Griffith and Martindale were well used to the pressures of playing as representatives of a community, long before they played international cricket.

Griffith personified progress in Barbados cricket. In 1913, he had been effectively excluded from top level club cricket on the island. He went away and, along with the other founding members, established a club that by 1916 was playing in the Barbados Cricket Challenge Cup. By 1921, Griffith was playing for Barbados in the Inter-Colonial Tournament. He was controversially omitted from the 1923 West Indies tour to England, but was selected for the West Indies' first test tour in 1928. Griffith had to borrow money to support his family whilst he was in England. In 1932 Empire won the Barbados Challenge Cup and in 1941 the forty-eight-year-old Griffith captained Barbados in a first-class match against Trinidad. Captaincy marked twenty-five years of increasing integration in cricket in Barbados.

But, at the same time, Empire's existence exemplified a Barbadian society that was essentially conservative. Combermere, the school Griffith attended, mimicked the institutions of a British public school, albeit in more modest surroundings. The school's headmasters prior to World War II were white men who had been educated at either Harrison College or The Lodge, the two elite schools in Barbados. Combermere played an important role in developing cricket in Barbados but was also a conduit for the trickle down of British attitudes. Similarly, although Empire was a self-administered club, it played cricket in a competition run by the island's establishment based around the Wanderers and Pickwick clubs. Members of the Empire club were equal on the cricket field but played no part in the Barbados Cricket Association.

The existence of the Empire club might challenge some views of what cricket in Barbados was about, but did not challenge the primacy of Britain in the life of the island[68]. The very name Empire was an indication of this; in case the point was missed, the club colours were red, white and blue and the union flag was raised whenever Empire played at home[69]. At this time and distance it is difficult to be sure of the exact meaning of Empire's British regalia, it may have been a realisation that wrapping the club in the flag made Empire less challenging to the liberal elements in the Barbados cricket establishment. Or perhaps it was down to a seam of Anglo centrism that ran through some sections of Barbados' society.

The idea that it's the taking part that matters wasn't part of either Griffith's or Empire's ethos but the club enthusiastically insisted on the respectability of its members. An Empire cricket club member who played for the first team in the 1940s and 1950s and dropped down to the intermediate side in the 1960s described his role in the junior team: "We brought them *(the younger players)* along as to how they should behave, the way they should dress. The way they should accept the crowd; the way they should

---

68 Although attaching nationalities to qualities and attitudes seems odd to me it is prevalent in some academic studies of colonial societies.

69 From the Empire 75th anniversary brochure.

accept senior people at other clubs."[70] Griffith in his role as club secretary "would bring down the hammer" if fees weren't paid, going through team sheets and putting a line through the names of defaulters.

HM Dalrymple in his book *50 Great West Indian Cricketers* suggests Griffith's exclusion from the 1923 tour of England was because he was suspected of communist sympathies. This may be true, but it seems unlikely Griffith was a communist. Indeed, it may be the case that at some point Griffith was enrolled in the militia, possibly during the unrest prevalent in Barbados from 1935-1937.[71]

By joining the league run by the Barbados Cricket Association, Empire accepted the Association's rules including the ban on professional cricketers. As professionalism equated with being employed as a groundsman and being a groundsman was the obvious route for a manual labourer to be involved in cricket, Empire accepted a certain group of black men would not be eligible to play for the club. Similarly, Griffith's insistence on membership fees being paid and the need to dress properly (i.e. play in cricket whites) imposed financial constraints on those wanting to play for Empire. There is also some evidence that players wanting to join Empire were turned down on the basis of their having insufficient status for the club[72]. However, the club's 75th anniversary brochure regards the Empire Club as a conduit

---

70 Author's interview with Horace King.
71 As for 66. Also, Tony Cozier has Griffith in the militia from when he left school in 1909.
72 Comments in *Cricket Social Formation and Cultural Continuity in Barbados: A Preliminary Ethnohistory* By Brian Stoddart.

for players who had started out in the lower status Barbados Cricket League to play in Barbados Cricket Association matches and a member of the club who played in the 1940s recalls some good players were effectively sponsored with benefactors paying their membership subscriptions and providing kit and equipment.

And although Empire may have accepted certain elements of colonialism, the club stood out in an undemocratic Barbados: Empire played against and often defeated establishment clubs and its integration into society was a two-way process. The club's black, lower-middle-class players were accepted as equals, not only on the cricket field, but also in the reciprocal hospitality that accompanied cricket matches in Barbados. The opposition of the Pickwick and Spartan clubs to Empire's existence showed significant elements of the Barbados establishment were hostile to these developments.

The admission of Empire to the Barbados Cricket Cup meant the game had a similar structure to cricket on other West Indian islands. That structure was segregated, with clubs defined by skin colour. Middle class, African, Indian and Chinese boys might go to schools such as Queens Royal College, Harrison and Combermere, but once they left they would graduate to the appropriate club for "their" race. But cricket was also, in a sense, integrated, as those teams would play against each other.

Racial segregation wasn't just a simple matter of black and white, there were also divisions of class within racial groups and these class differences might be accompanied by colour distinctions. In his book *Beyond a Boundary*, CLR

James catalogues how the cricket teams of Trinidad reflected the island's overlapping divisions with Queens Park, the dominant force in Trinidadian cricket, having only white members; Maple being the club for upper-middle-class non-whites, who generally had light skin colours[73]; Shannon was the club for lower-middle-class black men including Lebrun and Learie Constantine; and Stingo, "the club of the proletarian".

In a famous passage in *Beyond a Boundary*, James explains the significance of the successful Shannon club. "As clearly as it was written across the sky, their play said: Here on the cricket field as nowhere else, all men in the island are equal, and we are the best men in the island."

What applied to Shannon in Trinidad must have gone double for Empire in Barbados where racial discrimination was more pressing.

Although there were parallels in the structure of cricket in Trinidad and Barbados there were also important differences. There were two white-only clubs on Barbados, with Wanderers being for the upper echelons of the British establishment and the most prosperous Barbadians, and Pickwick for tradesmen and more junior civil servants. There was also no equivalent of Stingo in Barbados and opportunities for poor black men to play top level cricket were very limited prior to the introduction of the Barbados Cricket League in 1936[74]. George Francis, who opened the bowling with Manny Martindale in this first test match of

---

73 Although the dark-skinned James played his cricket at Maple.
74 Although even then the League had a lower playing status than the Barbados Cricket Association.

1933 and who had been one of the few successes of the West Indies 1928 tour, was excluded from the Barbados Challenge Cup and inter-colonial cricket as he was a groundsman and considered to be a professional.

Both Griffith and Francis were born in the nineteenth century[75], but represented two different models for the participation of black cricketers in a mixed-race West Indian team. Francis was talent-spotted by West Indian captain Harold (HBG) Austin. The selection shows Austin to have been an astute judge, but patronage was unlikely to be a consistently successful basis of selection. Griffith represented a different model, he played his cricket for a club run by its black membership competing in the top level cricket competition in Barbados and for the Barbados team. Furthermore, although he was a highly successful and important cricketer, his role as an administrator and founder of Empire was perhaps more important still. Griffith poured his time and energy into the quotidian tasks essential to grass roots cricket, collecting subscriptions, picking teams, making sure there is a pitch to play on. And, of the cricketers profiled in this book, Griffith was the most amateur of all, he had to pay to play cricket and his service to Empire was unremunerated. Griffith died in 1980 and lived to see the early years of West Indian cricketing dominance. He would have been justified in regarding the West Indian triumphs as a tribute to his competitive attitude, hard work and forthrightness.

---

75   Griffith was the elder of the two by four years.

Chapter 8

EMMANUEL ALFRED "MANNY" MARTINDALE

With England at 103-3 and the match in the balance, West Indian captain Jack Grant called on Manny Martindale for another effort.

Walters, on fifty, attempts to drive Martindale through the off side, the ball takes the edge, flies to second slip – who clutches at it but the ball tumbles to the grass. Next ball, Walters again edges a delivery that flies behind the stumps and this time is safely caught by wicketkeeper Ivan Barrow. England are 106-4 and the West Indies are on top.

Martindale was one of the three West Indian stars of 1933. Whilst George Headley and Learie Constantine remain familiar names, Martindale has been swallowed up by time, but he was one in a long line of world beating fast bowlers to come from the West Indies, and in 1933 and 1935 he was as good a quick bowler as there was in world cricket.

In photographs of the 1933 West Indian touring party, the twenty-three year old Manny Martindale is on the back row; next to the batsman CA Merry. At five feet and eight inches tall, Martindale stands shoulder high to the lanky batsman. But, although Martindale was not a tall man, he was still big, a heavyset frame with strong sloping shoulders. In its report on the 1933 tour, *Wisden* comments on how good the weather was; it doesn't seem the West Indian team agreed. They are generally rugged up in team photographs, with Martindale wearing a thick long-sleeved sweater. This might be the cause of what looks like a little excess weight around the middle or perhaps Martindale wasn't worried about a few extra pounds at the start of a tour where, in first-class cricket, he was to bowl 668 overs (almost three times the overs a county pace bowler now bowls in a first-class English summer and perhaps double the total workload taking one day matches into account) and take 103 wickets at just under twenty-one runs per wicket. In test matches he took fourteen wickets at an average of under eighteen.

It's not a surprise a relatively short man was able to bowl both quickly and effectively. Martindale was about the same height as Harold Larwood and Malcolm Marshall; in overall build and perhaps playing style Waquar Younis[76] might be a better comparison. RES Wyatt's biography includes a description of Wyatt in 1930: "Struck by a very fast ball from Martindale. Swinging in late as he played forward it landed full toss on the top of his foot breaking a bone." It wasn't the last time Wyatt was to have trouble with Martindale.

Bowlers with Martindale's physical strength often have perfunctory run ups, wrenching speed from their delivery, but with Martindale the power, obvious in his shoulders, was matched by long legs and a rhythmical, athletic approach to the wicket. Michael Manley described Martindale's run up providing "The impression of an express train. Everything seems to focus around an axis which provides the straight track for the smooth accelerating approach to the wicket[77]." The *Cricketer* said that Martindale included "a fashionable West Indian jump in the middle of his run up," and the *Morning Post* described: "A delightful action delivering the ball with an ease that gives no suggestion to the power behind it." This was perhaps a factor in Martindale remaining uninjured for pretty much the entire season and to be going strong in September, taking 8/141 against Leveson Gower's xi at Scarborough in the final match of the tour.

Martindale was a skilful bowler rather than a pure speedster. Reports on the summer of 1933 refer to his moving the ball away from the right hander but in the West Indies in 1935 he seemed to have predominantly moved the ball the other way. At times Martindale was ferociously

---

76   Although Waquar was six feet tall.
77   From *A history of West Indies Cricket* by Michael Manley

quick; *The Times* in May of 1933 dubbed him, only half in jest, the black Larwood, but on other occasions journalists reckoned Learie Constantine was faster. Martindale altered his approach depending on the state of the match and the pitch.

Although this was Martindale's first tour, he quickly established himself as a bowler of distinction. Before the first test, Martindale played nine first-class games in England and cut a swathe through English county batting, taking thirty-nine wickets at an average of just over twenty. Due to the paucity of first-class cricket in the West Indies, selectors sometimes had to base selection on hunch as much as hard evidence. Martindale was a hunch that paid off.

Manny Martindale was born on the 25th November 1909 in the parish of St Lucy, Barbados, although the family home was Selay Hall, in the parish of St. John, located in the south-eastern corner of the island[78]. Martindale was the child of William A. Martindale, a Shipwright, and Elvira Bishop, a Domestic Servant. Conditions in post-slavery Barbados were hard, but Martindale's family certainly wasn't at the bottom of the pile. They managed to raise enough money to send their son, Manny, to Combermere School, perhaps with assistance from a church scholarship. Unlike Learie Constantine, there was no history of cricket in the Martindale family, but Combermere was an institution that, along with the Empire club, played a central role in the development of cricket in Barbados and the West Indies.

---

78 This and other details come from Manny Martindale's grandson, Roger Martindale.

By 2017 the school had educated seventeen West Indian cricketers, including Frank Worrell, Clyde Walcott and Wes Hall.[79] Combermere's British-based curriculum with its emphasis on games was well established by the 1920s and the school competed in the second division of the Barbados Cricket Challenge Cup.[80] This gave Martindale the chance to play cricket, at a good standard, against men[81].

As a former Combermere pupil it was pre-destined that Martindale would go on to play for Empire and open the bowling with club captain, and Combermere alumnus, Herman Griffith. The Empire pitch, famously quick, was polished to a sheen by the club's groundsman and in 1932 the combination of the skilled, combative Griffith, the young pacey Martindale and those fast pitches won the club their first Barbados Cricket Challenge Cup. Griffith's influence on Martindale wasn't confined to the cricket field; like Griffith, Martindale was a Sanitary Inspector. It was a popular job for Empire players in the 1930s and Griffith was, presumably, pulling strings.

Some of Griffith's strong personality may well have rubbed off on the young Martindale. The MCC archive includes correspondence on payments to be made to Martindale, George Headley and Learie Constantine for the 1939 tour of England. It seems Martindale was representing

---

79 http://www.espncricinfo.com/magazine/content/story/868811.html; Rhianna also went to the school.

80 As per *Cricket Colonial Nurseries of Barbados* by Keith AP Sandiford, page 106.

81 The school was promoted to the first division in 1929-1930, by which time Martindale had left.

both himself and George Headley in negotiations with Richard Mallett, who was the WICBC representative in the UK. The negotiations were a three-sided process, being a struggle between the WICBC and the three black cricketers, and also pitting Martindale and Headley, who wanted equal pay for all three players, against Learie Constantine who was touchy about retaining his position as "senior pro". In his correspondence with Mallett, Constantine uses a jocular style, and at one point sends Mallett a signed copy of *Cricket and I*, his autobiography.

Martindale is much more straightforward: "My remuneration in a league season exceeds by a big margin whatever I shall receive for playing with the West Indies, with much less cricket. Therefore, considering all of the aforementioned circumstances, I feel I am doing West Indies cricket a great favour in deciding to play on tour, for which I must be paid £600 plus expenses." Martindale seems to have been like Griffith, a forthright man. He was also a pretty good shop steward. Constantine, Martindale and Headley all got their £600, plus expenses, plus an additional £50 as a kit allowance[82].

Martindale was able to use his success as a cricketer in the 1933 and 1935 series as a pathway to a better life. In 1936 he joined Learie Constantine and George Francis in Lancashire league cricket, although he was seemingly reticent about making the move to the UK. Martindale had first been offered the chance to play in the northern leagues

---

82 In actuality, Martindale and Headley initially had the better deal; the £50 kit allowance was extended to Constantine to prevent on tour ructions.

whilst touring England in 1933. But he had married Gillan Hunte of Church village Barbados in July 1932 and a move to the UK may have been a step too far for the newly married couple. The *Gleaner* reported in 1935 that Martindale was considering taking a job in Trinidad, but eventually the financial rewards of the Lancashire League won out and he signed a contract to play for Burnley. Martindale's *Wisden* obituary reports that his long stint in league cricket: "earned much popularity and respect, both on and off the field". He was a highly successful professional for Burnley, in one 1937 game against Learie Constantine's Nelson, Martindale bowled seventeen overs, took the first six wickets to fall (Constantine caught and bowled Martindale for nine) and then buckled on his pads to open the batting, score a fifty and take his team, most of the way, to their eventual victory.

Martindale made his final test appearances in 1939 but was not able to repeat the performances of 1933 and 1935. Perhaps he was hampered by the long gap between the final test in March 1935 and the series in the English summer of 1939. Like Constantine, Martindale remained in England during the second world war playing in numerous charity games. After the war he continued to play and coach in the Lancashire leagues and at his Burnley home, No. 4 Constable Avenue, playing host to visiting West Indian cricketers Seymour Nurse, Wes Hall and Charlie Griffith. The Martindales had six children: four girls, Norma, Carol, Yvonne and Pamela and two boys, Alfred and Colin.

In his 2008 biography of Learie Constantine, Peter Mason records a "vituperative correspondence" between Constantine and Martindale after their pay negotiations with the WICBC for the 1939 tour. Clearly relations improved subsequently because Martindale worked for a short stint with Learie Constantine in the managing of a hostel in Bolton, before working as a supervisor at Lucas' Electrical in Lancashire.

The Martindales returned to Barbados in 1964 and were joined by their daughter in 1966. Martindale's grandson, Roger Martindale, lived with his grandfather in Barbados and vividly remembers his grandfather taking him to the Merrivale Preparatory School, located at Pine Road, Belleville, St. Michael. Roger describes his grandparents as being "inseparable" and "living for each other and their six children." Martindale guided his children and grandchildren away from thinking of cricket as a career. He believed success in cricket was too dependent on the whims and fancies of selectors, regarding education as a more certain route to success. His descendants absorbed the message and his children were employed respectively as a secretary, teachers[83], a health educator, a solicitor and a professor. The grandchildren of Manny Martindale are active in a variety of professions in the UK, the USA and Barbados. There is, however, one famous sporting descendent, Leah Stancil (née Martindale), Manny Martindale's granddaughter. Sixty-six years after Manny played for the West Indies in the second test at Old Trafford, she came fifth in the women's fifty metre freestyle swimming at the 1996 Summer Olympics.

After his return to the Caribbean, Martindale was awarded a two-year contract as a cricket coach in Bermuda

---

83   Carol and Yvonne

and subsequently became manager of the newly built Barbados National Stadium. Gillan Martindale died in December 1971 and, after his wife's death, Manny Martindale's own health began to fail. He died on the 17th March 1972, aged 62.

Like most famous cricketers, Emmanuel Martindale lives on in his statistics: thirty-seven test match wickets at 21.72. But the success of the Martindale family shows how cricketing success was a way forward for West Indians to make a positive impression on society and a place in the world.

England are 106-4 but, with Griffith and Martindale rested, the West Indian support bowlers need to keep the pressure on. Ellis Achong bowls well on a pitch already taking spin and wrinkles out, Douglas Jardine and Maurice Turnbull to leave England on 155-6. Gubby Allen joins Les Ames and England are up against it. Ames comes down the pitch to Achong; the ball grips, turns and passes the edge of the bat with Ames out of his ground. But Ivan Barrow can't gather and the chance is missed. It is a vital moment. Griffith comes back to bowl, but Ames is cautious, letting deliveries pass outside the off stump; much muttering in the crowd. Allen is run out by Jack Grant for sixteen, with England on 194-7 and with the new ball due at 200 runs the West Indies are still well placed. But Ames changes his approach, now going for his shots and puts on partnerships of twenty-three with Walter Robbins forty-eight with Hedley Verity and thirty-one for the last wicket with George Macaulay, the number eleven batsman contributing just nine. Macaulay and Ames walk back to the pavilion with England all out for 296, Ames eighty-three not out.

England had nearly doubled the score they had reached for five wickets down. Although Les Ames was a technically accomplished and reliable wicketkeeper, it was generally accepted George Duckworth of Lancashire was his superior in that discipline. But Ames averaged forty as a batsman in test match cricket and was invariably chosen to play for England ahead of Duckworth. Behind Ames in the batting order came Allen with a batting average of twenty-four, Hedley Verity who averaged twenty-one and George Macaulay who averaged nineteen.

Martindale took the wickets of Robins and Macaulay to end with figures of 4-85 and establish himself as a test match bowler. The lack of wicket-taking bowlers other than Martindale was already becoming apparent, but the West Indies had shown they could compete against a strong England side.

Chapter 9

LIBERAL IMPERIALISTS

The success of Herman Griffith and Manny Martindale was not only due to the efforts of black cricketers and administrators. Of necessity, black cricket clubs and players had to interact with white cricketing elites. This sometimes had a negative impact, particularly in Barbados where racial divisions were more marked than on neighbouring Trinidad. But the impact of cricket's establishment on multi-racial cricket was, on occasion, distinctly positive. This chapter looks at three individuals who had a significant role in the establishment of West Indian cricket, Barbadian and West Indian captain Harold Austin, English administrator Richard Mallett and Pelham Warner, who we last saw in tears during the 1932-1933 bodyline tour.

The Warner's family colonial history goes back to the seventeenth century when Thomas Warner settled on St Kitts and amassed great wealth via the suppression of the native Caribs and subsequent repopulation of the island with African slaves.[84] [85] Warner's descendants remained a prominent plantation-running, slave-owning family, across a variety of Caribbean islands. The end of slavery in the British Empire in 1833 was no disaster for the Warners – slave owners were compensated for their "loss" and the family moved seamlessly into colonial administration with both Warner's father and brother being Attorney General of Trinidad.

Warner was educated at Harrison college in Barbados, Rugby school in the English midlands and finally at Oriel college Oxford. He was called to the bar in 1896 but realised he lacked the commitment to make a good living from the law. Money was important as Warner had upper class expectations but, as the youngest of sixteen children, distinctly limited means. But fortunately a position was opening up for a young man with: good cricketing skills, personal charm and links to the cricketing establishment in England and the West Indies. To understand why, we need to travel to Birmingham.

The annual banquet of the Birmingham Jewellers and Silversmiths Association. The members have eaten well; the gas lit hall fills with cigar smoke and the rise and fall of postprandial conversation. Two sharp raps on the table brings conversation to a halt and the guest speaker rises. The

84   http://en.wikipedsuria.org/wiki/Thomas_Warner_%28explorer%29
85   http://www.bbc.co.uk/dorset/content/articles/2007/03/07/slavery_warner_feature.shtml

fifty-eight-year-old politician cuts a spry, slightly dandified figure, but no one can have felt more at home than Joseph Chamberlain in front of a Birmingham audience in January 1895.

Although born and raised in London, Chamberlain made his financial and political fortunes in Birmingham. As Mayor, Chamberlain had organised the civic buyout of inefficient private suppliers of gas and water, improved sanitation and transformed Birmingham with new developments, art galleries and a council house.

When Chamberlain entered national politics, the "Birmingham Caucus", an alliance of small capitalists and skilled workers, was his base within the National Liberal Federation. Chamberlain was an avowedly middle-class politician but differed from his liberal predecessors in recognising British business required the assistance of government to meet foreign competition. It was no longer enough to concentrate on getting the state out of the way of business. And the pacifism of old-style radicals like John Bright was anathema to Chamberlain who shared the patriotism of his Birmingham constituents.

Chamberlain's nationalism had led to him pulling apart the Liberal party in a misguided attempt to prevent Home Rule for Ireland in 1885. Now, ten years later, the Liberal Unionists had entered a Liberal Conservative coalition without any noticeable damage to Chamberlain's Birmingham support.

However, some in the audience wonder what their man is doing. On entering the coalition, Chamberlain could have had any job of his choosing with the exception of Prime Minister and Foreign Secretary. But instead of one of the great offices of state, Chamberlain has decided to be Colonial Secretary – a bit of a comedown for the former mayor of the nineteenth century's capital city. Chamberlain, though, has the pure politician's instinct for power; Colonial Secretary gives him responsibility for governing 450 million people and the scope to run British foreign policy free of foreign office civil servants. Now Chamberlain explains his vision for the British Empire:

> "It is not enough to occupy great spaces of the world's surface unless you can make the best of them. It is the duty of a landlord to develop his estate."[86]

Chamberlain is speaking to two audiences at once. Assuring his supporters in the hall he intends to have a leading role in world affairs. But by referring to a landowner and his estate he is also speaking to the Conservative party, the economic interests of landowners made political flesh. Chamberlain is appointing himself the spokesman of a new imperialism.

---

86   http://en.wikipedia.org/wiki/Joseph_Chamberlain

The emergence of the doctrine of imperialism in the late nineteenth century appealed to the British upper classes. It was men educated at public schools, who governed the Empire as administrators and expanded it as soldiers. Imperialism stressed the economic importance of empire and concurrently elevated the maintenance and expansion of Empire to a moral act.

Although amateurism preceded the flowering of imperialism it too was an element of a world view formed in the public schools and, like imperialism, it was an uneasy mix of morality, expediency and a raft of unjustified assumptions about the superiority of the British upper classes.

The new imperialism had its counterpart in the expansion of cricketing contacts between English touring sides and cricket in the colonies and dominions. Lord Hawke of Yorkshire county cricket club and the MCC was at the forefront of this expansion touring India and Ceylon in 1889-1890 and again in 1892-1893; America in 1891 and 1894 and South Africa in 1895-1896. In 1895 South Africa was in tumult following the Jameson raid; a British sponsored attack on the Transvaal Republic. The touring party travelled to a tense Johannesburg and Hawke made his affiliations clear by dining with British nationals imprisoned by the Boer authorities[87].

The West Indies were generally considered amongst Britain's least important colonial possessions, but events in the 1890s brought the islands to Chamberlain's attention. The sugar trade was in sharp decline, tax revenues fell and

---

87 See *Sport, Cultures, and Identities in South Africa* by John Nauright.

the administrations of the various Caribbean islands faced bankruptcy. To decide how the West Indian portion of the British "estate" could best be managed, Chamberlain sent a Royal Commission to the West Indies in 1896.

Lord Hawke organised tours to the West Indies in 1894-1895[88] and 1896-1897 that bookended the Royal Commission and were a conscious attempt to augment the political and economic program of the new imperialism. The stated aims of the 1894-1895 tour were not only to play cricket but also to identify how the West Indies could best be developed as a tourist destination, reducing the dependence on sugar[89]. This sporting imperialism wasn't just an adjunct of economics; cricket, by emphasising and enhancing the common cultural inheritance of the British Empire, gave additional depth and substance to imperialism. In cricket, as in politics, conservatism at home was accompanied by an ambitious foreign policy.

Warner was a natural choice for the second of Hawke's West Indian tours. He had grown up in the West Indies, played cricket at Oxford and, via his mother, had links to cricket administrator Lord Harris. But there was a problem. Warner might have had the "breeding" and the cricket to go on the tour, but he didn't have the money. It was arranged he would submit reports to the *Sportsman* and *Wisden*, providing Warner with the dual cricketing role he was to fill for the rest of his life, participating as an amateur player and administrator whilst also being a cricket journalist for

---

88   Hawke eventually didn't make the tour of 1894-1895 and its was led by R Slade Lucas.

89   *Jamaica at the Wicket*, Arnold Bertram.

hire. In his biography, *Plum Warner*, Gerald Howat suggests Hawke might have provided Warner with some additional finance for the tour over and above Warner's earnings as a journalist. You might wonder whether that meant Warner should have been classed as a professional rather than an amateur, but it seems things didn't work that way.

Over the course of the tour, Warner struck up a valuable rapport with Hawke and, given the pre-existing relationship between the Warner family and Lord Harris, Warner now had links to the two most important figures in the late nineteenth century cricketing establishment. The two cricketing Lords had their respective fiefdoms in Yorkshire and Kent but were also influential figures within the MCC. In domestic matters both were cricketing conservatives.[90] The amateur vs professional distinction remained axiomatic and much of the correspondence of the MCC in the 1920s and 1930s concerns the arcane residency qualification that effectively stopped players moving between counties and limited the bargaining power of professional cricketers.

There were close links between the conservative cricketing establishment and the Conservative Party. Harris held positions in a variety of Conservative administrations as well as being Governor of Bengal, and Viscount Hailsham, president of the MCC at the height of the bodyline controversy, was a senior Conservative politician.[91] HDG Leveson-Gower, who toured the Caribbean alongside Warner

---

90   Cricket retained that Victorian flavour on into the 1960s
91   Alec Douglas Home, the only British prime minister to play first-class cricket, was on the Warner-led tour of Argentina in 1926-1927. He too became MCC president, but not until 1966.

in 1896-1897, was another aristocrat who went on to play an important role in cricket administration. The Leveson-Gowers were old school Whig grandees, but their strand of liberalism was subsumed by the Conservative Party and FNS Leveson-Gower was a minor figure in Chamberlain's Liberal Unionists who formally merged with the Conservatives in 1912[92]. As we have seen, Stanley Jackson was another cricketer who went on to be a Conservative politician and, like Harris, Governor of Bengal.

National politics in the first half of the twentieth century saw the rise of men (always men) from varied backgrounds. David Lloyd George, Ramsay MacDonald and the Conservative Prime Minister Andrew Bonar Law were, in many respects, more heterogeneous than their twenty-first century equivalents. But cricket's leading administrators continued to be drawn from an upper-class, tight-knit social group, and were, by nature, both conservative and Conservative. However, the development of political imperialism and its cricketing offshoot at the end of the nineteenth century showed conservatism did not equate to parochialism.

Warner had an instinctive identification with Hawke's cricketing project. By virtue of family background and education he was conservative. He had an emotional

---

92 In *The MCC Society and Empire* by James Bradley there is an analysis of presidents of the MCC by political affiliation for 1860-1914. For the period as a whole, 57% were Conservatives and 37% liberals, but after the split in the Liberal party of 1885 nearly all were Conservatives; perhaps an indication that the MCC's political centre of gravity was the liberal unionist tradition within the Conservative party.

attachment to the British Empire and was an enthusiastic Imperialist. His childhood experiences gave him a positive view of the West Indies' black population, a desire to see them perform well in world cricket and the knowledge they had the talent to do so.

The tour of 1894-1895 organised by Hawke but led by R Slade Lucas[93] had already provided an example of the practical importance to West Indies cricket of visits from British teams. Slade Lucas had met members of a recently formed team of black cricketers, the Jamaica Cricket Club, and provided them with some cricket kit. As a thank you for the gift, Jamaica Cricket Club changed its name to Lucas. Lucas went on to be one of the most successful and influential cricket clubs in Jamaica.[94] [95]

Hawke's tour of 1896-1897 emphasised the importance of black West Indian cricketers in improving playing standards[96]. Both British Guiana and Barbados picked all-white island sides to play against the tourists and Hawke's side remained undefeated against both. But in Trinidad, where racial prejudice was not so stark, the island team, captained by Aucher Warner, included five black players, amongst them Lebrun Constantine, father of Learie, and four exiles from Barbados, including star bowlers, Joseph "Float" Woods and Archie Cumberbatch. By the standards

---

93   Hawke having pulled out with illness.

94   *Jamaica at the Wicket* page 109.

95   George Headley, Frank Worrell and Chris Gayle have all played for the club.

96   Chapter five of Clem Seecharan's *Muscular* Learning covers this point in more depth.

of the Caribbean, Cumberbatch was a professional, being groundsman at the Queens Park Club. The multi-racial Trinidad team won both its matches against Lord Hawke's side with Woods and Cumberbatch taking thirty-seven of the forty wickets to fall, with two run-outs and one wicket for another exile from Barbados, Stephen Rudder.

As a journalist, Warner had a pulpit for the propagation of West Indian cricket and he lobbied for multi-racial sides. In his final article on the tour for the *Sportsman* he wrote:

> "The future of West Indian cricket is a good prospect, with an excellent climate and good grounds. The visit of a West Indian team to England is by no means improbable. Four or five natives should be included and the side would prove a good attraction."

Hawke's tour of 1896-1897 had clashed with another tour to the West Indies led by AA Priestley. With the MCC disinclined to become involved in cricket outside of the UK, Hawke used the sporting committee of the West India Club in London as an organising body to avoid similar duplication and, on his return from the West Indies, Warner acted as Hawke's aide de camp on the committee. His first task was to organise a visit to England by a team representing all of the British-ruled Caribbean islands. Warner, and more importantly Hawke, were both keen the team should include black and white players if it was to prove equal to playing English teams in English conditions and that the party should include the "professionals" excluded from top level cricket in the Caribbean. Warner's advocacy of multi-racial cricket was important. He could speak as a West Indian who also had a place in English society with the additional kudos of playing first-class cricket. And if he said the West Indies teams needed to pick professional players to be competitive, he was probably right.

When the tourists arrived in 1900 they had a party of sixteen players, including Warner's brother Aucher, who was Captain. There were six black players[97] in the squad, including Lebrun Constantine[98] and Delmont Cameron St Clair Hinds, the man who had been ostracised from top-level club cricket in Barbados when recruited by the Spartan club.

On the field, the tour was not a particular success. The West Indies played against county sides that generally included more second than first choice players and the tour record of five wins, four draws and eight defeats was hardly inspiring. Warner, however, did what he could to help. He turned out for the West Indies team for one game and in his press articles stressed the positive aspects of the tour and that black players, especially the bowlers Archie Burton and Float Woods, had performed well.

It is noticeable that after the tour of 1900 there was a general loosening of racial segregation in cricket across the West Indian islands. In 1901 the Lucas club was admitted to

---

97 As per Maurice St Pierre, *West Indian Cricket: a socio-historical appraisal*.

98 Lebrun Constantine also toured England in 1906, the first tour to be granted first-class status, and was caught and bowled WG Grace for nought in a game played at Crystal Palace.

the senior cup competition in Jamaican cricket[99] and black players first appeared in a Jamaican side in Inter Colonial cricket. Delmont Hinds was selected for a Barbados side in the Inter Colonial Tournament of 1901-1902[100].

The period from 1905 to 1939 saw five tours from the West Indies to England and numerous first class tours by English teams to the West Indies. These gave West Indian players exposure to a higher standard of cricket than was available domestically and were particularly significant for Jamaican players who did not play in inter island cricket due to the long journey time to the Eastern Caribbean. The 1906 and 1923 West Indian tours to England had equal numbers of white and non – white players and in 1928 non – white players made up approximately 2/3rds of the party; a ratio that was to remain broadly constant up to and including the 1957 tour of England[101].

Both the 1906 tour and the 1923 tour were captained by the same man, Harold (HBG) Austin of Barbados. Austin's family had been established in the Caribbean from the middle of the eighteenth century, owning black slaves and running several plantations. Austin was born in 1877, educated at Harrison College, alongside Pelham Warner and was a member of Wanderers cricket club. In 1897,

---

99   They were to win the competition in 1905, although not without a lot of acrimony along the way see Jamaica at the Wicket Arnold Bertram page 137.

100 Cricket Archive, although Hinds only made one appearance in the Inter – Colonial tournament and I get the impression there was still discrimination in island selection particularly for the intercolonial tournament.

101 Maurice St Pierre: as before.

Austin was selected for a West Indies representative team that included Aucher Warner and Lebrun Constantine to play against AA Priestley's tourists. Austin went in at four in that game with the score at 7 for 2 and scored seventy-five not out from a team score of 215, helping the West Indies to win the game. Austin continued to play first-class cricket for another thirty-two years, playing his final game in 1928. He remained an effective if never spectacular cricketer. In 1926, at the age of forty-eight, he scored forty-five and sixty-nine batting for the West Indies against an MCC touring team.

A photograph of Austin from 1906 shows a handsome man with a fine waxed moustache; even in an Edwardian photograph he bristles with energy. Austin was a successful businessman, Speaker in the Barbados Assembly and was, at various times, a member of the Board of Commerce, Swedish consul, chairman of the Barbados Board of Education and a founding member of the Barbados Museum and Historical Society[102]. He was president of the Wanderers cricket club and used his personal wealth to keep the club going during the early years of the twentieth century.

Austin ticked all the boxes to be a premier figure in the cricketing establishment of Barbados and the West Indies, he was white, independently wealthy, played cricket to a good standard and was prepared to give of his time. He would probably have been captain of the West Indies' first tour to England in 1900 had he not joined the British

---

102 Cricket Nurseries of Colonial Barbados: The Elite Schools 1865 – 1966 by Keith A.P. Sandiford.

army to fight in the Boer War[103]. Austin's involvement in the South African war demonstrated the tight spiritual bonds that held the British Empire together. Austin was, by descent, upbringing and adult occupation, Barbadian, yet was prepared to travel to the southern tip of Africa to fight the Empire's wars. If Austin had sat down with a Boer commando they might have had much in common, not least a dislike of "meddling" from London. But the culture of the British Empire was powerful and pervasive, and a part of that culture was, of course, cricket.

When a West Indies cricket team visited England in 1906, Austin was back from the wars and captained the side. However, the tour was something of a disaster; out of thirteen first-class games, the West Indies lost eight, winning three[104] and drawing two. The standard of opposition was perhaps higher than the West Indies experienced in 1900 and one of the three wins was a prestigious victory over Yorkshire,[105] but neither the results nor the poor attendance figures could be explained away. There were no other West Indies tours before the outbreak of World War I, and the next visit to the United Kingdom was in 1923.

Austin, now forty-five years old, was, again, captain. He also had a significant role in selection for the tour and took two crucial decisions. The first was to pick the "professional" fast bowler George Francis who was employed

---

103 Illness meant that Austin was sent home without reaching the front line.

104 Including a game against Scotland counted as first class.

105 Although Yorkshire's first innings of fifty all out suggests a rain affected pitch, or a really good night out.

as a groundsman preparing the pitch at the Bridgetown Oval and bowling in the nets to white cricketers. Because of his professional status, Francis hadn't played any first-class cricket or in the Barbados Challenge Cup. This contrasted with the situation of another 1923 tourist, the Trinidadian resident George John who was the groundsman at the Queens Park club but who played top level club cricket for Stingo and had appeared in two first-class matches for Trinidad against Barbados.

Austin's second selection surprise for the tour was the inclusion of Learie Constantine. Constantine was only twenty years old and had played just three first-class matches. In these, Constantine had dazzled in the field, shown promise with the ball, but not bowled many overs and had little success as a batsman. Austin decided on the slim evidence available it was worth taking a chance on the son of Lebrun Constantine. It was not the only time Austin intervened to assist Constantine's career and Constantine always acknowledged Austin's role in his own development and that of West Indian cricket in general.

The 1923 tour of England re-established West Indian cricket. George Challenor, the white Barbadian, proved himself to be the first outstanding batsman from the West Indies, averaging over fifty in first-class cricket for the summer. The other batsmen were not of Challenor's standard but the bowlers partially compensated for their deficiencies. The West Indies' first-class record was won six, lost seven, drawn seven a marked improvement on the tours of 1900 and 1906. The British press were generally impressed by the tourists and the West Indians were invited to the Scarborough festival to play against an HDG Leveson Gower XI that was not far from being a full England team. For Francis, the tour was a triumph, eighty-two wickets at an average of fifteen and he was well backed up by George John and Cyril "Snuffy" Browne. Learie Constantine had taken thirty-nine wickets at an average of twenty-two and was outstanding in the field. Austin's high risk selections had succeeded, the West Indies had shown that they could take on first-class counties and test match status was a realistic possibility.

But admission to test match cricket required the cricketing authorities of Jamaica, Trinidad, Barbados and British Guiana to come together and form a board to take control of West Indies cricket. A significant figure in establishing the WICBC was Richard Mallett, a British resident MCC member who travelled to the West Indies in 1926. Mallett had a lifelong connection with West Indian cricket managing the 1900, 1906 and 1923 West Indian tours to England, his behind the scenes work giving practical substance to Pelham Warner's oratory and Harold Austin's on-field contribution.

Right up to his death, in 1939, Mallett continued to act as the WICBC's "man in England" and was central to arrangements for the 1939 tour. There is no indication he received any payment for his services, indeed correspondents from the West Indies often felt it necessary to urge Mallett to claim his expenses. Like thousands of other, unrecorded, volunteers, Mallett gave his time because he liked to help and clearly had a great affection for cricket and West Indian cricket in particular. Jack Kidney, West Indies tour manager in 1933 and 1939, wrote to Mallett: "Who knows – your wishes may yet be gratified by seeing the West Indies win a test match at Lord's.[106]"

In 1926, the process begun by Hawke in the 1890s and sustained by Warner, Austin and Mallett saw the expansion of test match cricket, with the West Indies, along with India and New Zealand, being admitted to the Imperial Cricket Conference. Pelham Warner had retired from first-class cricket six years previously. As a player, Warner was good but not exceptional. But with his eye for cricketing talent, tactical appreciation, financial independence and the ability to make a speech extolling the benefits of cricket and Empire, he excelled as a captain. Warner's time as a player was bookended with two triumphs as a leader, the successful ashes tour of 1903-1904 and Middlesex's county championship of 1920.

After standing down as a player, Warner continued to work as a journalist for the *Morning Post* and subsequently *The Daily Telegraph* and established his own magazine *The Cricketer*. Warner took an income of £600 per annum from *The Cricketer*, made in the region of £200 from his work as a journalist and also published books.[107] His income from writing about cricket was at least comparable to Learie Constantine's earnings as a player and Constantine was widely seen as the best paid sportsman of the age. Warner married the wealthy Agnes Blythe in 1904, but from Gerald Howat's biography it appears he always considered

---

106 MCC archive.
107 He was paid £500 as manager of the bodyline tour – more than the professionals on the tour.

himself on the verge of penury. The England squad for the bodyline series bought Warner a thousand cigarettes at the start of the tour in the belief it would be cheaper than acceding to Warner's constant requests for a smoke. Similarly, anyone dining with Warner could be sure of hearing some good stories but could also be confident of picking up the bill.

Warner's journalism and influence within the MCC gave him the scope to act as a (very refined) cheerleader for West Indian cricket and the place of black men within it. CLR James writes of the 1923 tour of England: "PF Warner and a few others said quite openly that an English side of that year would have been glad to have Francis and John." This public relations work on behalf of West Indian cricket was important and contrasted with *Wisden*'s disapproval of the extension of test status to the West Indies. Warner's support of West Indian talent was not confined to cricketers. One of CLR James' first jobs as a writer in England was to produce a series of articles on West Indian cricket for *The Cricketer*, owned and managed by Warner, James' fellow Trinidadian.

But for British cricket historians, Warner's role on the 1932-1933 bodyline tour has overshadowed his championing of West Indian cricket and he is criticised for supporting Jardine in Australia whilst opposing bodyline whenever he was on English soil. Ironically, Warner commenced the bodyline tour by making one of his speeches on cricket as an uplifting and unifying element of the Empire. "An incautious attitude or gesture in the field, a lack of consideration in the committee room and a failure to see the other side's point of view, a hasty judgement by an onlooker and a misconstruction of an incident may cause trouble and misunderstanding which could and should be avoided. This is the aim of Marylebone Cricket Club, of which I am the humble if devoted servant, in sending teams to all parts of the world to spread the gospel of British fair play as developed in its national sport."[108]

Warner soon found himself trapped between his fine sounding words and Jardine's remorseless desire to win. Although Warner had championed Jardine for the captaincy of the 1932-1933 series, the pair had fallen out by the time the boat carrying the MCC had docked in Perth. Once on tour, the captain was the ultimate source of authority for his team, an authority buttressed by the players' support for the continuation of bodyline tactics after the Adelaide test. As Jardine was an amateur, Warner didn't even have the power to influence his future career.

Warner was also trapped because, for all his talk about the value of fair play and cricket as a foundation of the Empire, he was a sportsman and he really, really wanted to win[109]. Occasionally there is a sporting contest of such

---

108 From *Plum Warner* by Gerald Howat page 111

109 There's a marvellous story that, in the 1920 season, Middlesex, captained by Warner, were involved in a close race for the County Championship with Lancashire. With a couple of games to play, Lancashire looked set to win the championship on the percentage system used. Warner sent an anonymous letter (signed incredibly "Fairplay") to *The Times*, denigrating Lancashire's record and suggesting the percentage system now be abandoned and that the 1920 champion county be selected by the MCC (of which Warner was a highly influential member). Middlesex went on to win the last two games, obtain the best percentage and win the county championship; Fairplay's campaign for elected county champions was discontinued.

skill and excitement even the losers come out as winners, but far more often sport is a zero-sum game: for me to win you have to lose and for the game to be compelling losing has to hurt. For Warner losing to Australia in 1932-1933 would have been particularly painful. In his luggage for the tour was the MCC pennant he had carried as captain of the successful 1903-1904 tour of Australia, the first tour to be made under the auspices of the MCC. Warner didn't carry a Union flag; he didn't have a country but an empire and a class that found an administrative form as the MCC.

But, in contrast to their British colleagues, West Indian cricket historians do not view Warner solely in the context of bodyline. Hilary Beckles in the *Development of West Indies Cricket, The Age of Nationalism* sums up Warner as follows:

"The struggle for ethnic equality in West Indies cricket, therefore, had much to do with the application of the concept of fairness to the selection process. It is a narrative that runs through the story of Pelham Warner ... He was a defender of empire and an ambassador for cricket, but he was a West Indian who did the best he could, under difficult circumstances, to see that his fellow countrymen got the recognition they deserved."

As well as Warner's role as one of the founders of West Indian cricket, he often supported individual cricketers. Of those featured in this book: when Wally Hammond lay in a Bristol nursing home suffering from a mystery, near fatal, illness it was Pelham Warner who visited and convinced him he could recover and continue his cricket career. Warner would subsequently champion Hammond as an England captain. Douglas Jardine was another England captain whose appointment was engineered by Warner, although Jardine, unlike Hammond, never played the part of grateful protégée. When a young Learie Constantine first arrived in a grey and perplexingly cold England on the 1923 West Indian tour, Warner arranged for him to have coaching at Lord's.[110] Warner was Patsy Hendren's Middlesex captain for a number of years and supported his retention on the playing staff until the apparent journeyman professional blossomed as a world class batsman. And when, in January 1928, Bill Bowes went for a trial to be on the MCC ground staff, who should appear but the fifty-three-year-old Pelham Warner, wearing his Harlequin cap and carrying a cricket bat.

But there is another perspective on Warner and the role of the English cricketing establishment in the globalisation of the game, and that is an African perspective. A detailed description of the development of South African cricket lies outside this book but the interested reader will find a good starting point in an article by Andre Odendaal in *The Cambridge Companion to Cricket*[111].

South African cricket at the turn of the twentieth century was in a similar position to cricket in Barbados. Clubs were segregated racially but it was unclear how this would be reflected in touring teams representing South Africa. English

---

110 Although Constantine, who was no fan of coaches, doubted if it did him any good.
111 Cricket and representations of beauty: Newlands Cricket Ground and the roots of apartheid in South African cricket in The Cambridge Companion to Cricket edited by Anthony Bateman and Jeffrey Hill.

cricket tourists to South Africa noted the enthusiasm of the non-white population for the game and generally encouraged their involvement. WW Read's 1892 touring team played against a South African "Malay" side. There they spotted a young fast bowler, named Hendricks, who so impressed them that they suggested he be included in the party for South Africa's tour of England in 1894. Hendricks was selected initially but pressure from reactionary elements within South African cricket, supported by Cecil Rhodes, led to him being deselected. The exclusion of Hendricks was symbolic of the birth of a cricketing apartheid in the Cape Colony that preceded its political counterpart by over forty years.

MCC's response to South Africa's colour bar was to do nothing, a policy of inaction that was to persist until the 1960s. Perhaps the Boer War of 1899-1902 made the English establishment particularly unwilling to broach issues of participation in South African cricket. Warner was captain of an England team that toured South Africa in 1906-1907 and lost the test series four to one. As ever, he was quick to draw attention to links between cricket and Empire: "Step by step we have forced our way up north and the cricket pavilions that have sprung up along our track may almost be called the milestones on the nation's road to progress."

Of course, the cricket pavilions were closed to non-white players and spectators. Warner's goals were the unity of Empire and the development of cricket as the game of that Empire. Multi-racial participation was a good thing; it raised standards, brought more people inside the cricketing fort and chimed with Warner's genuinely liberal views on race. But if racial integration imperilled the objectives of Empire it could be quietly jettisoned.

There's a tempting, but ultimately patronising, tendency to say the past is the past and it is wrong to judge Warner and the MCC of the 1930s by the standards of the twenty-first century. But, reading through press coverage for the 1933 West Indies tour, I came across a short piece about a British Table Tennis Association demand that membership of the international Table Tennis association: "Be open only to those countries which affiliate all their nationals irrespective of race or colour." Similarly, the 1934 Commonwealth Games were relocated from Johannesburg to London when the South African authorities refused to admit black athletes.[112]

What would have happened if the MCC had issued a similar demand in 1933 or, better still, 1903, or when Hendricks was omitted from the first touring party to England? It would at least have allowed the MCC to occupy the moral high ground and avoid the humiliation of the D'Oliveira affair.

The curious rise of West Indian cricket was founded on the determination of men like Herman Griffith and Manny Martindale to make their mark in an unfair world. But it was also assisted by members of a white cricketing establishment such as Warner, Richard Mallett, Harold Austin and Lord Hawke.

These men were not perfect and, like most of us, embodied the faults as well as the qualities of their time and social class. They believed their position in the world

---

112 Although a South African team still participated.

required them to be of service to their islands and the wider British Empire but also expected the lower orders to know their place. In 1938-1939 there were negotiations between the WICBC and Constantine, George Headley and Manny Martindale over the fees to be paid for the 1939 tour of England. West Indian cricket was heading towards professionalism and Austin was prominent amongst a group in the West Indian establishment who saw this as ingratitude and suggested the tour go ahead without the trio.

Mallett, from his home in England, pointed out that there would be little interest in a West Indian team without its three principal attractions. But from Mallett's correspondence with the WICBC it is clear he too was unhappy with the change from black players relying on the grace and favour of white administrators to being equal participants in a free market for their skills. Neither man realised that if West Indian cricket was to continue to develop, West Indian cricketers and administrators who were not independently wealthy would have to be paid for their efforts.

But Austin and Mallett also showed an interest in the human qualities and benefits of cricket that stands out from current day cricket administrators and their focus on cricket as a commodity in a sporting market. Given the length and breadth of his involvement in cricket, it is perhaps inevitable that Warner's inheritance is also mixed; he too certainly shared some of the prejudices and failings of his era and caste. But he did many good things and if he lacked courage he didn't lack generosity of spirit. In 1945 there was a game between England and The Dominions at Lord's. Learie Constantine was in the Dominions team and was made captain. The other ten players in the team were white. Constantine who had so often played under white captains who were not qualified for the position wrote a heartfelt letter to the man who had selected him, Pelham Warner.

Chapter 10

HANGING ON
FOR A DRAW

At the end of the second day of the first test the West Indies are left with a tricky hour to bat. In fading light it is vital they make a sound start. Luckily for them they don't have to contend with Harold Larwood bowling from the pavilion end with no proper sight screen behind him,[113] but they do have to face Gubby Allen who is a genuinely quick bowler. Robertson Glasgow writing in the *Morning Post* judges him the fastest in the match. Douglas Jardine may be shorn of fast-bowlers, but he hasn't lost his instinct for the moment to attack, Allen has just one man in front of the wicket on the off side, two men close in on the leg, a square leg, a fine leg, three slips and a gulley – a total of six close catchers. With the three slips and gulley this is not a bodyline field but those two close catchers on the leg

---

113 Which continues to this day.

side are a sign a few short balls are going to be aimed at the batsman.

At the other end Jardine alternates his three spinners, the left arm Hedley Verity, the leg break and googly bowler Walter Robins and the off-spinner George Macaulay (who bowls with the new ball). The mixture of pace, spin and fading light is too much for the West Indies batsmen. Allen clean bowls Roach for nought: West Indies on 1 for 1. Verity gets Ivan Barrow, caught and bowled for seven: West Indies 17 for 2 . An astute change of bowling by Jardine sees Robins bamboozle Hoad; LBW for six: West Indies 27 for 3. A desperate situation becomes a disaster, Allen steams in from the gathering dusk to have George Headley LBW for thirteen: West Indies 31 for 4, Headley is the hope of West Indian batting; Oscar Da Costa and Cyril Merry fall to Robins and Macaulay respectively and the West Indies stagger from the second day's cricket at 55 for 6.

But oddly there was still hope, test matches in the English summer of 1933 were played over just three days and most of the first day had been lost to rain. The plasticity of playing regulations was an example of the uncertain status of test match cricket in 1933. In the Australian summer of 1932-1933, the bodyline series had been made up of five timeless tests, played until a winner was established, the crucial Adelaide test finished on the sixth day. Scheduling the 1933 West Indies tests for just three days was rather an insult to the West Indies; if both teams batted well the series could have been a nil – nil draw; clearly the West Indies weren't expected to bat well. But insult aside, if the West Indies' last fourteen wickets could hang on for the last day, they would avoid defeat in a test match in England, for the first time.

After the devastation of the second evening they made a decent fist of the third morning. Runs came slowly but it was time that mattered. Captain Jack Grant and spinner Ellis Achong held firm. The score moved, slowly, from fifty-six to eighty-seven. Then Hammond, fielding at slip, caught Achong off Verity and neither Francis nor Martindale lasted long against the spinners. Herman Griffith came to the crease. Prior to the first test, in the match between the West Indies and Middlesex, Griffith had scored sixty-two. If he and Grant could add a "mere" fifty-one more runs, England would have to bat again, taking more time out of an already truncated game.

With the last man in, Grant decides to take the initiative against Walter Robins. Grant plays back-right back waiting for the ball to come to him. When the ball is level with the stumps and inches from the keeper's gloves Grant, with wrists cocked, drops the bat on top of the ball, the late cut, finest of shots. But as the ball is heading to the third man boundary Grant is heading to the pavilion – he has played not just back but too far back and falls on his stumps nearly decapitating England wicketkeeper Les Ames in the process.[114] It is a bathetic end to a poor first innings, all

---

114 From *The Times*.

out for ninety-seven responding to England's 296. Douglas Jardine "asks" the West Indies to bat again.

The West Indies' second innings gets off to an awful start, George Macaulay opens the bowling and from the first ball of the innings Clifford Roach spoons up a catch to Herbert Sutcliffe. Out for nought, and Roach has a pair of noughts for the game. George Headley comes in to bat and attacks whilst Barrow defends. The English crowd and press are aware this is something special, "To all these excellent bowlers Headley played with contemptuous ease, made balls of quite reasonable length look short or over-pitched and altogether persuaded the onlooker that a test match can still provide the highest and most pleasant form of cricket.[115]"

Barrow is LBW to Robins and replaced by Teddy Hoad who takes on his role of diligent defence. As Headley bats on, the ground begins to fill with spectators, "who had rushed from all parts of London to see him make a hundred." They are to be disappointed. Headley gets to his fifty out of sixty-four runs scored before Allen takes his wicket again, this time clean bowled. Grant and Hoad hold out for a while but when Grant is LBW to Macaulay, the rest of the order goes quietly, barring a bit of a tail end thrash from Griffith and Francis. Hoad is ninth out for what with just a bit more assistance might have been a match-saving innings. Eventually the West Indies are all out for 172 at 4.01pm on the third and final day.

---

115 *The Times*, 28th June.

They had lost the game by an innings and twenty-seven runs. If they looked, at times, like they might get away with a draw, it was only because this was effectively a two-day game. It was their fourth test match in England and their fourth innings defeat and it was difficult for the supporters of West Indian cricket to argue that they were up to the standard of the English team in English conditions.

The English selectors were much more satisfied with the first test match. They had won the game comfortably and their spin centric attack proved too much for the West Indies. Although it was Allen who dismissed Headley in both innings; seventeen of the other eighteen wickets had gone to the three English spinners. Spin bowling was effective both as a cricketing tactic and as a means of supressing the bodyline controversy. English wickets were helpful to spinners in the summer of 1933. In the first class averages for the season the six lowest averages (for bowlers bowling more than 1,000 balls) were enjoyed by spin bowlers, the Yorkshire and England pairing of Verity and Macaulay being joined by Tich Freeman of Kent, James Langridge of Sussex, Tom Goddard of Gloucestershire and Harold Owen Smith of Oxford, The Gentlemen and South Africa.[116]

Cricketing administrators, both West Indian and English, also had cause to be pleased. The combined crowd over the three days was 46,449[117], particularly good given rain had restricted play on the Saturday. Receipts net of sales tax were £3,874 of which the West Indies took half. The

---

116 The six were to take 12,397 first-class wickets in their combined careers.
117 Just over 50% of the crowd who watched the first test against Australia in 1934.

total cost of touring England was in the region of £3,000, with the £1,937 share of the gate money for the first test and an additional £633 from the MCC game at Lord's, the tour had come close to covering its costs by the end of June. The question was whether this financial success could be sustained through the second and third test matches, given the poor performance of the West Indian batting in the first. Worryingly Neville Cardus, generally well disposed to West Indian cricket, summed up the first test match: "The time has come to ask the MCC to put an end to Test matches that are not Test matches.[118]"

One bit of good news for the West Indian team was that Learie Constantine would be available for the second test match to be played at Lancashire's Old Trafford ground. But although Constantine's appearance promised more competitive cricket, what impact would it have on the bodyline truce between England and the West Indies?

---

118 Writing in *The Guardian*

Chapter 11

BODYLINE AND LEARIE CONSTANTINE

The second session of the second day of the second test sees the reanimation of the bodyline controversy.

Grant uses first Martindale and then Constantine from the Stretford end both bowling short and targeting the batsman's body. Initially Martindale's fields are some way short of the ring of leg-side catchers seen in the winter tour of Australia. He bowls with a long leg, square leg, mid-on, deep midwicket and Constantine at forward short leg.[119] So, five on the leg with only one in a catching position but if the field isn't full on bodyline the line and length used by Martindale are.

---

119 From the *Manchester Guardian*. A similar but not identical field is described by Robertson Glasgow writing in the *Morning Post*.

Three, four or even five balls an over are short and rising into the batsman's ribs. In one over Hammond ducks the first two balls he receives. Then a delivery from Martindale strikes him on the arm, the next hits him on the back[120] and then Hammond tries to hook, gloves the ball into his chin, blood flows, and with a handkerchief pressed to the wound and a face like thunder he leaves the field. As often happens with bodyline, the surprise full straight ball takes a wicket when Martindale has Walters LBW. Hammond returns to the field and, with Martindale tiring, Constantine is on to bowl.

There was bad blood between Constantine and Hammond. They first met in 1923, when Constantine, twenty-one, was on his first tour of England and Hammond was just twenty. They had got on well. So well that when Hammond toured Trinidad in 1926 with the MCC, Constantine had gone to the Port of Spain docks to greet his friend. Quite what happened next is uncertain, but Constantine came away with the idea that he had been snubbed.

> "I got a strong impression that though I was good enough for a morning's fun in Gloucestershire, things were not quite the same where the colour bar was more pronounced."[121]

---

120 *Morning Herald.*
121 From *Cricketers Carnival* : Learie Constantine

It was the start of a seven year feud between the two men. In a 1928 match at Folkestone between the touring West Indies and an "England xi", Constantine had bowled a ball to Hammond "delivered from past the popping crease which reared past his chin. He didn't like that much and quickly surrendered to Griffith."[122]

Hammond again faces Constantine, this time in a test match. Another man is moved to the leg side making six in total. The game is "alive and passionate" [123]. Constantine makes up for the leg side bias of his field going after any ball in an arc from cover point to mid-on, justifying his Lancashire league nickname 'Electric Heels'. Constantine goes around the wicket to better target Hammond's body and the English batsman is struck again turning away from a short ball. Hammond counter attacks hitting two sixes from the occasional bowling of Headley.

But then Hammond attempts to swing away a full delivery from Constantine, the ball flies into the air off an outside edge to be caught by Martindale fielding at fine leg, Neville Cardus writes, "It was a triumph for bodyline, for Hammond does not usually make merely impulsive hits in test matches."

That evening, Learie Constantine is approached by Wally Hammond, his chin still covered in plaster. Hammond says:

---

122 From RES Wyatt, *Fighting Cricketer*.
123 *The Guardian*

"Let's make peace, Learie. It was nicer when we first met, wasn't it?"[124]

The switch to bodyline tactics for the second test merits explanation. It probably wasn't a response to Old Trafford being a faster wicket than Lord's; press reports are unanimous the pitch was slow, offering little for bowlers of any type.

The availability of Constantine for the Old Trafford match may have given a clue the West Indian bowling would be more aggressive than in the first test as Constantine had a history of short-pitched bowling. In 1926, Constantine bowled bouncers at members of the MCC team, including their captain Freddie Calthorpe,[125] in retaliation for the similar tactics used by the MCC[126]. Like the ACBC in 1933, Constantine acknowledged the requirement of fair play but never accepted everything English teams did was, by definition, fair; for him all teams had to be judged by their actions not their high-flown words.

1926 was by no means the only time Constantine used short-pitched bowling as a tactic. In a 1928 tour match a short ball from Constantine hit Bates of Warwickshire on the neck and the batsman was carried from the field. Bob Wyatt, the next man in, was twice hit on the head by balls delivered by Constantine, although he carried on batting. In the Lord's test match of 1928, Jack Hobbs

---

124 From *Cricketers' Carnival.*
125 *Beyond the Boundary*, CLR James.
126 Although the story is not in *Cricket and I.*

and, ironically, Douglas Jardine both made it clear they thought Constantine was bowling too many short-pitched deliveries.[127] Constantine and controversy continued to be closely linked and he was one of the first bowlers to use a form of bodyline in a test match. In the first test of the 1929-1930 series between England and the West Indies, England were chasing 287 runs to win on the final day of a five-day match. Constantine bowled outside of the leg stump with only two or three fielders on the off side and seven or six on the leg. Accounts of what exactly was going on differ, for Constantine the tactic was purely defensive, bowling outside of the leg stump and the batsman's body to keep the runs down. In Bob Wyatt's biography[128] he describes, "Constantine bouncing the ball at our batsmen." Whatever the exact line being bowled there is no doubt Constantine was combining a leg-side field with short-pitched bowling, or that one short-pitched delivery bowled by Constantine hit English batsman Andy Sandham. Although bodyline as used by the MCC in 1932-1933 was something new it was, to borrow a phrase from Constantine's autobiography *Cricket and I,* "latent" in the cricket that preceded the tour.

Throughout the summer of 1933, Constantine's sporadic appearances in the West Indies side coincided with the use of short-pitched bowling by the team. When early in the tour Martindale took 12 – 105 in the match against Essex, *The Times* commented on how refreshing it was to see a fast bowler who kept the ball up to the bat and looked to claim

---

127 *Cricket and I*, Page 186.
128 *Three Straight Sticks*: RES Wyatt

wickets bowled and caught behind. But when Constantine joined the West Indies team to play against the MCC, there was some criticism of the amount of short-pitched bowling, although the fields in this game were conventional with just one man in close on the leg side.

Constantine also played in the county match against Yorkshire, the only other time the West Indies adopted bodyline in 1933. Although the game was played in the midst of a spell of fine weather, the wicket was damp, perfect for Yorkshire spinner Hedley Verity. Neville Cardus in *The Guardian* commented: "Verity is a lucky bowler, he often gets to bowl on a sticky wicket, even in Harrogate, in a heat wave."[129]

The West Indians believed the state of the pitch was unfair and Constantine explains in *Cricket and I*[130] that Grant requested bodyline bowling as a form of retaliation. "The skipper I know was most upset and it was in the second innings that he came to me and told me to bowl fast with the men on the leg side. I replied that the wicket was too soft but he insisted." Constantine admits he was quite prepared to give England, in this second test, a taste of what they had given Australia, but that again the original idea and eventual decision were down to Jack Grant. Constantine's conclusion on bodyline and its place in the future of cricket is equally mild although, with a lawyer's discretion, he left himself with some leeway to return to the tactic in the future: "Finally, as far as I see my cricket in the future, I do not see myself

129 Quoted in *Cricket and I*, originally from *The Guardian*
130 Page 195.

bowling bodyline except under captain's orders or perhaps as retaliation."

In *Cricketers' Carnival*, Constantine states he subsequently heard Pelham Warner had asked the West Indies to bowl bodyline at Old Trafford in 1933 to demonstrate its iniquities to English cricket spectators. It is certainly possible such a request was made, Warner could have contacted Grant directly or used an intermediary such as Richard Mallett. However, there is no other evidence of such a request, neither Warner nor Grant refer to it, and, on balance, it is unlikely to have happened.

Given how the style of cricket played by the West Indies changed when Constantine was available, I suspect he was more involved in the decision to bowl bodyline than he lets on in his autobiographies. Prior to the first test match, CLR James wrote an article for the *Port of Spain Gazette*, commenting on the possible tactics for the test series.

> "Whether Grant will allow himself to be frightened by these English critics is an important question. If he breaks the morale of his fast bowlers by expressing doubts as to whether the tactics of Constantine and Martindale are fair, the West Indies should flay him alive."[131]

It's clear from this that James, Constantine's friend, feared Grant would object to short-pitched bowling by Constantine and Martindale. This hardly squares with Constantine's explanation that it was Grant who pressed him to use

---

131 Reproduced in *Cricket* by CLR James

bodyline, but ultimately this all must remain speculation: there is nothing in Jack Grant's memoir to suggest he was pressurised by Constantine to use bodyline tactics.

If Constantine was underplaying his true involvement in the use of bodyline he was wise to do so. Harold Larwood, on his return from the 1932-1933 bodyline series, had gone into print to defend bodyline and to accuse the Australians of a lack of courage and sportsmanship in standing up to it. As a result, Larwood the bowler was subsumed by Larwood the bowler of bodyline; he would have perhaps fared better taking the Constantine line: the skipper told me to bowl it so I did: let the amateur captain take the heat.

Although Constantine was not prepared to take a stand on bodyline, in his biography *Cricket and I*, he defended the use of short-pitched bowling.[132] For Constantine, the short-pitched ball was the key to the fast bowler's success; without it the batsman was free to walk across his stumps and play the fast bowler easily. Constantine was nuanced and realistic about the purpose of the short-pitched ball: it was not done to hurt the batsman but to make the batsman think he might be hurt.

Once that thought was in the batsman's head, the way he played would change, just as Bradman changed his style to meet bodyline. Such a clear distinction between bodyline and short-pitched bowling gives Constantine's arguments a

---

132 It is difficult to decide whether *Cricket and I* is by Constantine or James, it purports to be an autobiography and is written, unsurprisingly, in the first person, although James' assistance is acknowledged. I think it safe to assume that all the opinions expressed are Constantine's own.

clarity lacking in many other contemporary commentators who did not have Constantine's experience of top-level sport and had, perhaps, unrealistic expectations of what was, and was not, cricket.

Chapter 12

SPARTAN CRICKETER

The West Indian first innings at Old Trafford had seen their best batting of the series, dominated by a 200 run second wicket partnership between George Headley and wicketkeeper Ivan Barrow. Headley was his customary mix of style and control. Barrow had the nerve to take advantage of some good luck, reports differ on whether he was dropped two or three times in his innings, but he just beat Headley to a hundred and was the first West Indian to score a test century in England. The innings spluttered, but a quick thirty-one from Constantine and Headley's unbeaten 169 took the West Indies to a decent 375.

When Wally Hammond was dismissed by Learie Constantine, England were on 118 – 3 in reply.

Now the tall figure of Douglas Jardine comes in to bat. Not only is Jardine the captain of a team in a perilous position against a supposedly inferior side, he has to face, for the first time, the bodyline he invented. In 1928 he complained about the short-pitched bowling of Learie Constantine and in the 1933 MCC game the same bowler had him caught in close on the leg side off a short-pitched ball. We know Jardine can dish it out, but can he take it?

With Constantine tiring, Martindale resumes the bodyline attack. Wyatt goes to pull a ball on the leg side – makes good contact – but somehow the fielder at short leg gets his hands to the ball and manages to hold on, an amalgam of preternatural reactions, bravery and perhaps a little luck. It's Constantine, of course, who takes this remarkable catch, he might not be bowling but he isn't out of the game. England 134 – 4 still 241 runs behind. Can something remarkable be happening?

Jardine stands up to the attack. Stands up to it mentally, saying to Les Ames: "You get yourself down this end, Les, I'll take care of this bloody nonsense."[133] He also stands up to the technical challenge of facing bodyline. The Australian batsmen who had done well against bodyline had either attacked the short-pitched ball, McCabe at Sydney hooked, Bradman at Adelaide moved across to the leg and hit into the off or, like Woodfull, soaked up the punishment and let the ball hit them. Jardine certainly doesn't hook, he takes a few blows and lets a few whistle past his beak of a nose, but more often than not defends off the back foot using his height and the slowness of the pitch to play the ball down. His hands grip the bat lightly, the right hand attached only

---

133 From Christopher Douglas, *Douglas Jardine: Spartan Cricketer*.

by the thumb and forefinger, cushioning the impact of the ball and ensuring it will fall short of the gaggle of leg-side catchers.

Jardine and Ames survived and, with his two fast-bowlers tiring, Jack Grant reverted to Valentine and Achong and conventional fields. Neville Cardus believed Grant's decision not to persist with bodyline and dredge another spell from his best bowler Martindale was where the West Indies missed their chance of winning the match. Was this an example of Grant's lack of stomach for a war to the knife? What would Jardine have done? Probably the same, fast bowlers can only bowl for so long and with a second new ball available at 200 runs Grant's decision was reasonable. England, as they did throughout the series, prospered against the second tier of the West Indies bowling and Ames and Jardine saw England through to 200.

Bodyline bowling resumed with the second new ball and this may have been where Grant missed his chance. Vincent Valentine bowled at the other end to Martindale rather than Grant opening up with Constantine and subjecting England to an all-out bodyline assault. Similarly, Martindale and Valentine opened the bowling on the third and final day. In not bowling Constantine and Martindale at the same time Grant may have been dealing with the sensibilities of his star all-rounder. In the MCC archive there is a letter from Learie Constantine to Richard Mallett including the following complaint: "When I was an amateur and formed one of the contingent of West Indian cricketers on tour, and when I was the fastest bowler of the crowd, I have had to play "second fiddle" so to speak. I had to take the other end. That happened at Lord's and Old Trafford as recently as the 1933 tour." So, Grant may have acceded to Constantine's wish to bowl from the Stretford end.

With the second new ball, Martindale again made the breakthrough having Ames caught by Headley. With the game in the balance, Martindale was bowling to Jardine with four men in the leg trap – real bodyline. They must have thought, with Jardine, defending off the back foot, one ball would have to lob to a fielder, but his technique was too good. England reached 263/6 at the end of the second day still 112 runs behind the West Indies. With a day to go it was going to be difficult for the West Indies to win the match, but early wickets and a bold declaration would give them a chance. England also had a chance to win and their captain was only thirty-two runs short of a first test hundred.

The third and final day began with another burst from Martindale. Jardine played more shots than on the second day and, having proved his point, didn't have to face bodyline bowling on that third morning; all-rounder Walter Robins who had been so effective with the ball in the first test was not so lucky. Again, once Constantine and Martindale had been seen off, batting became much easier against Valentine and Achong. Jardine reached his hundred in characteristic style, tucking Ellis Achong away for a single. Now Robins looking for quick runs went down the pitch to Achong, failing to realise the left-arm spinner had bowled him a ball spinning from off to leg rather than in the usual direction for a left arm orthodox. Out stumped, Robins went back to the pavilion allegedly chuntering about being bowled by a bloody Chinaman; the term stuck and a "Chinaman" is a left-armed delivery that turns towards the legs of a right-handed batsman. Although, sadly, there is some doubt over whether this is the true origin of the expression.

Straight after Robins was out, Jardine was caught in the gulley by Constantine off Martindale. Even then he was reluctant to go waiting for confirmation the ball had carried from the umpire. He left the field to a standing ovation. Jardine had scored his first and only test match hundred and his reputation had never been higher.

For many English cricket supporters, the story of the 1932-1933 ashes series was one of an unbending captain and fine side outplaying Australia whose supporters and players had not been able to take defeat in an appropriate manner. Now Jardine had faced and faced down bodyline, he had seemingly strengthened his claim: bodyline was not an English excess but an Australian deficit, a lack of courage and decorum. He was vindicated as a captain. And vindicated as a batsman; after a run of poor scores in test matches his hundred was proof he was worth his place in the side. He was to average forty-eight in test match cricket. And he was vindicated because he had scored runs when the series was at its fiercest and had demonstrated the physical toughness he so valued. Christopher Douglas's biography of Jardine has a well-chosen subtitle, *Spartan Cricketer*. Jardine had taken the grounding of the English public school system and boiled it down to its essentials: boiled-off Christianity and "The Edwardian gesture and humbug of may the best side win,"[134] and reduced it to physical toughness and desire. For Jardine, test match cricket was a struggle and the struggle was at its keenest and best when a batsman faced fast bowling. He was contemptuous of batsmen who used protective equipment to reduce the possibility of physical injury: "Grown men who constrict their freedom with thigh pads and chest protectors are faintly ridiculous."[135] [136]

Another aspect of Jardine's cricketing philosophy was the amateur's view of cricket as a game for those who played it: spectators should passively watch, not participate. This was at odds with an Australian public whose democratic spirit was expressed in its raucous crowds and barrackers. Long before Larwood was counted out as he walked to the top of his run, "1-2-3-4-5-6-7-8-9-10 out yer bastard", the Australian crowds had developed a marked antipathy for Jardine, his harlequin cap and his style of cricket where what mattered was scoring runs not the way they were scored. During the 1930 tour to Australia after Jardine had faced constant barracking during a four hour innings at Sydney, Patsy Hendren, the English professional, had said to him, "They don't seem to like you very much over here Mr Jardine." "It's fucking mutual," Jardine had replied.

At Adelaide in 1933, Jardine had banned supporters from watching net practices contributing to the bad feeling that was such a part of the third test of the bodyline tour.

---

134 Neville Cardus, Jardine obituary.

135 From *Douglas Jardine: Spartan Cricketer*, page 90.

136 Although on the 1933-1934 tour of India Jardine encouraged his batsmen to wear solar pith helmets, to protect them against short-pitched bowling as well as the sun.

On returning to England after the tour, Jardine was to suggest bad behaviour in the crowd should be punished by a reduction in playing time; the Australians should be compelled to be more like (southern) English spectators.

Restraint was not only a feature of English spectators; English batsmen of the 1930s were, with a few exceptions, also pretty restrained. Run rates of a little more than two an over[137] were common and, of all the English batsmen of 1933, Jardine was probably the slowest scorer. As Christopher Douglas writes in *Spartan Cricketer*: "If the bowler threw down the gauntlet it was ignored, or occasionally pushed round the corner for a safe single." Jardine was known as a strong on-side player, skilled at blocking the ball with his pads secure in the knowledge he could not be given out if the ball pitched outside off, and seemingly happy to advise the umpire on any close decisions. In the Old Trafford test, his 127 runs came off 305 balls[138] or two and a half runs per over. In a game such as the second test when the cricket was tense and close, slow scoring almost added to the entertainment. There is something about seeing a batsman bring all his energy and concentration to a desperate fight against a bowler who has the upper hand. But in other circumstances, when batting was easy and Jardine's caution out of keeping with the need to win, slow scoring was simply boring. Boredom led to unrest in the crowd, which made not a whit of difference to Jardine unless to make the scoring slower still. If the crowd was unhappy, why should

---

137 *Spartan Cricketer* as before
138 http://www.sportstats.com.au/bloghome.html

an amateur cricketer like Jardine bother? He would have been quite happy with no crowd.

What Jardine stood for inside the boundary of the cricket ground cannot really be doubted. Cricket as a struggle played up to the limits of the written rules and not some vague ethos of fair play and 'it's just not cricket'. Cricket as a breeding ground for the manly virtues: a cricket where opponents were enemies, spectators an unwelcome intrusion and the press, right up to the point where Jardine took up journalism, an object of contempt.

There have been various attempts to put Jardine into context outside of the boundary as representative of wider historical forces. For some Australian commentators,[139] Jardine was an ambassador of rancour sent by the game's establishment to stir up and then put down the colonials, demonstrating English superiority on the playing fields of Australia. Such an argument does, at first glance, have some appeal. Jardine's family and upbringing were at the heart of the colonial establishment of the British Empire and had some parallels with Pelham Warner's. Both men were the sons of Advocate Generals, Warner's in Trinidad and Jardine's in Bombay and both had their earliest cricketing experiences being bowled to by family servants, in Jardine's case on the veranda of the family home in Malabar. Like many children of members of the British establishment working overseas, both Warner and Jardine had to endure the dislocating experience of being sent to Britain for their education. Warner went to Rugby school aged thirteen, but

---

139 Including the 1984 "Bodyline" Australian TV series.

for Jardine the transition was even earlier, at nine he was sent to live with his Aunt Kitty in Scotland.

But although Jardine was a product of the British establishment, he was rarely at ease with fellow members of his class and caste. The principal opponents of bodyline were the amateurs in the 1932-1933 touring party, Gubby Allen who refused to bowl bodyline and in letters home compared Jardine (unfavourably) to Hitler, and the Nawab of Pataudi who refused to even field in the leg trap. Jardine: "I see his highness is a conscientious objector."[140] Others, such as Pelham Warner and vice-captain Bob Wyatt, due to solidarity (and perhaps enjoying the results) didn't speak out publicly during the tour but expressed their private doubts when they returned to England.

Jardine often seems to have got up the noses of his upper-middle-class contemporaries. His captaincy of the Winchester school first eleven so disgusted one of its members, Cecil Verity, that he abandoned cricket for rowing. Although Warner had been an early advocate of Jardine's captaincy he worked behind the scenes to have Jardine removed from the position once he had returned to England. After he had left the captaincy, Jardine neither held a position at the MCC nor was he a national selector. By contrast Warner, who first supported Jardine and then opposed him, was knighted in 1937 for services to cricket.[141] Warner had played both sides of the bodyline controversy successfully.

---

140 http://www.espncricinfo.com/bodyline/content/story/316186.html
141 https://en.wikipedia.org/wiki/Pelham_Warner

To see Jardine as some sort of class warrior is generally mistaken, it was the large crowds at Lord's and Old Trafford who had been his loudest supporters whilst the cricketing establishment were always uneasy about the consequences of bodyline. But there is perhaps a scintilla of truth in the accusation that Jardine was a tool of the cricketing hierarchy. He personified an important truth people like Warner knew well but had difficulty in articulating. Winning mattered and winning against Australia really mattered.

For CLR James,[142] Jardine, far from being a relic of colonialism, was a very modern figure: "Bodyline was not an incident, it was not an accident; it was not a temporary aberration. It was the violence and ferocity of our age expressing itself in cricket." For James, Jardine was a part of a world changed: by the First World War, industrialisation and the erosion of amateur values. This is certainly more accurate than seeing Jardine as an agent of the British establishment.

Jardine failed to get on with his fellow amateurs but was generally and genuinely admired by the professionals who played in his sides. There is a picture of Jardine in Port Hacking, Australia, during the bodyline series. Jardine is in a swimsuit and sun hat, standing next to a boat and smiling. It's a picture at odds with the normal images of the bodyline series filled with *sturm und drang* and catchers on the leg side. What is also notable is that the man on the other side of the boat from Jardine is Herbert Sutcliffe, a professional cricketer. Amateurs and professionals often socialised

---

142 *Beyond a Boundary*

separately on overseas tours, but Jardine's cricketing friendships were with middle-class professional cricketers such as Sutcliffe and his fellow Yorkshireman Hedley Verity, who named one of his sons Douglas, after Jardine. Between Jardine and the unambiguously working-class Harold Larwood, there was a different dynamic, part officer and other ranks, part tempestuous marriage. Larwood seemed to spend most of the bodyline tour in a strop over something Jardine had done, played him, not played him, made him night watchman, tried to stop him going out at night, but whatever the techniques used, Jardine was able to get the best out of the strange mix of humility, pride and rage that made up Harold Larwood.

What bound Larwood, Jardine and the other professional cricketers of the time together was an acknowledgement that cricket was an important business. If Larwood had not been a cricketer, he would have had to earn his living down a mine and, in the 1930s, maybe even that wouldn't have been possible. Professionals needed a captain who could get the team to win and who was good enough to merit a place in the side rather than play as a specialist. Jardine didn't only win the respect of professional players on his own side, George Headley told CLR James that Jardine was his idea of a perfect captain.

Jardine's stubborn independence was sometimes echoed by the professional cricketers who played for him; both Larwood and Jardine were adamant that if they were to continue playing cricket after bodyline they must be able to use whatever tactics they thought appropriate. It was a point of principle that was to contribute to both men leaving test match cricket.

Although James' characterisation of Jardine as a product of a post-war professional age is persuasive, it is only persuasive up to a point. Jardine may have shared some of the points of view of professional cricketers, but their perspectives were very different. Jardine was a proper amateur, he didn't earn money as the secretary of a county, but rather put his career on hold to captain Surrey and England. And as his biographer Christopher Hill puts it: "In almost every respect – intellect, morality, even appearance – he was a nineteenth century man."

Ultimately, any attempt to reduce Jardine to an agent of economic or social forces is doomed to failure. He was a one off, driven to win by something in the depths of his complicated personality. Jardine was English cricket's captain Ahab, Don Bradman his white whale. And James is perhaps too reductionist in drawing parallels between test cricket and the world that goes on around it. Peace in cricket was brought about by the time Australia toured England in 1934 and it held pretty well until the emergence of Lindwall and Miller in the 1950s. But in the real world, 1934-1945 was a period of war, turmoil and holocaust. As James was amongst the first to identify, cricket is not isolated from society but, like any game, it can also be a place of retreat from the real world, to an alternative, well regulated, parallel existence.

Chapter 13

BODYLINE AUTOPSY

Although Old Trafford 1933 marked the high point for Douglas Jardine as a cricketer, the doubts over the sustainability of the bodyline tactics he had devised and developed became more widespread after the second test. Previously there was a concern that the continuation of bodyline might result in the cancellation of Australia's planned tour of England in 1934, but this was more a practical than an ethical issue. Now journalists had seen bodyline in action and, what is more, in action against English batsmen, doubts about the tactic became more widespread. A good example of how attitudes were beginning to change can be found in the 'Notes by the Editor' piece in *Wisden* for 1933 and 1934. The 1933 notes, written whilst the 1932-1933 ashes series was still in progress, starts with a clear expression of principle: "It may at once be said that, if the intention is to hit the batsman and so demoralise him, the practice is altogether wrong."

And an equally clear though mistaken statement: "That English bowlers, to dispose of their opponents, would of themselves pursue such methods or that Jardine would acquiesce in such a course is inconceivable."

However, rather than leaving it there, *Wisden*'s editor commences a discursive description of bodyline, its history and its place in the game that makes everything much less clear. In summary, *Wisden*'s position seems to be something like:

> Bowling to hit or intimidate the batsman is wrong.
>
> But that's not what happened in Australia.
>
> It can't have happened because an England side wouldn't do that.
>
> Even if it had happened, it would have been the fault of defensive batting techniques.
>
> And the Australian crowd.
>
> And the Australian press.
>
> Anyway, it's always gone on so why make a fuss about it now.

By 1934, after the visit of the West Indies, things were much clearer:

> "If there remained many advocates for its *(i.e. bodyline's)* use, what occurred in the test match at Manchester must have convinced them of its unwelcome nature. For this reason, as already observed, the tour of the West Indies, apart from the useful lessons it taught our visitors, rendered one great and, we hope, lasting service to English cricket."

The change in tone between 1933 and 1934 has a number of explanations. Firstly, the *Wisden* editor in 1933 was writing without having seen bodyline as practiced by Jardine's team. Secondly, *Wisden*'s editors had their view of bodyline in particular, and short-pitched bowling in general, skewed by who was bowling and who was being hit; they weren't alone in this. Finally, Stewart Caine, the *Wisden* editor of 1933, died soon after publication of the 1933 Almanac, being replaced by SJ Southerton for the 1934 edition.

Wisden was not alone in undergoing a bodyline conversion. Robertson Glasgow writing in the *Morning Post* included a clear statement of his change in views: "If at any time I have either purposely or by inference justified this type of bowling or served to defend it I am sorry for it and after ocular demonstration with wholeheartedness recant my opinion. It is simply warfare and not cricket."

There was also perhaps the first sign of some change in the attitude of the English cricketing public in the letters page of *The Cricketer*. Issue number fifteen of 1933 had four letters on bodyline, three of which were in favour of outlawing it and suggested various changes to the rules, whereas the fourth was in support of Douglas Jardine and his tactics. However, *The Cricketer* with its southern, public school and international slant was a particular subset of the cricketing public and its editor Pelham Warner was against bodyline. Warner, who had privately expressed his concerns over the events of the ashes series to an MCC enquiry earlier in the summer, now broke cover in a letter sent to *The Daily Telegraph*.[143] Which explained

---

143 *Bodyline Autopsy*, David Frith, page 361

his opposition to the tactic and his opinion that bodyline in the second test of 1933 was not equivalent to the tactics used by the MCC in the previous winter. The Old Trafford pitch was slower than the Australian wickets, Constantine and Martindale were not quite as fast as Larwood, bodyline was bowled from one end and the circle of men in the leg trap was only used for a short period of time.

Other press coverage was more ambivalent, for instance both *The Times* and Neville Cardus writing in the *Manchester Guardian* noted how exciting the cricket of the second test had been.[144] But both papers also expressed concern over whether cricket could be sustainable if bodyline was to become the principal tactic of the game.

There was also a split between the newspapers aimed at a section of the middle-class and the mass circulation press. *The Daily Herald* continued to regard the bodyline controversy as a problem not of English tactics, but an inappropriate Australian response. "The plain truth of the matter is that we and the West Indies treated this type of bowling sanely and calmly whereas Australia did not."

The Herald, with its links to the trade unions had no instinctive deference to the cricket establishment and it was impatient with any suggestion that fair play and the maintenance of colonial ties should be placed ahead of the need to win.

There is some evidence this attitude was shared by cricket spectators, or at least those in the crowd at Old Trafford.

---

144 Cardus, although he wasn't in Australia in 1932-1933 had opposed bodyline from the outset.

The crowd got restive during a slow passage of play in the England first innings and, according to *The Daily Herald*, called on Grant to, "Try some more bodyline."

Of course at Old Trafford it wasn't Australian batsmen facing bodyline now it was two black bowlers who were making white English batsmen duck, weave and wince. With assumptions of white superiority coming up against the facts of burgeoning Afro-Caribbean success in boxing and athletics, was this another reason for the change in attitudes towards bodyline?

Well it might have been but reading press reports on the second test there's no evidence this was the case. Journalists agreed that, whatever they thought about bodyline, the West Indies couldn't be blamed for adopting tactics the MCC had developed. Neville Cardus in *The Guardian*: "Grant deserves approbation for his courage in treating English cricketers to a taste of the new fast bowling." However, there is one piece of isolated evidence that the bowling of bodyline in the second test served to crystallise racial animosity. Constantine received a letter posted in the Lancashire town of Colne and dated the 26th of July (i.e. the day after the second test had finished). Nelson were to play Colne on the 8th August, the letter included racist abuse and ended: "If you start bumping them on Saturday you will get bumped, not half, so try to play the game – and remember you are playing among white men."[145]

The letter was significant for Constantine who retained it in his private papers. He took 7/35 in the cup victory

---

145 From Peter Mason's *Learie Constantine*, page 40.

over Colne. But it remains unclear how widespread the racism expressed in it was and how much those attitudes were influenced by the second test and the West Indies' use of bodyline.

Two things were clear though: Firstly, the bodyline controversy had not gone away and was now dividing the English newspapers as well as Australia and Britain. Secondly, there was a good competitive test match being played with any result possible on the third and final day.

Captain vindicated: Douglas Jardine raises his cap, having scored a century at Old Trafford in the 2nd test.

A young Pelham Warner, Warner was involved in cricket throughout the first half of the twentieth century as player, administrator, journalist, publisher and selector.

West Indies team 1933: Back row left to right Jack Kidney (Manager), Herman Griffith, Cyril Christiani, Ivan Barrow, Ellis Achong, Cyril Merry, Manny Martindale, Archie Wiles, George Headley. Front row, left to right: Jack Grant, Clifford Roach, Ben Sealey, Vincent Valentine and Oscar Da Costa

Harold "HBG" Austin, Early West Indian captain much admired by Learie Constantine. Taken in 1906.

Manny Martindale, shows them how to do it.

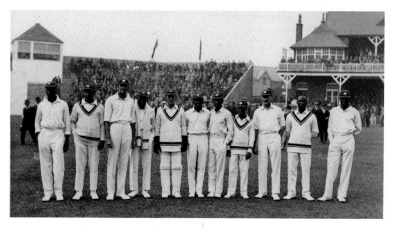

The West Indies team of 1928, Herman Griffith is giving you a stern stare from one in on the right and Learie Constantine is dead centre stood next to captain and wicket keeper Karl Nunes.

Charles Marriott bowls
to Oscar Da Costa
3rd test at The Oval in
1933.

Bob Wyatt, Captain
of the 1934 - 1935
MCC tour of the
West Indies.

Captain Bob Wyatt carried from the field, unconscious at Sabina Park, Kingston Jamaica 1935. Learie Constantine holds Wytatt's head. To the extreme left of the photo is Derek Sealy. Jack Grant (I think) has his back to us and in pads, on the left of shot, is David Townsend. The two players between Grant and Townsend I can't recognise.

George Headley at Aigburgh in 1933

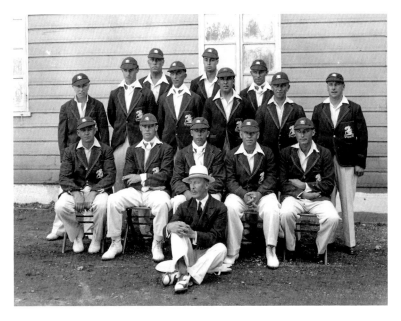

MCC tourists to the West Indies 1934 – 1935, Back three, left to right: Jim Smith, Ken Farnes, George Paine. Second row left to right: Eric Hollies, David Townsend, Jack Iddon, Les Ames, Maurice Leyland, Bill Farrimond. Front row left to right, Wally Hammond, Errol Holmes, Bob Wyatt, Patsy Hendren, William Harbord. Seated on ground Carlton Levick (Manager).

Learie Constantine, in the nets on the 1933 tour.

Chapter 14

OLD TRAFFORD DAY 3 AND LEARIE CONSTANTINE

England were eventually all out for 374,[146] just one run behind the West Indies. There probably wasn't time for the West Indies to win the match but, given their uneven batting line up and susceptibility to spin, there was time to lose it. Macaulay was unable to bowl in the second innings but selection for the second test of Sussex spinner James Langridge allowed Jardine to use three spin bowlers with leg spinner Walter Robins opening the bowling. At the other end was Northants left arm quick Nobby Clark who bowled to bodyline fields. Jardine was not going to let the West Indian side get away with bodyline; it was tit for tat, bruise for bruise and if the MCC had been hoping for a

---

146 Macaulay's injury meant he didn't come out to bat

peaceful series they were to be disappointed. Clark struck early having Ivan Barrow caught by James Langridge in the leg trap. Then Roach was hit by a ball delivered by Clark and the game had to be stopped whilst he recovered.

But Clifford Roach responded to bodyline by going on the attack; attack was generally Roach's way. With George Headley all watchful calm at the other end, any possibility of a humiliating defeat seemed to have been averted. Even when Roach was out having scored sixty-four of eighty-six second innings runs, the presence of Headley seemed to guarantee safety. But, disaster, Headley was out caught and bowled by Langridge and with three hours left in the game it suddenly seemed possible that, despite a strong first innings performance, West Indies would be defeated for the fifth time in five test matches played in England.

The soft white underbelly of the West Indian batting was exposed. Hoad and Grant determined to block out the remaining time but Langridge was bowling well and had Hoad caught by Wally Hammond fielding at slip. This brought in Archie Wiles who was making his test match debut at forty-two years of age. Langridge snaffled him up – stumped Ames for two – two more than Wiles scored in the first innings of his only test match.

Constantine is next man in – generally an unsuccessful batsman in test match cricket – but surely he can apply himself, one hour's batting, dogged defence, will be enough to see the West Indies through to a draw. But wickets continue to fall; first Grant and just six balls later Da Costa is caught by Sutcliffe off Clark. At 4.15pm West Indies are 132 – 7 and, with more than a session to play, defeat is rushing towards them.

With the West Indies ahead on the scoreboard, runs are as important as time and Constantine decides attack is the best means of defence. First, he uses his feet to Langridge slamming three fours in an over. "Swift as lightning and swifter, he cracks the bat like a whip, using forearms as flexible as they are powerful."[147]Constantine faces the final two balls of the next over from Clark, both are short, both hooked to the boundary. Jardine reverts to his most trusted and parsimonious spinner, Hedley Verity, and Constantine plays the Yorkshire man with a bit more restraint. Nobby Clarke bowls the final over before tea and tries Constantine with another bouncer. Despite the state of the game, Constantine can't resist the hook shot, this time the ball just clears the field and trickles away for four. The next ball is driven through the off side for two more and the last ball before tea solemnly blocked, no point in taking risks. Constantine goes in for tea having scored thirty-four runs off twenty-seven balls and the onrushing locomotive of defeat is halted. After tea, Constantine carries on batting with brio, he and Achong put on fifty-nine runs, of which Achong contributes just ten. Constantine is ninth man out for sixty-four off fifty-five balls and the West Indies are all out in their second innings for 225. England need to score a theoretical 227 to win. But, the decision to limit the 1933

147 *Good Days:* Neville Cardus

test matches to three days deprives the Manchester public of an exciting finish, instead, "A most imposing notice was paraded around the ground to say that the cricketers were to be allowed to catch an early train."[148]

The West Indies hadn't won but for the first time they had avoided defeat in England, they had saved the match. And how they had saved it, the West Indies scored at 3.7 runs per over in the second innings. A good rate in twenty-first century test cricket and a marked acceleration on the usual stately progress of the 1930s. The match was saved through aggressive batting, West Indian batting; the batting of Learie Constantine.

It's sometimes said a cricketer's behaviour on the field reveals his character but with Constantine the inter-play between the cricketer and the man is more complicated.

To English spectators and journalists such as Neville Cardus, Constantine was defined by his vivid athleticism, his clearly expressed enjoyment of his own powers and his aggressive to the point of reckless batting. Cardus wrote in his introduction to *Cricket and I*: "We know that his cuts and drives his whirling fast balls, his leapings and clutchings and dartings – we know they are the consequences of impulses born in the blood, a blood heated by the sun and influenced by an environment and a way of life much more natural than ours."

---

148 *Daily Telegraph*

Constantine was certainly blessed with a prodigious athletic talent, CLR James believed, a spectator could pick out Constantine as exceptional just by watching him walk onto the field. But as James and Constantine knew, it took a lot of time, effort and practice to be a "natural" cricketer. The practice started early for Learie Constantine, son of one West Indian cricketer, Lebrun and nephew, on his mother's side, of another, Victor Pascal. The garden of the Constantine family home included a matting cricket pitch and the games played on it were fun, but the serious fun of sporting application.

But cricketing success did not come automatically to Constantine. After the West Indies 1923 tour of England he found it hard to reconcile playing sport and making a decent living. There was no support from local businesses for a cricketer of talent and he found it hard to get steady work in Port of Spain; without Harold Austin's intervention he may not have played against the MCC tourists in 1926.

Eventually, Constantine went south to Fyzabad to work as an administrator for an oil firm, but he was now unable to play many games in Port of Spain where competition was at its strongest. Constantine married in 1927 and his daughter was born in 1928. With another tour of England and Wales scheduled for later that year, Constantine saw he had one chance to make it and began to recreate himself as a cricketer. Previously Constantine was a medium pace bowler. He decided if he was to make the breakthrough and become a professional cricketer in England he would have to add pace and he set to work on his endurance and strength. To do this he would run a two-mile circuit, starting off running as fast as he could and, when he could run no more, walking as fast as he could before running again. In peak condition, Constantine reckoned he could, pretty much, cover the two miles at a flat-out run.

Constantine also decided if he was going to be a premier bowler he would have to give up fielding at cover and determined to become a slip fielder of distinction. Again, he trained for the role, and skipping was added to his exercise regime to build strength in the legs. To aid flexibility and balance, Constantine would "place a cricket ball on the floor at the limit of his reach and would pick it up balancing on one leg."[149] All of this was supplemented by hours on the slip catching machine.[150]

The work paid off, Constantine was selected for the 1928 tour, acknowledged to be one of the fastest bowlers in test cricket[151] and as good a fielder at slip as he was in the covers. Constantine had a fine summer in first-class cricket, excelling in the game against Middlesex where he scored a rapid eighty-nine, took seven for fifty-three followed up with a breakneck 103 and a three wicket win. On the basis of this performance he was offered a professional contract by Nelson. His professional cricket career had begun, but Constantine was no teenager, he was twenty-seven years old in 1928.

---

149 The author would encourage anyone trying this exercise to ensure the surrounding area is clear of any objects that might cause an injury in the event of a fall, such as the sharp edge of a TV stand, for instance.

150 Constantine's regime is described in pages 209-211 of *Cricket and I*.

151 From Peter Mason, *Learie Constantine*, page 27: Jack Hobbs thought Constantine was as quick as anyone he faced.

Constantine's re-invention as a quick bowler had a limited duration. Wickets in the Lancashire League didn't favour pace bowling and, although successful against first class batsmen, he was not, early in his career, a consistent test match bowler. A third bowling Constantine emerged, one who varied his pace bowling the odd quick delivery or spell in amongst an assortment of spin, swing and cut. By the time he played his final first-class season in England in 1939 he was pretty much a spin bowler, but one with a quicker ball a little quicker than possessed by most spinners. It was his most successful season as a bowler, 103 first-class wickets at an average of just under eighteen, four for forty-two in the second innings of the Manchester test match and five for seventy-five in the first innings at the Oval.

The adaptability and application Constantine demonstrated as a bowler and fielder was also apparent in his career outside of cricket and his position as a representative of his community. Constantine was characterised by principle, strong ambition and patience. When he came to Nelson he was one of only three black residents and life was difficult in what seemed a very grey England. But, encouraged by his wife Norma, Constantine stuck at it, winning the town over with his down to earth nature away from the cricket pitch and his prodigious feats on it. By the time he left Nelson he was a local hero.

Arriving in England, Constantine hoped to progress a career in the law, which had been stymied in race-conscious Trinidad. Cricketing success and celebrity impeded his legal studies, which don't seem to have come easily to Constantine, but he persisted, studying for the bar exam in the evenings. By 1945 Constantine was in his mid-forties and his days as a first-class cricketer were behind him. He enrolled in Middle Temple and in 1954 he was called to the bar; it marked the end of a process that had started in the offices of Jonathan Ryan in Queen Street Port of Spain, thirty-seven years previously. Constantine did practice as a barrister but never shone in court and, in any event, could earn well as a broadcaster on the BBC and as a cricket coach. The impression is becoming a barrister was what was important to Constantine, it was the career he had started on leaving school and he was determined to progress; if the way society was organised and his sporting talent meant it took a little longer, very well, he could endure, take the long way round without losing sight of his goal.

Constantine's goals weren't always personal, he also had a keen appreciation of his position as a prominent Trinidadian and a representative of a wider black Caribbean community. At the end of the 1939 test match series between the West Indies and England and with war imminent, Constantine, like Manny Martindale, made the decision to remain in the UK rather than return with the rest of the team to the West Indies. Having spent nine years in the UK, Constantine thought it inappropriate to leave and prepared to enlist. Instead, he was offered the job of welfare officer for the Ministry of Labour and National Service in Liverpool, working with West Indians employed in the British munitions industry.

The involvement of Constantine and other West Indians in the war effort still left them susceptible to racism. In 1943, Constantine visited London to play a charity cricket match at Lord's. Constantine, accompanied by his wife and daughter, had booked a hotel in London for the weekend. On arrival, Constantine was told he and his family could only stay for one night on account of their skin colour. It would have been understandable if Constantine had responded furiously to being turned away. He could have refused to play in the charity game as a protest against a society happy to have West Indians in its factories and on its cricket fields but which would not treat them as equals outside of those areas. He might have simply found the whole incident, played out in front of his wife and daughter, so painful that any response other than checking in to another hotel and trying to forget his treatment became impossible.

What Constantine did was to find a way between rage and humiliation, allowing him to protest but still remain as a government employee and a man starting to be a part of the British establishment. Constantine, the aspirant barrister, sued the Imperial Hotel, not under a race relations statute, no such statute existed, but rather for breach of contract. Constantine won, received £5 in damages and earned a small place in legal history.

Although his wartime role and the Imperial Hotel's case marked Constantine as a personality in British society, he returned to Trinidad in 1954 and became party chairman of the People's National Movement (PNM) established by Eric Williams. Constantine was Minister of Communications Works and Utilities in the first William's government and returned to Britain in 1961 as High Commissioner.[152]

---

152 In 1961 Trinidad was still a British colony.

Remaining in Britain after his time as High Commissioner, Constantine became, in 1969, Baron Constantine of Maraval in Trinidad and Nelson in the county Palatine of Lancaster. Constantine had become, like Jack Grant and Pelham Warner, a man of the British Empire. "Local Boy Makes Good" was the headline in the Nelson Leader.[153]

So, there we have it, an interesting study of the gap between the perception of Constantine as an athletic natural and the real character, diligent, hard-working and patient, in his cricketing career, professional life and as a public figure.

But the more nuanced view isn't entirely correct. Alongside Constantine's patience and diligence there was a passionate desire to compete, a stern competitive instinct that would have been recognised by Herman Griffith and the Yorkshire dressing room. On the cricket field Constantine wanted to win, to win right now not in some distant point in the future and it was foolish to be too nice about the methods adopted. Insults were to be promptly and fully avenged; justice of the eye for an eye variety.

In a Lancashire league game between East Lancashire and Nelson, the East Lancashire professional was a white South African cricketer, Jim Blanckenberg, who refused to shake Constantine's hand. Throughout Blanckenberg's innings of seventy-seven, Constantine bowled short to the South African who was continually hit on the thigh and in the ribs by the rising ball. At the end of the game, Blanckenberg came into the Nelson dressing room wearing only cricket boots and a raincoat. He removed the raincoat

---

153 From *Learie Constantine* by Peter Mason

and said to the Nelson captain, "Look what your bloody pro has done to me." The left-hand side of Blanckenberg's body from knee to shoulder was a mass of bruised flesh.[154]

As we have seen, this was no isolated incident. Bouncer controversies were a feature of Constantine's fast bowling years and Blanckenberg wasn't the only opponent who experienced Constantine's wrath. There is an impression Constantine might have been more popular with spectators than his fellow professionals. Like Herman Griffith, if he felt there was a batsman he could get out without too many problems he would let the batsman know all about it.

So now we have it, natural athleticism, hard work and patience but animated by a competitive spark that could cause conflagrations. But there seems to be another side, another level to Constantine as a cricketer, Constantine the batsman, that doesn't bear any relation to our much-revised formula.

Constantine was an explosive run getter. Against Middlesex in 1928 he had reached fifty runs in just eighteen minutes of batting in the first innings and 103 in an hour in the second to win the game. In 1931 on the West Indies tour to Australia he scored ninety-seven in an hour and a half against Queensland and was out trying to hit a six to reach his hundred. But the days when Constantine came off were, in first-class cricket, relatively rare. He averaged just nineteen as a batsman in test matches, twenty-four in all first-class matches, a meagre return for a player who many felt could have been a dominant batsman. And if

---

154 *Cricket and Race* by Jack Williams

Constantine's bowling was constantly adapting, his batting stayed constant; in his final test match at the Oval in 1939 Constantine scored seventy-nine in less than twelve overs at the crease, including eleven fours and "an astonishing stroke off the back foot"[155] to hit Perks for six into the Vauxhall End.

One explanation for Constantine's thrilling refusal to play the percentages is that it was a calculated money-making decision. Constantine was paid to bring the crowds to Lancashire league cricket and the crowds came to see him bat in a high-wire act where power and improvisation could always be undermined by disaster. But can that be all the explanation? In *Beyond a Boundary*, CLR James describes a group of well-meaning Trinidadian friends going to Constantine urging him to fulfil his talent and to bat properly. But Constantine didn't take any notice of James and co, even though a career in league cricket was a distant prospect. Similarly, most famous hitters, Ian Botham would be a good example, have batted defensively when saving a game rather than trying to win it was the only possibility. But there is no record of Constantine ever playing for a draw. Constantine's batting stands in contradiction not only to his constant adaptation as a man and cricketer but also to his competitiveness.

What animated Constantine's batting has to be a matter of conjecture, but I wonder if it was motivated by the desire to keep something that was truly his. Ever since he first played on the matting pitch at his father's house,

---

155 *Wisden* Match report

this son and nephew of West Indian cricketers was marked for cricketing greatness. Becoming a professional cricketer brought Constantine financial success and a place in the world but with that came responsibilities, not just to himself but to a West Indian team making a mark in the world game. As a black man in a largely white country, Constantine was a representative of Caribbean society; if he failed, his countrymen failed with him. And he carried all this, brilliant fielder, canny adaptive bowler, fierce competitor, through cricket games, public service, court cases and the long journey to qualify as a barrister. But his batting, there he drew the line that was him, instant, unmediated even by the requirements of the match position. When he went out to bat at Old Trafford in 1933 for the West Indies was he thinking his team was lurching to defeat and a few quick runs were the way to go, or was he relishing the forthcoming simple joy of a ball sweetly struck?

Chapter 15

INTERLUDE

At Old Trafford, the West Indies avoided defeat in a test match in England, for the first time, and had shown they could give England a game, even allowing for some vagaries in selection. But Old Trafford was to be the high point of the tour and in the final test of the series, played at the Oval in London, they suffered another innings defeat. Learie Constantine was not available and a pattern was emerging, the West Indies were competitive when Constantine played but struggled without the all-rounder. Constantine's non-appearance in the third test is a bit of a mystery story in itself.

The original expectation was Constantine would only appear in the second test of the series, but *The Guardian* had carried an article in mid-July stating a compromise had been reached with Nelson who would release Constantine for the Oval test in exchange for Stan Nichols of Essex playing for Nelson whilst Constantine was with the West Indies.

Nichols was available to stand in as his county, Essex, did not have a game on the day concerned.

However, that arrangement fell apart when on the 1st August England selected the team for the third test and included Nichols. Writing about these events, Constantine commented: "Rumour has it that Jardine immediately requested Nichols to play for England! That settled that."[156] The rumour that the selection of Nichols was intended to prevent Constantine from playing in the third test match has continued ever since, and it may be true, but it is, I think, unlikely to be true. There is no documentary evidence to suggest the selection of Nichols was a blocking manoeuvre, but then you wouldn't expect to find any, such things could easily be done with a nod and a wink.

However, the MCC had attempted throughout the summer of 1933 to arrange for Constantine to play in the test matches. Additionally, although Jardine had been co-opted to the selection committee, he did not have the final say in selection. Chairman of selectors, Lord Hawke, had many faults, but he was no-one's patsy and had shown himself to be a friend of West Indian cricket. Finally, Nichols was a good cricketer, and was included in the party to tour India in 1933-1934 which was announced on the same day as the team for the third test, it was not as if England had selected him out of the blue, which would have been suspicious.

The MCC's approach to the selection of Nichols seems to me of a piece with their approach to the West Indies side in general. They were well disposed towards cricket in the

---

156 Page 60 of *Cricket in the Sun.*

West Indies and would, in a slightly detached way, help where possible, but the real focus of the MCC (as distinct from individuals such as Warner, Mallett and Hawke) was on English cricket. They weren't going to leave Stan Nichols out of the team for the third test to ensure Learie Constantine could play.

Whatever the reasons behind it, Constantine's absence saw the West Indies slide to defeat in a very similar manner to the first test of the series. England won the toss and chose to bat. Martindale was hard to play in his first two spells and took three of the first four wickets to fall, with Valentine chipping in with the vital wicket of Hammond. The England team was tottering at 68 – 4. But Fred Bakewell who had come in to the side played a crucial innings of 107. Bakewell was a professional cricketer who played for Northamptonshire and didn't have much to do with the MCC coaching manual. Even in an era of two-eyed stances, Bakewell was remarkably "open" at the crease, "with the right shoulder so far round that it seemed almost to be facing mid-on."[157] He crouched down low and had one hand at the top of the bat handle and the other at the bottom; it must have been quite a sight. In county cricket Bakewell was an aggressive opening batsman who often didn't come off, but when he did could shred an opposing attack. In this match, however, he was a different character, his hundred taking five and a half hours; a long haul given the rapid over rates of the 1930s.[158] But Bakewell's self-denial provided a foundation

---

157 From his *Wisden* obituary
158 For instance 108 overs bowled in the first day at the Oval.

for the innings. Langridge, Ames and the debutant Nichols all made contributions and positions 6 – 11 in England's batting order made 173 runs compared to just 139 from the top five (with Bakewell making 107 of those). Martindale ended with five wickets, but the other six bowlers used only took four wickets, Barnett being run out by Jack Grant.

The West Indies started their first innings on the morning of 14th August in overcast conditions. The left-arm fast bowler Nobby Clarke was even more effective with the new ball than Martindale was on the Saturday; having Ivan Barrow caught behind, before Clifford Roach and Oscar Da Costa were both out fending short balls to fielders close in on the leg side. Clark also sent down plenty of other short stuff, hitting George Headley on two occasions. It was a tough time for Headley. He had come into the match carrying an injury and the news that the aunt who had taken care of him since his return from Panama had been killed in flooding that had swept through Jamaica. It must have been a terrible blow for Headley but, as he always did, he carried on batting.

And Headley was still in when Charlie ("Father") Marriott came on to bowl. Marriott was an amateur cricketer who turned out for Kent during the summer holidays at Dulwich College. Now at thirty-seven years of age he was making his test debut for the injured Walter Robins. There is a picture of him bowling in the Oval test and in terms of unorthodoxy he is a good match for Fred Bakewell. Coming in to his delivery, Marriott has both feet pointing down the pitch and slightly off the ground. He was a long-limbed man and somehow his right arm is so far round that he is showing the ball to the batsman from the left side of his body, as if he were about to bowl underarm and behind his back. In getting into that position he would bang his right forearm against his back with sufficient force for the batsman to hear the smack from twenty-two yards away. His action was described as "high with a free, loose arm"[159] and there must have been a tremendous amount of work on the ball as he unwound from this position to deliver from past his right ear. Although the terms leg-spinner and wrist-spinner are often synonymous, Marriott span the ball from out of his fingers[160] and though his variation was a conventional off-spinner rather than a googly, batsmen found it hard to spot.[161] Not surprisingly, he was the sort of leg-spinner who could be unplayable, or could be rubbish. As with many losing sides, the West Indies didn't have much luck in 1933 and this was to be one of Marriott's good days. First Headley confronted by this Heath Robinson contraption of a bowling action decided attack was the best response, came down the pitch, missed and was stumped by Les Ames. The West Indies were 44 – 4; and looking defenceless. Unlike England there was no recovery from the lower half of the order, Marriott swept away the rest of the batting as the West Indies scored a round 100 all out in just twenty-nine and a half overs with Ben Sealey, "who cares little for the set form of test match cricket,"[162] top scoring with twenty-

159 Per his *Wisden* obituary
160 Muttiah Muralitharan would be an example of the reverse: an off-spinning wrist-spinner.
161 As per *The Times* report on the test.
162 From *The Times* match report.

nine. At the start of the second day the West Indies had been in the game, twenty minutes before lunch they had already been bowled out and asked to follow on.

Clifford Roach opened the batting and played one of his scintillating innings. In the five overs before lunch, the West Indies took their score to 38 for 0. Roach went on to score fifty-six in three quarters of an hour; reaching his fifty in thirty-three minutes, the fastest fifty scored by a West Indian to that point and the fastest fifty by any batsman to open an innings, a record Roach continued to hold until 2014.[163] He "swept" the distinctly rapid Clark for six and got his own back on Bakewell who had caught him in the first innings by hitting him on the knee (with the ball) whilst Bakewell fielded at short leg; Roach apologised. When Ivan Barrow was out, George Headley was still in the pavilion recovering from the blows received in the first innings. Grant took his place at three, but Clark hit him as well, striking him on the arm and forcing him to also retire hurt. Even though the summer of 1933 lacked the rancour of bodyline or the ball on head violence of the MCC's tour of India in 1933-1934 there were still a succession of batsmen who were struck whilst batting, and Grant joined Hammond in being forced from the field by injury. Both Headley and Grant recovered and returned to bat, although Headley was out for twelve and Grant for fourteen.

This time the West Indies lower order at least hung around for a bit and with the help of a couple of rain breaks forced the game into the third day, but it only took England

---

163 *Wisden Book of Test Cricket*, Bill Frindall.

two overs of that final day to finish the West Indies off and bring to an end what was described in *The Times* as, "A match which had never quite carried the atmosphere of a test match." Marriott took 6/59 in the second innings and 11/96 in the match; the second-best bowling analysis by an England test debutant of all time.[164] Although he toured India in 1933-1934 he didn't play another test match, so was left with a test average of just under nine runs per wicket. He was another member of the illustrious club of bowlers who took more first-class wickets than they scored runs.

Although Douglas Jardine had missed the final test of the West Indies series he was back, fit and in charge, for the subsequent tour of India. But the MCC minutes for 10th July 1933 record that Lords Hailsham and Hawke had a "talk" with him. The inference is that the MCC were anxious the tour should be a diplomatic success at a time when Indian demands for independence were becoming ever more pressing. But Hawke and Hailsham weren't able to temper the competitiveness that was the essence of Douglas Jardine. Hopper Levett, who toured with Jardine in India in 1933-1934, said, "He appeared to me to approach a test match as if he was going to fight a battle in which one's life was at stake."[165]

It was to be another overseas tour with plenty of short-pitched bowling from the representatives of the "Premier Club" who played fast bowlers Nobby Clark and Stan Nichols in all three tests. The first Indian national sides lacked quality

---

164 *Wisden Book of Test Cricket*, Bill Frindall
165 From *Douglas Jardine: Spartan Cricketer* by Christopher Douglas.

spin bowlers but, with Mohammed Nissar and Amar Singh, were able to retaliate, bouncer for bouncer to English short-pitched bowling. Both sides used bodyline fields on occasion in the series.[166] Dilawar Hussain was hit by Nichols in the second test and had to be carried from the pitch but was able to return to bat later in the innings. But, in the third test, Naoomal Jeoomal, was hit by a ball from Nobby Clark that he edged into his face, and was out for the rest of the match. Clark followed up by bouncing the Yuvrajah of Patalia, there were shouts of bodyline from an angry crowd, and a stone was thrown at Clark whilst he was fielding in the deep.

Controversy wasn't limited to short-pitched bowling: There was also a serious spat between Douglas Jardine and the former Australian and Middlesex professional cricketer, Frank Tarrant, who umpired in the first two tests between England and India. Jardine felt Tarrant was giving too many LBW decisions against the England batsmen and was unduly influenced by his connections to various cricketing maharajahs. As in 1932-1933, telegrams were sent to and from Lord's but this time their content was, and has remained, secret. Tarrant, however, was asked to stand down for the third test by the Indian Cricket Board of Control. In Tarrant's account of the incident, Jardine's protests weren't only motivated by LBW decisions, but also by Tarrant instructing Jardine to replace Clark in the second test for too much short-pitched bowling.

Towards the end of the tour, the MCC party spent two weeks in Sri Lanka that even by the standards of Douglas

166 David Frith, *Bodyline Autopsy* as before.

Jardine were notable for the bad feeling between hosts and the visiting team. It has been said Jardine's approach to the bodyline tour arose from his having a peculiar enmity for Australians – but this would be to underestimate the breadth and impartiality of Jardine's hostility. If there was any nationality that particularly seemed to annoy Jardine, it was Sri Lankans. During the fortnight-long stop off, Jardine first insisted on play being held up during a game in Colombo whilst a group of spectators who were barracking him were thrown out of the ground, and then turned up two hours late for a game in Galle in protest at the condition of the car used to drive him down the coast.

The Sri Lanka excursion reached its nadir when Nobby Clark, whilst batting, began to, deliberately and obviously, use the studs on his boots to rake up the pitch. It's not possible to link Jardine to this incident as he had taken the game off, leaving the Kent amateur Bryan Valentine as captain, but Clark's action was sufficiently serious for Valentine and Charles Marriott to go to the Sri Lankan dressing room and apologise.

However, for all the disputes and controversy, Jardine's biographer, Christopher Douglas, stresses that the Indian tour was conducted in a good spirit[167] and Jardine was much more comfortable in India than he had been in Australia the winter before. In the first test match, Jardine prevented wicketkeeper, Harry Elliot, from running out Indian captain Cottari (CK) Nayudu who had left his crease to see off spectators who had run onto the field, the only

---

167 Presumably he was overlooking the Sri Lankan extension.

example I have found of a "sporting gesture" by Jardine in a game of cricket. Rather more typical of Jardine was the result of the series. England won the first and third tests of the three matches and forced India to follow on in the second, which ended in a draw. When, at the end of the tour, Jardine brought his test match career to a close, he had been England captain in fifteen test matches; England had won nine of those games, drawn five and lost only one.[168]

All in all, it was quite a way for Jardine to end his time as test captain. Starting in October 1933 and going through to March of 1934, a touring party of fourteen players and manager played thirty-four games, from Peshawar close to the border between modern day Pakistan[169] and Afghanistan, to Galle on the southern coast of Sri Lanka. They experienced bodyline bowling, pitch invasions, stone throwing, a test match boycott,[170] an umpiring controversy, arguments about a pitch being rolled for too long,[171] halts in play whilst barracking spectators were ejected and two cases of malaria. They injured two Indian batsmen with short-pitched bowling and were guilty of a flagrant, and unpunished, bit of pitch doctoring on their own account. It wasn't all work; Jardine in particular was quick to accept the hospitality of Maharajahs and enjoyed numerous hunting expeditions, bagging "a lion, a tiger, a panther, several stags,

---

168 http://stats.espncricinfo.com/england/engine/records/individual/
   most_matches_as_captain.html?class=1;id=1;type=team
169 At the time part of British India.
170 Of the second test in Calcutta due to the absence of Bengalis from the
   Indian side.
171 MCC vs Viceroys XI

a bear and innumerable smaller creatures."[172] Tours were different in those days.

Whilst Jardine brought his own style of cricket to his "home" of India, the debate about his methods continued in England and a tentative cricketing peace process was in motion. The first step was taken via the Advisory Cricket Committee (ACC) in November of 1933. This committee, under the auspices of the MCC was made up of captains and other representatives of the first class counties and declared "Any form of bowling which is obviously a direct attack by the bowler upon the batsman would be an offence against the spirit of the game". The Imperial Cricket Conference passed an identical resolution in its meeting of July 1934, extending the sentiment from county to test match cricket.[173] However, there was no change to the laws of the game; the statements of the ACC and ICC were guidelines to the sort of behaviour that constituted cricket.

The "spirit of the game" statements were part of a delicate diplomatic process that saw Australia agree to tour England in 1934. Jardine did not play a part in that series. In the *Evening Standard* of 31st March, he announced, "I have neither the intention nor the desire to play cricket against Australia this summer." It marked Jardine's retirement not only from test but first-class cricket. In part, this was a response to the ACC statement of November 1933 on direct attack bowling. This was the phrase used by the Australian Cricket Board of Control to describe bodyline

---

172 Christopher Douglas, *Douglas Jardine: Spartan Cricketer*, page 181
173 Frith, as above.

in its discussions with the MCC. So the clear implication of the ACC statement was that bodyline simply wasn't cricket. Jardine was very tetchy about his cricketing honour and didn't want to carry on playing under the new settlement. Perhaps just as importantly, financial considerations were pushing him away from cricket. Jardine had become engaged prior to the India tour and, on his return home, had to take up the responsibility of providing his family with an upper-middle-class lifestyle. It wouldn't be possible to do that if he continued to devote the majority of his time and energy to playing cricket, but the *Evening Standard* was prepared to pay him a good rate for writing about the 1934 series. Jardine was thirty-three years old when he retired from cricket, but it was quite common for amateur players to have shorter careers than their professional counterparts.

On the second day of the second test match of the ashes series of 1934, the cricket was dominated by Bills, Bill Bowes of England bowling to the Australian openers Bill Woodfull and Bill Brown. As was generally the case in the English summer of 1934, pitches were good for batting and Australia were proceeding smoothly after an England first innings of 440 all out. Bowes was becoming a medium pace bowler who relied on skill and control but in 1934 could still get the ball through and he let both batsmen have a few bouncers. There was no hint of a bodyline field and this was test cricket as it had been played since at least the 1920s when the Australian fast bowlers Jack Gregory and Ted McDonald had dominated ashes series with a mixture of skill, pace and intimidation. It was probably the way that test match cricket had been played since it began. But it was still too much for Australian tour manager Harold Bushby, who voiced his concerns to the three England selectors during the tea interval. As the players went back onto the field for the final session Wyatt sidled across to Bowes and explained that he had been handed a note saying "Tell Bowes not to bowl short". Bowes asked what Wyatt wanted him to do. "Well," said Wyatt, "if they want it friendly perhaps they better have it that way."[174] [175]

Australia won the series 2-1 and it was a more emphatic result than the one test margin would imply. England were greatly assisted by the weather: Hedley Verity bowled on a rain-affected pitch at Lord's to give them their only victory, and rain saved England from defeat in the fourth test at Headingley. As in 1933, English wickets assisted spin bowling and in Bill "Tiger" O' Reilly and Clarrie Grimmet Australia had two of the best. Bob Wyatt felt that the pitches were "over prepared" and "featherbeds" with the inference being they were designed to keep fast bowling out of the game.

Prior to the second test match, Harold Larwood had joined his erstwhile captain in announcing he didn't want to be considered for selection against Australia. Bill Voce was still effectively exiled from test match cricket even though he was back in form for his county Nottinghamshire and averaged twenty-two runs per wicket in first-class cricket in

---

174 David Frith, *Bodyline Autopsy*, page 403

175 In his biography *RES Wyatt Fighting Cricketer*, Bob Wyatt confirms that he deliberately restricted the numbers of fielders on the leg side when Nobby Clark was bowling round the wicket for fear of Australian protests.

1934. Don Bradman had an uncertain start to the English summer of 1934 but was back to form by the end of the series, scoring a triple hundred in the Headingley test and 244 off 275 balls in the final test. With Bill Ponsford matching Bradman for runs if not rate of scoring and Grimmet and O'Reilly dominant with the ball, Australia won the deciding, timeless, test by 562 runs. The English public felt, with some justification, that Australia were having an impact on English selection, tactics and pitches. Douglas Jardine, in his new role as journalist, noted that the gate for the Old Trafford test was "10,000 down on what was expected". But although it may not have met with the universal approval of the English cricketing public, cricketing peace had been re-established and test match cricket between England and Australia was to continue.

The one serious break in the peace treaty came not in a test match but instead in Australia's county game against Nottinghamshire. Nottinghamshire captain Arthur Carr is sometimes credited with having been the inventor of bodyline and Nottinghamshire remained a bodyline outpost in 1934. Both Don Bradman and Harold Larwood missed the Australia Nottinghamshire game, but Bill Voce didn't and bowled bodyline complete with a ring of short-leg fielders taking 8/66 in the first innings, followed up with a particularly nasty second innings spell in front of a delighted crowd. But when the third day's play started, Bill Voce did not come out onto the pitch, he was unavailable, officially due to an injury but it was generally believed because the Australians had threatened to forfeit the match if he continued to bowl.

Voces' bowling at Trent Bridge gave support to the Australian claims that the spirit of the game statement from the ACC was insufficient to exclude bodyline from cricket. Harold Bushby, the Australian party's manager, made further representations to the MCC at the end of the tour. The Australians were supported in their anti-bodyline stance by English counties who had experienced the tactic in their fixtures against Nottinghamshire in 1934. Lancashire had already announced they were not going to play against Nottinghamshire in 1935 and other counties were close to releasing similar statements.

The MCC finally conceded the point they had been fighting against since January 1933 and tacitly accepted something had gone wrong in their 1932-1933 tour of Australia by introducing, in November 1934, law 43, defining a direct attack on a batsman as "Persistent and systematic bowling of fast-pitched short balls at the batsman standing clear of his wicket". Such bowling would result in a warning for the bowler and then the captain. If neither warning were heeded, then the bowler was to be taken off."[176]

The rule change was limited in its scope. Short-pitched bowling was only against the laws of the game if the batsman was standing clear of his wicket, i.e. presumably the ball would have to be on a line outside of leg stump if it was to be considered a direct attack. This imported one of the key arguments of the bodyline apologists into an anti-bodyline rule. It had always been claimed bodyline was a response to

---

176 As per *The Times* 6th March 1935, the rule change was approved by the Advisory County Cricket Committee in November 1934, see http://mcc.adlibhosting.com/Details/archive/110000626

modern negative batting where batsmen moved across their stumps and a batsman who continued to do this would receive no protection from the new law. Additionally there was nothing to outlaw bodyline fields, the circle of short legs that were a feature of bodyline at its most contentious.[177]

Law 43 wasn't introduced in isolation; the MCC also introduced a revision to the LBW law so a batsman could be out to a ball pitched outside of the off stump (although the point of contact with the pad still had to be in line with the stumps for the batsman to be given out LBW). The two laws taken together were an attempt to return batting to its pre-First World War state, batsmen should keep their right foot fixed and bat from a point outside of the leg stump, and then they would be safe from both LBW and bouncers.

Whatever the limited theoretical impact of the new law, it marked an emerging consensus between English and Australian administrators and players as to what was and wasn't cricket. Between 1935 and 1939 any bowler using the bouncer on a consistent basis was likely to draw a protest from an opposing captain.[178] Peace in our cricketing times, probably.

But the West Indies hadn't been a part of the negotiated truce. The Imperial Cricket Conference (ICC) reiterated the MCC's and ACC's description of direct attack bowling as against the spirit of the game and extended its ambit to international cricket. But although the West Indies were

---

177 The rule limiting fielders behind square on the leg side to two was not introduced until 1957 and was aimed at defensive not intimidatory bowling.

178 Frith as above, pages 414-417.

members of the ICC they, along with other recent joiners India and New Zealand, only had one vote to the two votes held by the three founder members, England, Australia and South Africa[179] . Even more importantly, the absence of air travel meant it was difficult for the non-English members of the ICC to attend meetings that were always held at Lord's. Instead, MCC luminaries such as Pelham Warner and Richard Mallett would represent other nations in ICC meetings.

With Larwood and Voce exiled from the English team, the West Indies had the best opening attack in international cricket in Martindale and Constantine. There was an MCC tour of the West Indies in 1934-1935. Would the West Indies accept that bodyline was over?

---

179 http://resolution1514.wordpress.com/2013/05/08/17/

Chapter 16

THE WEST INDIES 1935 AND CAPTAIN CIPRIANI

CLR James came to Britain in 1932 bringing with him two manuscripts. One was a biography of Learie Constantine, published in 1933 as *Cricket and I*. The other was the biography of Captain Arthur Cipriani, Trinidadian politician, labour leader and in James' own words: "national hero".

Cipriani had an unusual background for a people's champion. The descendent of Corsican immigrants, he worked as a jockey and itinerant supervisor on cocoa estates. The First World War changed the course of Cipriani's life when he recruited for and joined The British West Indian regiment. As white West Indians who wanted to fight typically enlisted as officers in the British Forces,[180] Cipriani's fellow

---

180 In *Beyond a Boundary*, CLR James tells the story of his unsuccessful attempt to enlist in the British army for the First World War.

volunteers were, generally, black West Indians. Cipriani was posted to Egypt where the regiment was confined to a support role as British high command believed it could not be trusted in battle.[181] Cipriani was prominent in successful protests against this limited role. On his return to Trinidad, the jockey was reborn as a labour leader and the hero of Port of Spain's barefoot man; Cipriani led the dockyard strikes of 1919 and in 1923 was elected as president of the Trinidad Workingmen's Union.[182] The union dated back to the late nineteenth century, had 15,000 members and became Cipriani's power base. In 1929, Cipriani was elected mayor of Port of Spain, a position he held on seven subsequent occasions. He was also an elected member of the legislative council from 1925-1945.

On 13th March 1935, the sixty-year-old Cipriani is in a police car heading south from Port of Spain, towards the town of Couva. Cipriani hasn't been arrested; he and Detective Inspector Liddlelow have the same aim; to prevent a Hunger march from the town of Fyzabad reaching the capital.[183] There are only 100 or so marchers, mostly former employees of the Apex oilfield. They had struck

---

181 https://www.iwm.org.uk/history/the-story-of-the-british-west-indies-regiment-in-the-first-world-war

182 That was rebadged as the Trinidad Labour party in 1934.

183 Fyzabad was originally founded by Kenneth Grant, grandfather of West Indian cricket captains Jack and Rolph Grant, as a mission for his appointed task of converting Trinidadians of Indian descent to Christianity.

over low wages,[184] the practice of checking pay[185] and the dismissal of one of their colleagues. But the strike has not been a success. The manager of the Apex oilfield Colonel HCB Hickling declares it illegal and replaces the striking workers. This is easy to do in Trinidad in 1935, the island's economy is dependent on the export of sugar and petroleum and particularly susceptible to the ongoing economic depression. The strikers are not only out of a job, they are blacklisted and denied work anywhere else in the oilfields of southern Trinidad. In a seemingly hopeless position they march to get their jobs back and to demand a commission of enquiry into their grievances.

Cipriani remains a progressive force in Trinidadian politics, but was never a revolutionary and his interest in, and enthusiasm for, strikes and direct action has waned over time. His electoral success, and the limited nature of the Trinidadian franchise, focuses his attention on the emergent black and "mulatto" middle classes and their self-help friendly society organisations. The hunger marchers may expect the leader of the strikes of 1919 to be on their side, but Cipriani sees his role as helping to avoid the violence he thinks[186] might break out if the marchers were joined by the "roughs" of Port of Spain. The firebrand of 1919 tells the marchers of 1935 that "The trouble was they had gone the wrong way about it."[187]

---

184 A reduction from $1.08 per day to $0.8 at the same time as duties were increased.
185 Levying fines for lateness and other real and imagined infractions.
186 Fourteen people died in the Trinidadian labour unrest of 1937.
187 *Port of Spain Gazette.*

Cipriani suggests that, rather than marching in to Port of Spain, the marchers appoint a delegation to meet with the governor of Trinidad. Although one speaker tells Cipriani that if "They did not get their grievances righted they would make a sacrifice of their lives," Cipriani's offer and the promise of free rail transfer back to the South is sufficient to halt the march short of its intended destination.

The delegation does get to meet the governor, first, briefly on 14th March and again on the 20th March, this time HC Hickling[188] is also present. The governor "Concluded that the men had not made out a case for the appointment of a commission of enquiry, but he would instruct the Warden of the District to inquire into the state of unemployment in Fyzabad and to endeavour to find employment for the men who were out of work."[189] In other words, nothing is to be done.

Viewed as a part of the broad sweep of history, the most significant aspect of the hunger march of 1935 was the presence of Uriah (Buzz) Butler in the delegation that met the Governor. Butler was a member of the Cipriani led Working Men's Union but the two were very different. Butler was a Grenadian who had come to work in the oilfields of Trinidad, whereas Cipriani came from a well-established family of Trinidadian planters. Butler's power base was in the

---

188 Downgraded from colonel to honourable.
189 *Port of Spain Gazette.*

oilfields of the south, Cipriani's in Port of Spain. Butler was a black man, a minister in the proscribed Spiritual Baptist church and radical to the point of eschatology. Cipriani was white, catholic and a reformer.

By 1936, Butler had left the Cipriani led Trinidad Labour party and in 1937 led the oilfield workers of Fyzabad and the surrounding districts out on strike. The strike spread to all of Trinidad's major industries and became a near revolt against British rule; a British navy ship was sent to the island and troops brought from Barbados.[190] Strikes leading to riot and revolt were a common feature of the Caribbean in the second half of the 1930s. At the same time as the Fyzabad hunger march of 1935, Cuba was in the midst of a violent general strike and there were strikes and unrest in St Kitts, St Vincent and St Lucia in 1935, Barbados in 1937 and Jamaica in 1937-1938.

The Trinidad hunger march of 1935 could be seen as a staging post between imperialism and self-determination. But the Fyzabad oilfield workers of 1935 marched out of current desperation, not in the interests of history. The *Port of Spain Gazette* reported the marchers hoped they would be taken on to work on planned improvements on the Port of Spain docks. It was a forlorn hope, the harbour works were one of a number of schemes the governor and legislative council discussed for the alleviation of poverty in Trinidad. The discussions were long but produced little of substance.

---

190 https://libcom.org/library/labour-rebellions-1930s-british-caribbean-region-colonies-richard-hart

The governments of Britain and the other western democracies were overwhelmed by the depression of the 1930s, and their representatives in the West Indies even more supine in the face of the slump. The nameless protestors of 1935 were abandoned, abandoned on an island stained by historical cruelty and benighted by economic conditions.

The historical cruelty was, of course, slavery. Emancipation in 1833 was a transformative event but the black population of the British Caribbean islands remained in a parlous condition. Money that should have been devoted to compensating the victims of slavery went to compensate slave owners. In 1846 the Sugar Duties Act equalised tariffs for sugar imports to the UK, imposing competition on West Indian sugar exports. There were eight years between slavery and the free market. And there was little ordinary West Indians could do to collectively improve their position. Under the Crown Colony[191] system effective power in each island was in the hands of the British governor and his British staff. There was a perfunctory nod to representative government in the presence of elected members on the legislative council, but they were in a minority and were voted for by a limited franchise. British governors were more or less talented, more or less inclined to consider the material status of their subjects, but all governed with British interests as a priority.

---

191 There was no standard system for British administration in the Caribbean: Barbados differed from the other British Caribbean islands and retained its elected assembly. British Guiana became a Crown colony in 1928.

As a result, the growing prosperity experienced in British society in the late nineteenth and early twentieth centuries was not replicated in its colonial possessions. In 1920, average life expectancy in Jamaica was thirty-five years[192] compared to sixty years in the UK.[193] Looked at another way, life expectancy in Jamaica was a statistical smidgeon higher than in the Palaeolithic era.[194] 10,000 years of history had improved the lot of the people of Jamaica by a couple of years.

Of course, life in colonial Jamaica was very different than in a hunter-gatherer society, but it's not clear that it was any better. The people of Jamaica had less chance of a violent death than their ancestors, but sickness is more prominent in agricultural societies, particularly when once localised diseases are transmitted by global trade. And although British government brought Shakespeare, Thackeray and Dickens alongside law and order, it also brought with it a stultifying hierarchy that generally confined its black subjects to inferior positions.

The 1930s added economic dislocation to the historical burdens of the inhabitants of the British Caribbean, many of whom either worked in export industries or who exported

---

192 From the appendix to *Poverty and Life Expectancy: The Jamaica Paradox*, by James C Riley
193 From the ONS https://www.ons.gov. uk/peoplepopulationandcommunity/ birthsdeathsandmarriages/lifeexpectancies/articles/ howhaslifeexpectancychangedovertime/2015-09-09
194 https://en.wikipedia.org/wiki/Life_expectancy: although hunter gatherer life expectancy was generally better than in the first 11,800 years of agriculture.

themselves. When the crash came, those working on sugar plantations, oil fields and on construction sites in the USA were particularly vulnerable; there was no shortage of causes for the protests and labour disputes that flared up in the region in the late 1930s.

There is no escaping the facts: British rule in the Caribbean, even after the abolition of slavery, was not a benign experience for the islands' inhabitants. But, even during the immiseration of the 1930s, there were pockets of limited progress. In some islands, Jamaica in particular, the end of slavery had seen the emergence of a class of land-owning peasants who couldn't stomach employment on the plantations and moved instead into the island's interior.[195] It is estimated that by the mid-1840s, 100,000 Jamaicans earned a living farming privately-owned smallholdings. Although life on the margins was hard, it offered a degree of independence.

Also, in the second half of the nineteenth century there was a limited recognition by the British establishment that it had responsibilities to the majority population, although improvements were meagre compared with the (negligent) mother-country. Education was the most obvious beneficiary of this social concern. By the early twentieth century, most Caribbean children had some formal, government-supplied education; in terms of quality and duration it often wasn't much, but it was something. The expansion of education required teachers, and the black schoolteacher became an important figure in Caribbean society, CLR James' father

---

195 Sometimes supported by church grants.

was one example. Teachers joined small scale capitalists and peasant farmers in what might (very) loosely be termed a black middle class.

And a black middle class that could vote. A 20th February 1935 picture of the elected representatives of the Jamaican legislative assembly shows most to have been black men. These men had limited power, but newspaper reports demonstrate they were keen to bring roads and other funded projects to their constituents and their very presence in the legislative council might have encouraged a more activist government policy.

Perhaps more importantly the non-white population of the Caribbean was prominent in church groups, friendly societies and charities that were also forces for progress in the islands, whilst the working classes united in the Labour organisations that became, on occasion, influential in the period after the First World War.

On some issues, the combination of progressive forces and central government action could bring about distinct improvements. As measured in James Riley's *Poverty and Life Expectancy: The Jamaica Paradox*, improvements in sanitation and public health saw average life expectancy increase from thirty-five years in 1920 to forty-four years in 1935. Herman Griffith, Manny Martindale and other Empire club regulars were employed as sanitary inspectors in Barbados; it may have been that their biggest contribution to society was made in the sewers rather than on the cricket pitch.

The inter-war period also saw the emergence of the Caribbean as a unique cultural force. In *Beyond a Boundary*, CLR James credits his 1933 biography of Learie

Constantine, *Cricket and I*, as the harbinger of a "West Indian renaissance." In the period after World War II James was followed by writers such as VS Naipul and Derek Walcott and academics including Stuart Hall. But if James had defined culture a little more widely, he would have seen he was not the only pioneer. In 1935, the *Port of Spain Gazette* reported Calypso artists Attila the Hun, Growling Tiger and Lord Beginner had travelled by ship to New York to record. In Jamaica, the black nationalist Marcus Garvey was director of the Kingston-based Edelweiss Amusement Company featuring black Jamaican entertainers Bim and Bam, who specialised in comic courtroom musical dramas[196] and dramatist Randolph Williams. Together with their Trinidadian calypso contemporaries, these men were the forerunners of a West Indian popular culture that in the second half of the twentieth century had an influence far beyond the small islands where it was formed.

Cricket was another type of culture where a West Indian aesthetic, present in the 1930s became globally prominent after the Second World War. But should cricket be placed alongside other West Indian art forms? Or is it best regarded as a part of a separate culture of compromise?

Whereas Caribbean music was something new and distinctive, cricket was a game developed in the UK and exported to the West Indies. The spread of cricket was linked to imperialism and the benign attitude of the British government to cricket contrasted with official opposition to other forms of black expression. In 1935, a legislative

---

196 Presumably the inspiration for The Specials' 'Stupid Marriage'.

act was introduced in Trinidad providing: "No stage play or song shall be presented which is insulting to any individual or section of the community referred to by name or otherwise." The *Port of Spain Gazette* did not doubt that the provision was aimed at the carnival tents where calypso artists saw everyone, British governors and administrators included, as a source of material. Similarly, the British government proscribed the Shouter Baptists, a church that combined African and Christian religious practices and where politician Buzz Butler was a minister.

In Barbados, where cricket was particularly popular, sports historian Brian Stoddart credits (or blames) the game for "creating virtually without protest a consensual Barbadian society".[197] And across the Caribbean there were links between what might loosely be called The Establishment and the spread of cricket. The amateur ethos, a belief in the virtues of the British ruling classes, linked education and sport. In his excellent *Jamaica at the Wicket*, Arnold Bertram tracks the dispersal of cricket in Jamaica by the Anglian church, responsible for the development of the influential Clovelly Cricket Club, and how, in outlying areas of Jamaica, teams were established by factory and estate owners and managers.

British administrators also associated themselves with cricket. The island's governors paid a state visit to each of the test matches of 1935 in the same way that George V visited the Lord's test match of 1933. The intertwining of

---

197 *Cricket, Social Formation and Cultural Continuity in Barbados: A Preliminary Ethnohistory.*by Brian Stoddart

the British state and cricket was not only evident at test matches. The *Gleaner* from 11th February 1935 includes a report on the McPhail and McNee Cup, for cricket teams playing in St Catherine's parish. McPhail was the parish Custos (a sort of magistrate) and McNee the legislative assembly representative. The winning team was the prison second XI (presumably staff only) and the awarding of the cup was preceded by the singing of the (British) national anthem.

But although the British establishment made use of cricket there was no establishment plot to infect the Caribbean islands with the game. Visitors to the Caribbean in the second half of the nineteenth century often noted the ubiquity of cricket, with the game being played in remote villages, with homemade bats and oranges for balls. Crowds of black spectators flocked to watch Wanderers and Pickwick play. This popular explosion of cricket rather puzzled British observers; these weren't people who had cricket thrust upon them, they were determined to play and watch despite the practical impediments.

The adoption of cricket by the non-white population of the West Indies was welcomed by some but not all of the cricket establishment. The snobbery that often accompanied amateurism was exemplified by the exclusion of "professionals" from inter-colonial competition and the attempts of Pickwick and Spartan to deny Empire entry to the Barbados Cricket Challenge Cup. For many white people living in the Caribbean, sporting apartheid was a preferable model to multi-racial cricket. And although cricketers were playing an English game, clubs such as

Empire and Shannon, run by their black members, were an early example of secular self-organisation in the Caribbean.

This confused picture of the interaction between cricket and Caribbean society is repeated in the cricketing backgrounds of disparate Caribbean politicians. We have already seen the close personal and cricketing bonds between Learie Constantine and CLR James. But James was a Marxist and Constantine a moderate black nationalist. Grantley Adams, prime minister of the ill-starred West Indies Federation and staunch monarchist, was a member of Spartan cricket club and played one first-class match for Barbados. In Jamaica, the effective deputy leader in Norman Manley's socialist People's National Party was Noel "Crab" Nethersole, one-time Jamaican cricket captain. And whilst James, Constantine, Adams and Nethersole all played roles in a, broadly, democratic post-World War II Caribbean, the cricket committee room became a hideout for the proponents of continued white domination. Grantley Adams might have been Prime Minister of the West Indian Federation, but the captain of the West Indian cricket team was a white man, right up to the appointment of Frank Worrell in 1960.

CLR James wrote in *Beyond a Boundary*, "The British tradition soaked deep into me was that when you entered the sporting arena you left behind you the sordid compromises of everyday existence. Yet for us to do that we would have had to divest ourselves of our skins … Thus the cricket field was a stage on which selected individuals played representative roles which were charged with social significance." James was right, of course, but the pervasiveness of cricket in the West Indies meant very different individuals were playing representative roles in the same game. When West Indians crossed the boundary's edge they were all actors in the same play, but didn't necessarily agree on the plot. Sometimes the result was a game of cricket that resembled a farce.

Chapter 17

JACK GRANT, "THE MAN WHAT LOST THE TEST MATCH"

Writing this book has meant a lot of time scanning CricketArchive for scorecards of games long gone. Sometimes the replication of runs scored and wickets lost summons up a mental picture of what the game must have been like. When I saw the scorecard for the first test between England and the West Indies in 1935 I decided this was clearly a case of match fixing, but rival bookmakers had suborned both teams to lose.

England won the toss and gave the West Indies the opportunity to bat first, the West Indies must have worried they were getting into a strong position when George Headley was dropped twice and rattled up forty-four. Was George not in on the plan? A well-judged run out put paid to Headley and the rest of the West Indian batsmen played their part to leave them in a near impregnable position of 102 all out. But England took up the gauntlet and responded with 81 – 7; captain Bob Wyatt had a trick up his sleeve and promptly declared, still twenty-one runs behind on first innings. Two could play that game; Jack Grant called a halt to the West Indies second innings on just 51 – 6 leaving England a scarcely credible seventy-three to win. Back and forth the two giants traded self-inflicted blows and, as England slumped to 48 – 6, the game no-one wanted to win hung in the balance.

But, captains Jack Grant and Bob Wyatt were both in their different ways highly principled men and the shenanigans of the first test were down to pitch conditions and miscalculation, not bribery. The fall of wickets and seemingly inexplicable declarations were the result of the strange practice in 1930s cricket of not covering the wicket once the game had started. This both unnecessarily disadvantaged spectators, who wanted to see players play, not sit in the pavilion, and introduced an element of pure chance into what was supposed to be a test of skill. For instance, in the second test of the 1934 ashes series, Australia were 192 – 2 at the end of the second day in reply to England's 440 and must have felt they could not lose. But rain on the Sunday completely changed the pitch; when cricket resumed on the Monday Australia were bundled out for 284, and following on, were bowled out again for 118. It was an Australian defeat but it was the English weather more than the team that was victorious.

The Barbados test of 1935 was plagued by bad weather. It had rained before the match began, it rained on the evening of the first day and it rained again on the second evening. The uncovered pitch was always wet. Wet wickets in the West Indies were rather different from their English counterparts. Firstly, the heat of the Caribbean sun meant they were unlikely to stay wet for long, whereas in a traditional English summer a wet pitch could stay damp for several days. Also, English sticky wickets were the preserve of the spin bowler,[198] but in the West Indies it was fast bowlers who dominated when the wicket was wet. With a good length ball often rearing at the batsman, a fielder close in on the leg side always had a good chance of a catch. True to form, Ken Farnes, the amateur pace bowler, "making the ball lift awkwardly[199]" took the first four West Indies wickets to fall but George Headley, with the help of two dropped catches, managed to survive the opening spell. He was going well when he called Cyril Christiani for a quick single. Wicketkeeper Christiani, twenty-one years of age and playing his first test sent Headley back, Headley slipped and was run out. Christiani was not out for nine when the West Indies were all out for 102; it must have been a long walk back to the dressing room to George Headley and his other team mates.[200]

When England batted, Manny Martindale produced another of his dominating new ball spells and took the first

---

198 Two of the best bowlers on wet English spinners were Hedley Verity and Derek Underwood; both conventional slow left-armers, who pushed the ball through.

199 From the 1936 *Wisden* match report .

200 Although Kenneth Farnes in *Tours and Tests* reckoned it was an impossible run.

three wickets, leaving England on 28 – 3. But late on the first day, with the sun drying out the pitch, was the best time to bat in the match; the Barbados Advocate believed "The wicket rolled out easy" for the English batsmen. With Wally Hammond not out on forty-three, England ended the first day on a comparatively prosperous 81 – 5.

The night brought more rain and play could not start until after tea on the second day. On a wet wicket drying in the sun and wind, Leslie Hylton was next to unplayable; he dismissed Wally Hammond with the first ball after play resumed and had Errol Holmes caught by Ellis Achong in the same over. Wyatt determined the conditions were so favourable for bowlers he would forgo the last three England wickets and he declared without a single run being added to the overnight score of eighty-one.

Jack Grant responded to this unconventional piece of captaincy from Wyatt by sending in his brother, hard-hitting Rolph Grant, to open the batting with Leslie Hylton, who had now opened both the batting and the bowling in the same match for the West Indies. Presumably Jack Grant hoped his brother could rattle up some quick runs. But conditions were terribly difficult. In the first over a ball from Ken Farnes reared from a length, straight over Hylton, over the head of England wicketkeeper Les Ames and away for four byes. Grant was dismissed by "Big" Jim Smith with the score at 4 – 1. Martindale and Achong were also pushed up the order, both were promptly dismissed by Smith and the West Indies were 4 – 3 and just twenty-five runs ahead in the match with seven second innings wickets left.

With Cyril Christiani, the man who had run out George Headley in the first innings, next in, the tactics changed from attack to desperate defence in the hope Christiani and Hylton could bat through the final hour and the pitch might be easier for the proper batsmen on the next day. They managed to fight it out, the tall Hylton perpetually gnawing away at a toothpick, in what was described by their captain as "An amazing exhibition of skill, pluck and gamesmanship"[201]. The skill came in not playing a shot at good length deliveries, instead allowing them to pass over the top of the stumps, the pluck was necessitated by the number of blows the two batsmen took and the gamesmanship was the amount of time it took them to recover from those blows and generally pat down the wicket and so on, all of which took them closer to the end of the day. But rather than being rewarded by better batting conditions, more rain fell overnight and once again the West Indies had to bat on a wet, but drying wicket. 33 – 3 quickly became 47 – 5 and when George Headley was caught off Farnes for nought, Jack Grant declared, setting England just seventy-three to win the match.

There was some logic in this seemingly incredible decision. It might be harder for England to make seventy-three runs on a drying pitch than 200 on a dry one. But Grant was giving up four wickets worth of batting and as he sent his bowlers in at the top of the order those wickets included Grant himself, Clifford Roach and Derek (JED) Sealy. The innings might have only lasted for another half

---

201 *Jack Grant's Story* By Jack Grant

an hour and thirty to forty runs could have been added. Also, there was always the prospect of yet more overnight rain if the match were forced to its fourth and final day. So, with the benefit of eighty-four years' worth of hindsight, it was probably an incorrect decision but not an egregious one. It was certainly a brave decision. To understand why it was such a brave decision and how Jack Grant came to make it, it is necessary to dive into the racial and national distinctions in West Indies cricket in the 1930s and consider the remarkable Jack Grant.

Jack Grant captained the West Indies for three series: the 1930-1931 matches against Australia, the 1933 series in England and this 1935 series against England in the West Indies. And yet he was regarded with suspicion by many West Indian cricket followers. This was not surprising as Grant's appointment was on the basis of skin-colour rather than experience: he was ushered into the captaincy neither having played in a test match nor an inter-colonial game. Learie Constantine, one of the best West Indian players of Grant's generation, believed, with good cause, he and not Grant should be captain and this must have had an impact on other players Grant was supposed to lead.

Suspicion of Grant wasn't purely racial. Learie Constantine had great admiration for HBG Austin, the white captain of early West Indian sides. But Austin's life was intimately wound up in the West Indies and West Indian cricket in particular. Grant was cut from a different cloth; he was a man of the British Empire rather than any one country, the Grants originally came from Scotland and had emigrated to Canada before Trinidad and used the freedom of movement afforded by the empire to move between the three countries. After the 1931 tour of Australia, the West Indian team took the boat to New Zealand, all except Grant who boarded ship for Rhodesia where he planned to marry his fiancée and start life as a teacher. It seemed his time as a resident of the West Indies and an international cricketer had ended. Then he received an offer from the British Colonial Office to work at Queens Royal College in Trinidad (where both Grant and CLR James had been pupils). It was not a fortunate coincidence that Grant's offer of employment in Trinidad allowed him to captain the 1933 tour to England. Grant was sure the offer was made with the captaincy of the West Indies in mind and at the instigation of his brother Fred, who was president of the WICBC.[202] What is more, Grant received "duty leave" – he continued to be paid both for the trial games that preceded the tour in January of 1933 and the full six months of the tour of England. Grant was really being paid to be a cricketer and what was more he was being paid to be a cricketer by the British government. By contrast, his players were on thirty shillings a week expenses and sometimes had to give up hard-to-find jobs in the West Indies in order to tour.

Grant's inexperience as a cricketer also meant there were doubts about his cricketing acuity. Learie Constantine makes it clear in *Cricket in the Sun* that, although he had no personal animus against Grant, he didn't think much of him as a tactician. Constantine's doubts weren't just about Grant's lack of tactical nous but also that as a white West Indian embedded

---

202 Jack Grant's Story pages 49 – 51

in the apparatus of the British Empire he might lack the desire for the "War to the Knife" of test cricket.

Grant was soon aware of the difficulties in captaining a mixed race team as a young, white man. He admitted, "Consciously or unconsciously, I was heir to certain assumptions on race" and "On one occasion when things were not going well, I 'ticked off' a player in anger and I did so, inadvisedly, in front of the others. He replied in language that savoured of 'White man, stop talking to me as a black boy'. It was as upsetting as it was helpful."[203]

The racial divide wasn't the only issue Grant had to contend with. The West Indies cricket team is a rare sporting beast taking its players from a variety of Caribbean islands and the South American mainland, rather than being based on a nation state. Inter-island rivalry was significant, particularly in a home series. In the West Indies first home test series, the 1929-1930 tour by MCC, sensibilities had been assuaged by allowing island selectors to pick the team for "their" home test and by revolving the captaincy so a home captain was in charge for each match. By 1935, the WICBC had managed to assert enough control over the individual island federations for Grant to be appointed captain for the entire series. Of course, the novelty of a Trinidadian as captain for all four tests found little favour outside of Trinidad and as Grant's brother Fred was president of the WICBC there was a feeling nepotism was afoot.

But despite all these problems, Grant seems to have found a way of leading the team. The English Cricket

---

203 Jack Grant's story page 30: it's probably worth reading twice.

writer, Sir Home Gordon, paid Grant an unintentional compliment when he wrote: "Latterly, a Cantab, GC Grant, undertook captaincy adequately, though to some English eyes the familiarity he permitted from some of his coal-black professionals seemed rather strange.[204]"

Grant does seem to have made an effort to break down the distance between him and his black players. During the 1931 tour of Australia Grant, on occasion, shared a room with George Headley, a bold step given the psychological distance generally pertaining between black and white West Indians.[205] He was also prepared to take advice from black cricketers who played in the teams he captained. His autobiography[206] includes an account of the fifth test in the 1930-1931 series against Australia where Learie Constantine approached asking "Skipper, change places with me". Grant, "Did not hesitate, for I could trust his judgement in these matters." Constantine standing in Grant's old position at mid-off went off to take a remarkable catch to swing the game.

Grant also had the gift of being able to communicate to spectators the sheer fun he got from playing cricket. In its review of the 1933 season *Wisden* had much to say in praise of Jack Grant, including: "Above all, Grant himself played the game, and insisted on those under him doing so, in the most sporting spirit. As the natural outcome of this, the team were always welcome wherever they went and left

---

204 Quoted in *Cricket in the Sun*, Learie Constantine, page 63.
205 Bridgette Lawrence, *Masterclass: The Biography of George Headley*, page 117.
206 Jack Grant's story

behind them a fine impression of keenness, combined with modesty and unfailing good temper."

And it wasn't only *Wisden* who noted Grant's good humour and enthusiasm; CLR James wrote:

> "The fielding was brilliant and Grant at cover is as good as Roach and Valentine were elsewhere. He picked up and threw a batsman out in a most brilliant way and then grinned and was very happy about it in a most likeable manner. He is rather nervous and runs after balls which he should not. But he is very, very keen and, though excitable, when the situation is serious, pulls himself together and bats like a hero."[207]

James' description may make Grant sound like an over-enthusiastic Labrador[208] but when the editor of *Wisden* and a leading Trotskyite theorist believe you are a good chap, you must be doing something right.

But Grant's good humour was only one side to his personality, he was also an intensely moral man. On the tour of Australia, Grant would take the protestant players to church on a Sunday morning whilst the tour manager would arrange an equivalent visit for the Roman Catholic players. It is not recorded how the players regarded this use of their one day off. Another good indication of Grant's style

---

207 From an article in the *Port of Spain Gazette* reproduced in CLR James Cricket page 34-38.

208 I wonder if James was having a bit of fun with English commentators who sometimes made comments about the childish natures of black West Indian cricketers.

of captaincy comes in a letter from Jack Kidney, manager of the West Indies tours of 1933 and 1939, sent to Richard Mallett. Grant was offered the captaincy for the 1939 tour of England but had turned it down; Kidney reflected that it might all be for the best as: "He has certain views about the conduct of the team that cannot be overcome with ours or any other team."[209]

Indeed, Grant's morality and his desire to work as a lay missionary meant he had almost as many doubts about his suitability for the captaincy as his many detractors. His fiancée, Ida, (they had fallen in love at a Students' Christian Movement conference), wanted to return to Rhodesia after leaving Cambridge University and Grant himself was uncertain if playing cricket could be reconciled with his active Christianity. Eventually cricket won out and Grant captained the West Indies in 1930-1931 but it wasn't a decision he was entirely happy with.[210]

Grant continued to be uncomfortable in his role as West Indies captain. He played cricket as a game and, as a member of one of the most prosperous families in Trinidad, had no interest in a career as house professional of the British Colonial Office. He attempted to resign in January 1934 but was persuaded to captain the West Indies in the 1934-1935 home series against England. Then he retired from international cricket at the age of twenty-eight. After the Second World War, Jack Grant and his wife Ida worked in education and as missionaries in South Africa, Nigeria and

---

209 MCC archives.
210 *Jack Grant's Story* pages 22-23.

Rhodesia. As he explains in his autobiography, the couple questioned the attitudes they had grown up with in Africa and the Caribbean and integrated into black congregations. Grant was appointed headmaster at Adams College in South Africa, where most of the pupils were black.

The Grants were not politically radical but their high-minded morality was to bring them into conflict with the racist regimes of South Africa and Rhodesia. Adams College was closed by the government and the Grants denied leave to remain. Moving to Rhodesia they became increasingly involved in the work of the Christian Council that spoke out in favour of a democratic multi-racial country. Eventually, the Grants received the notable double distinction of being barred from Rhodesia and from South Africa and they moved to Cambridge, England, where Jack Grant died in October 1978.

It took a steady nerve to stand up for what was right in apartheid era Rhodesia and South Africa and his underlying toughness was also expressed in the way Jack Grant captained a cricket side. It requires fixed and steady purpose to insist on moral conduct in a team environment and, for all his on-field amiability, Grant was prepared to play to win. He adopted bodyline bowling in the second test of the 1933 series, I suspect Learie Constantine might have had more to do with this decision than subsequent accounts allow, but it's also clear Grant wouldn't have gone along with a tactic he disapproved of. Similarly, although there were no bodyline tactics in the 1935 series, Grant, with one specific exception, seems to have let his fast bowlers get on with their business even though, as reported in *Wisden*: "Some of the England players complained of occasional attempts at intimidation in the matter of short-pitched deliveries and full-tosses directed at the batsmen."

Another, smaller illustration that Grant was not a plaster saint comes in his description of Christiani and Hylton's time-wasting tactics at the end of the second day of the first test. "I continue to marvel at their skill, to admire their pluck, and to blush at their gamesmanship. More correctly I naughtily smile at their gamesmanship."[211] Douglas Jardine was the product of a Muscular Christianity with the Christianity removed, Grant put Christian faith above sporting success but still played to win.

With seventy-three needed to win and in a game of unconventional decisions Wyatt sent bowlers Ken Farnes and Jim Smith in to bat at the start of England's second innings; they joined the West Indian Leslie Hylton in opening both the batting and the bowling in the match: the only time in the history of test matches three players have done both in the same game.[212] Wyatt's decision to reverse the order didn't meet with success as both makeshift openers were quickly dismissed and England were 7 – 2. England's recognised batsmen decided they needed to go on the attack, but continued to lose wickets to Martindale. Holmes was out for six, made with a single scoring shot and when Martindale had Maurice Leyland caught by Rolph Grant England were 29 – 4 and still forty-six runs from victory.

---

211 From Jack Grant's Story page 175.
212 stats.espncricinfo.com/ci/content/records/282801.html

England's hopes rested with forty-five-year-old Patsy Hendren and their best batsman Wally Hammond. The two experienced batsmen were able to adapt to the difficult conditions. Hendren stood outside of leg stump reducing the risk from a ball that reared from the pitch on a leg stump line. Hammond used his incredible eye and strength to play a succession of tennis style shots over the head of mid-off, forcing the field back. Hammond used the shot repeatedly against Hylton who began to lose his length. Although the partnership was only fourteen runs, it tilted the game back towards England. When Hendren was dismissed for a rapid twenty, first George Paine and then Wyatt blocked at one end whilst Hammond continued to score at the other. Hammond finished the match with a clean hit six. England reached their target of seventy-three with six wickets down and had scored the seventy-five runs off just sixteen overs and three balls. It had been a remarkable test match, with only 309 runs scored, the fourth lowest aggregate in a test match that has finished in a positive result and the second lowest in a game in which there have been four innings.[213] Jack Grant's gamble had failed: all over the West Indies he was known as "the man what lost the test match".

---

213 http://stats.espncricinfo.com/wi/content/records/284008.html

Chapter 18

WALLY HAMMOND

The man who won the test match was Wally Hammond; he had scored seventy-two of the 309 runs in the game and been not out in the second innings. Hammond had dominated the 1928-1929 ashes series (905 runs at an average of 113.12) and still held the record for the most runs in a test innings (336) scored in New Zealand in 1933. But his performance in Barbados, made on a difficult pitch and against the quality fast bowling he sometimes struggled against, was one of the best in his career.

On his previous tour of the West Indies in 1925-1926, Hammond had contracted a mystery disease, quite possibly syphilis,[214] although described at the time as blood poisoning. Whatever the cause of the illness, in the pre-

---

214 The syphilis theory is set out in David Foot's *Wally Hammond: The Reasons Why*. The author concedes that there is no conclusive evidence, although venereal disease was consistent with Hammond's lifestyle and not inconsistent with the reported symptoms.

penicillin era it was serious; Hammond was very ill during the long voyage back to England and doctors considered amputating his leg.

Hammond recovered, kept his leg but missed an entire English summer of cricket in 1926. He was back for 1927 and scored a thousand first-class runs by the end of May. Many of those runs came from his famous cover drive, his left foot moving unerringly alongside where the ball pitched followed by a long free swing of the bat with all of Hammond's weight behind it. A combination of loose-limbed grace, and precision. Hammond had remarkable cricketing gifts, hand to eye coordination, balance and what David Foot described as a Grecian athleticism. In the words of a colleague, he was "built like a heavyweight but able to move like a flyweight."[215] As a child, Hammond had lived in Malta and swam every day: George Headley, another cricketer whose physique was compared to a boxer's, also swam every day as a boy, part of his self-imposed fitness programme.

Hammond's one weakness as a batsman was a susceptibility to fast, hostile, accurate bowling. It wasn't that he couldn't compete against such bowling, his first great innings in county cricket came when he hooked and pulled the bowling of Ted McDonald[216] to take a hundred off Lancashire. In 1932 he walloped Bill Voce and Harold Larwood when they were bowling at their fastest for

---

215 From wicketkeeper Arthur Wilson quoted in *Wally Hammond: The Reasons Why* by David Foot, page 132.

216 McDonald was an Australian quick bowler who turned away from test match cricket to play first for Nelson and then Lancashire.

Nottinghamshire. But Hammond didn't like fast bowling. In general in cricket he was in control; canny Australian slow bowlers like Clarrie Grimmet and Bill O' Reilly could restrict him by bowling on his leg stump, but that didn't bother Hammond unduly, he responded by cutting back the number of shots he played and grinding out the massive scores necessary in Australia's timeless tests. But fast bowling took away Hammond's sense of mastery, he had given up the hook early in his career as it was not a percentage shot and thereafter he was forced to duck, weave and dodge the bouncer. In the second test of 1933 he had been hit by both Martindale and Constantine. So to come through in such trying circumstances against Manny Martindale and Leslie Hylton in the first test of 1935 was a particularly impressive achievement.

Hammond was a talented if somewhat reluctant bowler and, with his hand to eye coordination and balance, unmatched as a slip fielder. For a touring captain such as Bob Wyatt, Hammond was a tremendous asset as a player, but needed careful management as a teammate. Hammond was a loner, the important relationships in his life, sexual or otherwise, were with women. He wasn't one for sharing a drink after the day's play or, more importantly, helping a young player along with advice or a kind word. From Bill Bowes' account it is clear a young Yorkshire cricketer would get a great deal of advice from senior players. Although the old pros were quick to slap down any youngster who thought he had the game sorted they would be supportive when things were tough. A young Yorkshire professional did not lack for cricketing fathers.

But young Gloucestershire players could go through an entire match without hearing a word from Hammond. David Foot speculates Hammond's curmudgeonly nature may have been the result of an ill-advised attempt to treat his syphilis with mercury,[217] but Hammond had a difficult childhood that might have influenced his behaviour as an adult. After his father's death Hammond had become a border at Cirencester grammar school and rarely returned home to his mother, instead spending holidays with friends. Money was tight and Hammond wasn't any great shakes academically, but fortunately for him his headmaster was a cricket enthusiast, so to an extent Hammond was a professional cricketer and captain of his own destiny from his early teens. Perhaps that made him disinclined to help others.

It is also possible that Hammond's isolation at Gloucestershire was a function of an indeterminate position in cricket's social hierarchy. The distinction between gentlemen and players gives the impression the class structure of the 1930s was frozen. But the very obsession with status was the product of a world where people could move between classes with, for those in a privileged position, unnerving ease. Hammond's soldier father had started out in the ranks, but by dint of his discipline, hard work and the impersonal slaughter of the First World War, rose to the rank of major. The Hammonds had gone up in the world. His father's death, near Amiens, in 1918 was a financial as

---

217 Although this is a speculation as to the potential treatment for a possible disease.

well as emotional blow to Hammond and there wasn't the money for him to play cricket as an amateur when he left school. His initial attempts to establish himself as a cricketing professional were set back by the insistence of Lord Harris that Hammond serve a two-year residency period before turning out for Gloucestershire.[218]

Whilst he qualified as a resident of the county where he had been educated for five years, Hammond added to his Gloucestershire staff salary[219] by playing for Bristol Rovers in the winter. He rarely made the first team and turning out for the reserves in a struggling third division south team was a sporting low point. But even then, Hammond stood out from the crowd. Despite his limited wages he rented a room in upmarket Clifton and arrived for training in a car. Cars were important for Hammond. In 1933 he was given a job as a sales promotion manager with West Country car dealers, Caters, on a salary of more than £1,000 per year.[220] Applying a simple retail price factor to this amount gives it a present-day worth of £63,000, but this ignores the fact the world was a much poorer place in 1935 than it is in 2019. Applying an earnings index Hammond's £1,000 was worth over £170,000 by 2019 standards. And that was only one element of Hammond's income; his cricket-related earnings were likely to have been another £1,000 or so. Hammond combined sporting aesthetics with success in

---

218 Lord Harris had close connections with Kent, the county of Hammond's birth.

219 He would play for the county from time to time but not in first-class games.

220 *Wally Hammond: The Reasons Why*, as before, page 230.

a way only Dennis Compton[221] has replicated in post-war English cricket. By the standards of modern-day sportsmen his earnings were not remarkable, but the figures show the image of pre-world war professional cricketers as underpaid working class lads to be rather partial.

Most of what Hammond earned, he spent: on fast cars, women and drinks with his coterie at the golf club. The Hammond fortunes were on the rise again and Wally had his sights set higher still. As a young cricketer he had copied his flamboyant captain Bev Lyon, ensuring that he was always immaculately turned out; the message was clear: Hammond wasn't just another professional cricketer. In 1930s cricket, players would often stay with members of the opposition during a county game as a way of eking out expenses. The unwritten rule was that amateurs stayed with amateurs and professionals with professionals. But Hammond invited the amateur Bob Wyatt to stay with him when Warwickshire played Gloucestershire.

It may have been Hammond's unwillingness to respect the unwritten rules that made him stand out in the conformist world of cricket. As far as journalists of the 1930s were concerned, cricketers were allowed to come in one of two types, the stroke-playing amateur with a sense of noblesse oblige and the county professional who knew his place in the scheme of things but had a store of wisdom, pungently expressed, preferably in a strong dialect that could be reproduced phonetically. But a lot of cricketers didn't fit into either category; amateurs like Douglas Jardine weren't

---

221 And, hopefully, Joe Root.

dashing representatives of fair play, professional cricketers often saw their sporting success as a pathway to a better life and some players didn't fit neatly into a class-based scheme.

Hammond, upwardly mobile, and too gauche to hide it, nettled other important figures in the Gloucestershire team. Charles Barnett openly disliked Hammond; this owed something to Hammond's consistent infidelity, but there were other differences between the two men. Barnett was a member of the Beaufort and the Berkeley Vale Hunt, and the son of a former Gloucester amateur cricketer, but played as a professional and after retirement became a school cricket coach. The Barnetts were dropping down the social ranks and it may be this also inspired his animus towards Hammond who was travelling in the opposite direction.

Another factor in the breach between Hammond and his team mates was that Gloucestershire were, and remain, a famously and prodigiously unsuccessful sporting side. Hammond was a serious cricketer, romantics like Neville Cardus mourned the loss of the Hammond of the early years but he was a batsman prepared to give up a stroke if he believed it involved too much risk for the runs gathered. By contrast, Barnett retained his "aristocratic hauteur" and disdain for function despite his professional status. On his day he was a very fine batsman, good enough to play for England on twenty occasions, but a first-class average of thirty-five shows his day didn't come around often. For Hammond, so much more talented than Barnett, it must have been galling to see the man at the other end trapped in a cricketing adolescence.

Wyatt's management of Hammond would be crucial for the success of the 1935 tour. Hammond was the most talented England player, but Wyatt had to integrate the sometimes difficult all-rounder into his team, whilst retaining an atmosphere in the touring party that would allow them to play their best cricket.

Wyatt had certain advantages in managing Hammond: the two men got along quite well[222] and Les Ames, also on the tour, was a friend of Hammond's. Indeed, Hammond generally had decent working relationships with top cricketers. There was another factor that may have inclined Wally Hammond to be a good team man in the West Indies in 1934-1935; it is possible he was thinking he could become captain of the side.

The England captaincy wasn't a realistic ambition whilst Hammond remained a professional, but his job at Caters had shown that he could convert his cricketing fame into earnings from ostensibly non-cricketing sources. He had Pelham Warmer on his side and there is one other piece of circumstantial evidence Hammond might have been thinking of playing as an amateur. The England season of 1934 had been Hammond's benefit year and he had made £3,000. With that one-off payment safely in the bank the financial disadvantages of reinvention as an amateur were reduced.

The early signs were good. Hammond's starring role in the first test match was accompanied by a double hundred in

---

222 Also Hammond's brother "Lofty Hammond", the tallest man in the British navy, was on a ship that was in harbour during the Barbados test: source the *Barbados Advocate*.

a warm up game against Barbados. Off the field, Hammond seemed to be a part of the team, appearing with Maurice Leyland as a pair of convicts in the Christmas day fancy dress party. Vice-captain Errol Holmes went so far as to describe Hammond as a "great leg puller",[223] rather a contrast to the dour, ill Hammond portrayed by David Foot. But there was one sign of the other Hammond. The 1934-1935 touring party included the twenty-three-year-old Warwickshire leg spinner, Eric Hollies. Hammond played spin brilliantly and, perhaps as one of those leg pulls, took to massacring Hollies' bowling in the nets. Wyatt had to tell him to "Stop that Wally,"[224] but the young spinner had already been dealt a blow, by one of his own side.

---

223 *Flanelled Foolishness*, page 68.
224 From *Wally Hammond: The Reasons Why*, David Foot, page 264.

Chapter 19

TRINIDAD:
LAST MAN STANDING

The first test match of 1935 finished in Barbados on the 10th January and by the 15th the MCC were playing in the first of two matches against Trinidad, which preceded the second test in Port of Spain.

Learie Constantine had missed the Barbados test, instead playing in the Indian Gold Cup for the Freelooters side put together by Maharaja Kumar Ali Rajpur. Top professionals often played in the tournament. Indian cricket paid well and Constantine was following Jack Hobbs and Harold Larwood to India. Constantine had not been invited to play in the test series until he returned from India to England and agreed to participate in the West Indies once "terms had been agreed",[225] so it would seem that he was paid to play in the tests of 1935. He arrived in Trinidad just before Wyatt and the MCC team.

225 *Cricket in the Sun*, page 70

The return of Constantine strengthened the West Indies and Wyatt did not have a first choice England side to put against them. At the end of the first test match of the 1933 series, Neville Cardus wrote, "English cricket ought always to be strong enough to find a second eleven good enough to beat the aspirants from the West Indies." In selecting a side to tour the West Indies in 1935, the MCC selectors didn't pick a second team but rather gave Wyatt a squad of fourteen players pretty evenly split between first xi England players, second xi England players and rounded out with a couple of competition winners.

The core of the touring party was strong, including four batsmen who had featured in the 1934 home ashes series: Wyatt as captain, Wally Hammond, Patsy Hendren and Maurice Leyland. The invaluable Les Ames was one of two keepers chosen, Farrimond the Lancashire second xi wicketkeeper being the other.

Spin bowling for the 1935 squad was provided by George Paine and Eric Hollies who, like their captain Wyatt, played for Warwickshire in the English county championship. Paine was an experienced bowler, Hollies at the start of his long career; both were prolific wicket takers in county cricket who were often passed over for test matches.[226] The Lancashire all-rounder Jack Iddon was another good if not exceptional cricketer.

---

226 Both had pretty good test match figures in the few games they played, Hollies averaging thirty and Paine twenty-seven. Hollies was another man who took more wickets than he scored runs in his first-class career joining Bowes and Marriott.

The first clear-cut weakness in Wyatt's squad was quick bowling. The amateur Ken Farnes provided some pace and hostility and Cedric "Big Jim" Smith who averaged 19.25 runs per wicket in his first-class career; quality medium-fast support. However, there was an array of other English fast bowlers who didn't tour the West Indies in 1934-1935: Larwood, in international retirement; Voce, ostracised; the amateur Gubby Allen, business interests to take care of, and Nobby Clark and Bill Bowes – overlooked. In the 1932-1933 ashes series, England had taken four fast/fast-medium bowlers to Australia.[227] In this 1935 selection, Stanley Jackson and his fellow selectors were overlooking the strong West Indian pace attack, and West Indies pitches which often favoured pace over spin. They were also banking on neither Farnes nor Smith being injured. But Farnes didn't even survive the voyage to the Caribbean unscathed, ricking his neck on the way out.

The amateur batsmen selected for the tour, Wyatt, Holmes, Townsend and Harbord, included some very strange selections. Bob Wyatt was a tough, technically accomplished player. Errol Holmes, who had succeeded Douglas Jardine as captain of Surrey, had a first-class batting average of less than thirty-three, an acceptable return for a county cricketer but not really test standard. His role on tour was to be vice-captain ready to step in for Wyatt and prevent the dire necessity of a professional captain. David Townsend, had only played first-class cricket for Oxford University (he and Farnes played against each other in the

---

227 Larwood, Voce, Bowes and Tate.

famous bodyline varsity match of 1933). He was the last cricketer to play for England before playing for a first-class county.[228] William Harbord played cricket for Yorkshire, the county of both God and chairman of selectors Stanley Jackson but had little else to recommend his selection. He generally played for the Yorkshire second team and his first-class career batting average was just eighteen. During his time at Oxford, Harbord had not been selected for the Varsity match but now he was on tour with the MCC. Harbord's one notable cricketing achievement was scoring a hundred in a minor counties vs Australia match in 1934. Not the only occasion when a one-off performance has resulted in a poor selection for a touring party.

Money may have been a factor in the selection of Harbord and Townsend. Wyatt had typically received £100 or £125 as expenses for an MCC overseas tour.[229] With the average annual salary for the period in the region of £200 this was a decent return for a winter's work but hardly lavish. Most professional cricketers would earn £200-£300 for a summer and overseas test tours were relatively well paid.[230] So the amateur's expenses were probably a little more than just expenses (although the complaint was always that it didn't cover out of pocket expenses) but not equivalent to a professional's wage. However, for the 1934-1935 tour of the West Indies not even this was available; Wyatt was told by Lord Hawke that there would be no payment made

228 In fact, he never played for a first-class county.
229 See *RES Wyatt: Fighting Cricketer*.
230 £400 plus a bonus is the figure quoted in David Frith, *Bodyline Autopsy*, page 56.

to amateurs. The Hawke of 1934 was obviously a sterner figure than the man who, in 1896, had made under the table payments to allow Pelham Warner to tour the West Indies as an amateur. Eventually Wyatt was able to obtain an amateur expenses payment of £25, but any amateur making the 1934–1935 tour would be doing it for love of the game. There seems to have been an unofficial rule that a certain number of amateurs were needed on tour and Harbord and Townsend, both young men with no family commitments, may have been the best of what was available.

The other problem with the selection of the MCC touring party was opening batsmen; remarkably the England selectors had picked a squad without a single player who regularly opened the batting for his county or university side. The lack of opening batsmen exacerbated what some observers saw as a general weakness in England's batting against pace. Writing to Wyatt after the end of the tour, Douglas Jardine asked: "Was there anyone who didn't run away bar yourself and Maurice Leyland?"[231] With the Australian attack so dependent on spin bowlers, facing West Indian quicks in helpful conditions was an unusual challenge, even for batsmen with test match experience. As with the 1934 ashes, the impression is Wyatt put up with a side Jardine would not have countenanced.

As well as having to contend with a somewhat ramshackle squad, Wyatt's position as England captain was under threat. Wyatt first captained in England in the final test of the 1930 ashes, controversially supplanting Percy

---

231 Quoted in *RES Wyatt: Fighting Cricketer*, Gerald Pawle, page 150.

Chapman. England lost that match and with it the series, and Wyatt was not to return to the captaincy until the final test of the 1933 series against the West Indies. In the intervening period, Chapman and Jardine both captained the England side. The rapid turnover in leaders was in part a result of certain amateurs being available for certain tours but also because the selectors were quick to change captain if things weren't going well. Wyatt had been the captain of the losing side in the 1934 ashes series and there was no certainty he would remain captain in the English summer of 1935. Certainly Douglas Jardine thought the vultures were gathering: in a letter sent to Wyatt after the tour he commented, "Poor Bob, Warner's efforts on behalf of Gubby and Leveson Gower[232] on behalf of Errol Holmes' bid fair to make the season interesting." Of course, Errol Holmes was Wyatt's vice-captain in 1935 so it might have been both Holmes and Wally Hammond had their eyes on Wyatt's position – he needed a successful series if he was to hold on.

With such a wide spread of talent in the side it was vital for Wyatt to get the tourists to bond together, but there were some indications the reverse was happening. The governor of Trinidad had a dinner for the England touring party but only made invitations available for six players plus Wyatt as captain. Wyatt allocated three of the six invitations to the amateur players in the party with the other three going to senior professionals. The professionals

---

232 Leveson Gower was Holmes' father-in-law and there were rumours Warner was Allen's father.

who hadn't been invited felt slighted and refused to attend a governor's garden party offered by way of compensation. Although really nothing more than a spat, such an incident was important to a tour. Evening entertainment was a chance to eat free food, drink free drink and meet women. And on a more spiritual level it is always upsetting to feel left out. Wyatt should have known what to do in the circumstances; he had been on the 1925-1926 MCC tour of India when British expats in Calcutta had offered the amateur members of the team lavish hospitality whilst excluding professionals. Tour captain Arthur Gilligan made it clear invitations not made to all team members must be turned down; the good folk of Calcutta decided they could perhaps squeeze a few more guests around the table and the problem was solved. But Wyatt failed to take Gilligan's example, instead forcing all players to attend the consolation garden party.[233]

There are also some indications of splits in the party in the detailed account of the tour in *Tours and Tests* by the amateur fast bowler Ken Farnes. It is notable that whenever he went out in a small group it was with the other amateur players. The one exception is when Farnes, Townsend, tour manager Carlton Levick and Wally Hammond went ashore in Caracas. Farnes refers to the group as, "Hammond, Carlton, David and I." Referring to the professional Hammond by his second name and the others by their first seems like a snub, although it may have been unconscious, and that it should be applied to a man who was older than

---

233 Both stories taken from *RES Wyatt: Fighting Cricketer* by Gerald Pawle.

Farnes and a much better cricketer is indicative of a strong dividing line between officers and other ranks.

The Trinidad xi, reinforced by Learie Constantine came close to beating the MCC in the two island games that preceded the second test match. The first match was an absolute thriller. MCC batted first and rattled up a score of 348 all out, in a little over two sessions during which sixty-eight overs were bowled. Wally Hammond at his very best scored a hundred before lunch and Jim Smith smashed fifty-four runs, at one point swinging so hard the bat flew out of his hands and landed at the feet of the square leg umpire. It seemed as if MCC had decided to persist with the attacking cricket that had proved successful in the second innings of the first test.

But although Trinidad didn't match the tourists for flamboyance, they more than matched them for runs scored, Jack Grant declaring their first innings on 371 for seven. The twenty-six-year-old Arthur Maynard, on his first-class debut, opened the batting and scored exactly 200 of those runs. He became an instant local hero, a public subscription was started in his name whilst he was still batting, he was promised an entire cricketing outfit by HAP O'Reilly KC and the Len Wooley orchestra invited him as a special guest of honour to a party at the Belmont home of Miss Elsie Richards, where they played a song written to commemorate his achievement.[234] Maynard was also made the subject of a speech of political propaganda in favour of the separation of Trinidad from the British Commonwealth of Nations.[235]

---

234 *Port of Spain Gazette*, as is all description of the matches in Trinidad unless another source is specified.
235 Ken Farnes, *Tours and Tests*, page 80.

The heartfelt response to Maynard's success illustrates how West Indian cricketers were sustained by their communities. Cricketers on tour to England were sometimes financed by those at home and there were numerous small acts of kindness that allowed talented cricketers to progress. This informal support was particularly important as there was no formal funding for cricketers. The West Indies have generally been too small to sustain proper professional cricket and the colour bar in West Indian society meant successful West Indian cricketers were not provided with the equivalent of Wally Hammond's well-paid directorships.

The shock of seeing their first innings score easily bested by an island side and a debutant score two hundred not out may have been the pivotal event of the whole tour. The MCC abandoned their brief experiment with attacking cricket. 200 – 6 in the second innings came off ninety-one overs and Wyatt only declared when it seemed impossible MCC could lose the game. But Trinidad still tried to get the 178 needed to win. Learie Constantine sent in to bat at number three, promptly hit a six over the St Clair Oval's galvanised fence and into Elizabeth Street. He then hit consecutive deliveries from George Paine for six over square leg, he was out for twenty-five, scored in ten minutes and his partnership with Cyril Merry put up forty runs. Once Merry was out, George and Rolph Grant continued the attack. Rolph Grant was a dashing batsman, football goalkeeper and amateur heavyweight boxer, well equipped for quick scoring. He raced to thirty-five, the first four balls he faced went for two, two, four, four, including a shot sending a ball pitched outside the off stump to the fine leg boundary that sounds very similar to the Learie lift for six seen at Lord's in 1933. The West Indian style of cricket does not seem to have been confined to black West Indians. But, although the runs were coming quickly, wickets were falling as well and any result seemed possible. Eventually, Trinidad reached 159 – 8 off twenty-three overs when the game ended as a draw.

The attacking cricket that Trinidad, and in particular Learie Constantine, played, forced Wyatt onto the back foot and he was to remain there for the rest of the 1935 tour. In the first game between MCC and Trinidad any result was possible towards the end of the final day's play, but by the end of the second island game MCC were holding on for a draw. In fact, it seems as if a draw was on Bob Wyatt's mind since the game started. The MCC had ground out 226 all out off ninety-six overs in their first innings, but Trinidad had responded with a positive 230 – 9 off sixty-five overs by the end of the second day. Maynard, the hero of the first MCC island game, scoring just four. Rain fell overnight and it seemed Wyatt was in no hurry to resume. Not for the last time on the tour, he accompanied the umpires on their inspection of the damp outfield, drawing attention to places he felt were unfit for play. But the match resumed at 2.12 pm with Trinidad declaring on their overnight score. MCC were bundled out in their second innings for just 103, with Ben Sealey taking five wickets for twenty-six. However, MCC had managed to use up forty-eight overs in their second innings and the time taken was extended when the batsmen asked the ground staff to "fix" the matting. Trinidad were left to score 100 runs in twelve overs to win the match. By the genteel standards of 1930s cricket it was an impossible task, but Trinidad gave it a proper go. Learie Constantine thumped twenty-five, including what sounds very like another Learie lift: "He bent over towards point and hit the ball over the fine leg boundary for six,"[236] then quick wickets fell leaving Trinidad at 37 – 5 with the Grant brothers, Rolph and Jack, at the crease. They carried on trying to reach the target; with a maximum of two overs left they still needed thirty runs with Rolph Grant on strike. Now he bludgeoned eighteen runs from five balls to make the unlikely seem possible, but his dismissal saw the match end in a draw.

Ken Farnes and Eric Hollies, who had played in the second island game, were both injured and unable to play in the test match: a hard schedule was taking its toll on a stretched squad. With Farnes and Hollies injured and Harbord not remotely up to standard, the England squad of fourteen had been reduced to eleven, making selection a straightforward process. Reserve wicketkeeper Bill Farrimond came in to the side, Les Ames playing as a batsman and the amateur batsman David Townsend opened the innings with Wyatt. This left England with only two specialist bowlers, in George Paine and Jim Smith. What West Indian team would line up against a weakened England xi?

---

236 From *Jack Grant's Story*, page 174

Chapter 20

ROOM FOR ONE MORE?

The second MCC Trinidad game finished on the 22nd January 1935. The players were given one whole day off before the second test match started on the 24th. Given his selection difficulties, it is unlikely England captain, Bob Wyatt, enjoyed his free day.

By contrast, Jackie Grant captained a West Indian team that was close to being a truly representative side. In 1935, teams for each of the four test matches were selected by the WICBC rather than an island selection committee picking the eleven for its "home" test. WICBC members were nominated by island associations but the Board could refuse to accept a nominee. The self-selecting aspect of the WICBC helped insulate it against island-level provincialism and Jack Grant was appointed as captain for all four test matches. It also provided consistency in selection with: George Headley, Derek Sealy, Jack Grant, Grant's brother Rolph, wicketkeeper Cyril Christiani and fast bowlers Leslie Hylton and Manny Martindale playing in all four test matches and Learie Constantine playing in the second, third and fourth tests of the series. This core of eight players contrasted with 1930 when only two players; George Headley and Clifford Roach played for the West Indies in all four test matches.

But island loyalties hadn't gone away and still influenced selection outside of the core eight players. Such attitudes were, perhaps, particularly prevalent in Jamaica and Guiana. The eastern Caribbean islands of Trinidad and Barbados are relatively close to each other and could expect to have at least two players included in any West Indian side picked on merit. Trinidad had four players in the eleven for both the first and second tests, Barbados had three in the first test and two in the second. Generally, Barbadian and Trinidadian identification with the West Indian team was sufficiently close that it overcame, or at least damped down, island loyalties.[237] But it seems that in British Guiana and Jamaica the West Indies side was seen as a vehicle for their national players regardless of the impact on the West Indies team.

There were two striking anomalies in the West Indies team that played in the Port of Spain test match of 1935. Firstly, the inclusion of Charles Jones of British Guiana (who played in the first three tests of the 1935 series). Jones was not up to the standard required for test cricket having a first-class average of just twenty – two. His inclusion meant the luckless Ben Sealey didn't make the team although he

---

237 For instance, the *Barbados Advocate* suggested, incredibly, that Manny Martindale might not be a good choice for the first test match. This might have been a reprise of racist attitudes in Barbados that made some uneasy at the prospect of black Barbadian fast bowlers.

was a better batsman than Jones and also provided his very useful bowling.

However, it does not seem that Jones' inclusion was a case of the well-to-do white West Indian selectors favouring one of their own. Jones played for the Malteenoes club in George Town and was the first player from the working-class club to represent Guyana or the West Indies.[238] Jones' selection was to ensure British Guiana had two players in the test team. There is a report in the Jamaican newspaper, *The Gleaner*, citing an unnamed informant, that the British Guiana Cricket Board of Control brought two players (Jones and Christiani) to Barbados and had stated that unless both players were selected both would return to British Guiana.

The second anomaly was Oscar da Costa, another player with a poor test and first-class record (not as dire as CEL Jones) and who seems to have been shipped out to Trinidad to get Jamaican representation in the team for the second test up to three.

But race may have had less impact on selection for the West Indian team than in previous periods. Of the eighteen West Indians that played in the 1935 series I have tentatively[239] identified eleven black players,[240] four white,[241]

---

238 http://guyana-cricket.com/org/malteenoes-sports-club

239 Quite a lot of this involves looking at black and white pictures to work out if people are black or white – it's a perilous business.

240 Roach, Carew (purely on the basis that he went to Combermere school), Headley, Sealy (based on photo only) Hylton, Christiani (photo only), Martindale, Neblett (photo only), Mudie (photo in the *Jamaica at the Wicket*), Constantine and Fuller (picture in *Cricket in the Sun*, page 33).

241 Two Grants, Da Costa and Barrow.

the ethnically Chinese Ellis Achong, Ken Wishart, who is described in Michael Manley's *A History of West Indies Cricket* as non-white, and one whom I have been unable to categorise.[242]

White West Indians made up approximately 3% of the populations of the islands in the 1930s. So, four of eighteen players being white was still anomalous, but the proportion of white players was lower than applied on West Indian cricket tours to England and may have had has much to do with the inherent racism ground into West Indian society, as specific bias in selection. It is a feature of cricket that a disproportionate number of test players come from elite private schools where coaching and facilities are at their best and in the West Indies private school education was mainly a white privilege.

Of the eight players who were the test regulars in 1935, only the Grant brothers, Jack and Rolph, were white. The Grant family had something of a strangle hold on West Indian cricket in the 1930s; Fred was chairman of the WICBC, Jack was captain of the team and the continuation of the direct Grant system assured by the selection of brother Rolph who went on to captain the West Indies in the 1939 tour of Britain. Although it is natural to be suspicious of the selection of not one, but two, brothers of the president of the WICBC, both Grants had decent test records by the standards of West Indians playing test cricket in the 1930s.[243] They weren't outstanding players

---

242 Jones.

243 Jack Grant test batting twenty-six, Rolph Grant batting twenty-two, bowling thirty-two.

and there may well have been black players who were just as good, Derek Sealey springs to mind, but their selection was not egregious.[244] Whilst at Cambridge, Rolph Grant had been more prominent in football and boxing than cricket, but in one of his two appearances in inter-colonial cricket he had scored 152 against a strong Barbados bowling attack, an innings that had been interrupted when Grant had been knocked unconscious by a ball delivered by Manny Martindale, and carried from the pitch. He had returned, setting about the bowling with characteristic gusto and it is understandable if his brothers believed he had the temperament for big cricket.

Arthur Maynard, who had scored two hundred on his first-class debut, had been injured when he and Learie Constantine collided going for a catch in the MCC's second innings of the second island game and was probably not available for selection. Maynard was not selected for either the third test in British Guiana or the fourth test in Jamaica. It seems as if the travelling contingent of West Indian cricketers was chosen in advance and Maynard was not added to it. Trinidad did not play another first-class game until 1936 when Maynard was overlooked, and he seems to have lost his enthusiasm for cricket as a result. In any event, it was difficult for Maynard to combine first-class cricket with the demands of his job as a teacher. And that was it; Maynard lived to fifty but didn't play another first-class game and ended up with a first-class average of 206.

---

244 Their being appointed as captain, however, was clearly racially motivated.

In English cricket, professionalism gave cricketers time to develop: Patsy Hendren was touring the West Indies in 1935 at forty-six years of age,[245] and had only played his best cricket once past thirty. Even Wally Hammond, a true natural cricketer, took a couple of years of county cricket to turn his stylish shots into consistent run scoring. But because West Indians couldn't make a proper living playing cricket they often had to put professional and family lives before sporting careers and there was not always time for a player to develop. This was particularly an issue for black players who generally lacked the resources to self-finance their careers. The emergence of Constantine as a star professional in English league cricket showed other players how the need to earn a living might be reconciled with sporting excellence.

Along with Maynard, the other notable omission from the West Indies team for the second test was Trinidadian Clifford Roach, the opening batsman who had played in the first test in Barbados. Generally, if a West Indian played in an "away" island test match they were sure to be selected on their home ground. Roach was a decent batsman with an average of over thirty, and two test match hundreds to his name. But he didn't play in the second test match and was also unavailable for the second MCC vs Trinidad game. Clearly something was afoot, but it's not clear what. The *Port of Spain Gazette* reported gnomically: "The absence of Mr Clifford Roach from the Colony team was the subject of much speculation. Enquiries failed to elicit the real cause but there is every reason not to attribute it to the Selectors."

---

245 He turned forty-six whilst on tour.

For all the difficulties faced by the West Indies, they were much closer, in terms of averages, to the 1935 England touring party than they had been touring England in 1933. Recalculating the eleven player averages used earlier in this book, West Indies still had a negative score, but were now around minus thirty compared to the minus fifty of 1933. England's score had come down from over a hundred to fifty-six. So the gap was closing but on paper England still seemed to possess the stronger side; the question was how would a theoretical advantage bear up in the tense atmosphere of test match cricket.

Chapter 21

TRINIDAD, TO THE WIRE

After two exciting MCC vs Trinidad games, the test match was eagerly anticipated. Claud Hollis, British governor of Trinidad, appreciated the platform provided and on a radio broadcast the night before the second test welcomed the MCC team and took the opportunity to give an upbeat, perhaps downright misleading, survey of Trinidad's economic prospects.[246]

Crowds for the first day were estimated at 8,000 to 9,000.[247] Precise attendance figures do not seem to be available and in any event would have been difficult to audit; The *Port of Spain Gazette* included a report of the summary trial of a gateman at the St Clair Oval, who had

---

246 Although I haven't been able to work out where the governor was when he made the broadcast, Barbados had (at least) one radio station that broadcast updates from the test match but in Trinidad broadcasts seem to have been picked up either from the UK or the South American mainland.

247 *Port of Spain Gazette.*

been taking admission money at the gate but not handing out tickets. The retained tickets were then passed to an accomplice outside the ground who sold them to members of the public.

Adding to the crowd inside the ground were lorries parked in the road outside the Oval. Spectators, paying a small fee, could climb on top to watch the game. By the second day, one entrepreneur had jerry-rigged a small stand to the top of his vehicle, but it's not clear whether its patrons were included in the estimated attendance.

In Clifford Roach's absence, wicketkeeper, Cyril Christiani, and Charles Jones opened the batting for the West Indies and they got the chance to bat straight away, despite England captain, Bob Wyatt, winning the toss. Trinidad's matting wickets ensured playing conditions would be constant for a four day test match, so there was no particular advantage to bowling first and the conventional decision would have been for England to bat. The *Port of Spain Gazette* reported: "No small astonishment was occasioned" by Wyatt's decision.

The West Indies' makeshift openers both went early leaving the West Indies on 38 – 2, bringing together George Headley and Derek Sealy. Headley was caught by Errol Holmes off the spin bowling of George Paine for just twenty-five, but Derek (JED) Sealy was in and batting well. Sealy was only twenty-two years old but already had test match experience having made his test debut in 1930 aged seventeen.[248] He had scored a fifty in that game and was

---

248 He remains the youngest West Indian test debutant. espn cricinfo

expected to do great things as a cricketer. Instead, he was to become one of those players whose achievements never quite match their talents. His *Wisden* obituary says: "He epitomised the natural cricketing ability of so many West Indians, his cap at a rakish angle, the bat seeming to be an extension of himself, often smiling, always friendly." Perhaps he was a little too friendly for the stern work of test match cricket? Or maybe the lack of first-class cricket for West Indian players prevented him from developing the necessary edge. Sealy only made eighty first-class appearances spread over a twenty-one-year career. The 24th of January 1935, however, was a day to enjoy Derek Sealy's talent, not to be frustrated by his shortcomings; he scored ninety-two runs including thirteen fours. The other significant innings for the West Indies came from Learie Constantine who reached his best ever score in a test match, out for ninety with last man Manny Martindale at the other end. Tellingly, Constantine didn't adopt his usual tactics of all-out attack from the get-go. The *Port of Spain Gazette* reported in mock horror that his first ten runs took twelve minutes. But, once Constantine was in, it was business as usual: "Constantine did not hesitate to take risks, and he timed the ball perfectly in vigorous drives, pulls and hits to leg."[249] The influence of Sealy and Constantine was such that West Indies reached their final total of 302 off ninety-five overs; a good rate for a 1930s test match.

England shared those ninety-five overs between six bowlers, Jim Smith took 4 – 100 and his makeshift new

---

249 From *Wisden* match report.

ball partner, Captain Bob Wyatt, did a sterling job, sending down seventeen overs and taking 3 – 33. Wyatt had experience of bowling on matting wickets from a previous tour of South Africa and used this to good effect. Wally Hammond, often a renowned non-bowler, put his shoulder to the wheel bowling fourteen overs for twenty-eight runs and no wickets; clearly at this stage of the tour he was still engaged.

Matches on matting wickets often provided a good contest between batsmen and bowlers and a score of 300 in just over one day of a four-day match left any result possible. But the West Indies had the three fastest bowlers in the match, a record crowd of 11,000 supporting them and England were quickly in trouble in their first innings. Hylton took the wickets of Wyatt and Hammond, both undone by fast short-pitched deliveries, which were fended off and caught by Rolph Grant standing in close on the leg side. The catch to dismiss Wyatt was "a beautiful low right hand running away catch."[250] Constantine had Townsend LBW for five and celebrated his wicket, racing down the pitch and vaulting the stumps at the batsman's end, "because I knew I could feel in my bones – that everything was going to be all right."[251] Rolph Grant took his third catch of the innings, another spectacular effort, at short leg to dismiss Ames off the bowling of Martindale. Constantine had Maurice Leyland leg before wicket, although Leyland made it clear he thought he had hit the ball first. England were

---

250 *Port of Spain Gazette.*
251 *Cricket in the Sun*, page 70.

23 – 5, the crowd roared, it felt as if the course of the series had been defined.

But it was a series of reverses in fortune. Manny Martindale left the field with an injured hand and Jack Iddon, playing in his second test match at thirty-three years of age, put on seventy-two runs with the forty-five-year-old Patsy Hendren. After Hendren was out, Iddon and Errol Holmes, a specialist batsman in at number eight, put on a further seventy-three before Rolph Grant took his second wicket, having Iddon caught by George Headley to leave England on 168 – 7. Holmes, and the tail end batsmen, took the score to 200 – 8 at the end of the second day, still 102 behind the West Indies' first innings score but a good recovery from 23 – 5. Not only had England limited the first innings deficit, they had taken time out of the game. For the *Port of Spain Gazette* there was, "only one conclusion, the game would be a draw." Such pessimism would have pleased Bob Wyatt. Both Jack Grant and Learie Constantine[252] believed that Wyatt had, from the start of the second test, planned on three draws and winning the series 1-0. It wasn't an unreasonable tactic; the 1935 test matches were only four days long and a 1-0 series result was not uncommon in 1930s cricket.

The rate of scoring in England's first innings supports suspicions Wyatt had at least one eye on the draw. At the start of the third day's cricket, Farrimond was the first wicket to fall, dismissed by Derek Sealy's first ball of the match.

---

252 *Jack Grant's Story*, page 176, *Cricket in the Sun*, Learie Constantine, page 72.

Farrimond had scored sixteen runs in one hundred minutes and faced ninety-nine balls and, when George Paine was last man out, England had scored 258 off 121 overs.

With the best part of two days left to play, the pressure was back on the West Indies, and Jack Grant in particular. With a lead of forty-four and one-nil down in the series, the onus was on the West Indies to win the game. If Grant was too cautious in his tactics, the man who had been traduced for losing the first test match would be characterised as being too timid to win the second. But poor batting or an injudicious declaration could hand England a match they seemed to have lost on the second day.

George Headley, almost inevitably, was the mainstay of the West Indies second innings batting. His ninety-three scored in almost three and three-quarter hours wasn't particularly rapid, but as he batted through the third day and on into the fourth, he steadily moved his side to a dominant position. Learie Constantine and Rolph Grant played typically expansive innings and the West Indies accelerated towards a declaration which came at lunch on the fourth and final day at 280 – 6. With roughly seventy overs of play left in the day, England would have to score 325 runs to win the match, but as quickly became apparent their aim wasn't to win but not to lose.

It takes England half an hour to score their first seventeen runs. The defensive tactics aren't surprising, but the batting order is. Despite the eight batsman in the side, Bill Farrimond who had batted at number ten in the first innings opens in the second. When Farrimond is first man out with the team score on fourteen, Wyatt sends in George Paine who had batted at eleven in the first innings.

For a while the change of tactics seems to work. Townsend is dropped and he and Paine grind their way to 53 – 1 when Ellis Achong dismisses Townsend. Wyatt continues with his inverted batting order sending in Jim Smith who had batted at nine in the first innings. But disaster is stalking the English batsmen – Paine plays back to the off spin of Rolph Grant – treads on his stumps – out hit wicket.

Wally Hammond comes in and anxious to get on strike calls Smith for a quick single. What Hammond hasn't realised is with Manny Martindale off the field the ball has gone to substitute fielder Elias Constantine, Learie's brother. Fine fielding is a Constantine family trait and Big Jim Smith, built for comfort not for speed; is run out by a distance. With runs irrelevant, to give away a wicket to a run out is the height of folly. In a perilous position, sixty-two for four; England at least have their best batsmen to come. Scoring slows, then stops as Hammond and Hendren concentrate on keeping the ball out.

Wally Hammond is on strike and, desperate for a wicket before tea, Grant brings Hammond's nemesis, Learie Constantine, on to bowl. With only the second ball of his new spell,[253] Constantine scatters the stumps of England's best batsman. England hang on for four more overs and take tea at seventy-five for five. They have to bat for one complete

---

253 Z Cricket stats.

session to save the match, West Indies must take five wickets to win it. Their chances are improved by the return to the field after tea of Manny Martindale who has not bowled in the second innings due to his injured hand. Constantine opens the bowling after the tea break and in just his second over he has Wyatt caught one-handed and high over his head by George Headley in the slips.

Constantine is bowling at his fastest now, generating great pace from his short, furious run up. He lets a bouncer fly at Les Ames who ducks, then another bouncer. Ames weaves. Umpire Arthur Richardson asks West Indian captain Grant to come across. The two confer, no-one in the crowd knows about what. Ellis Achong bowls the next over. And then, Constantine off, Martindale on, Constantine who was winning the game for the West Indies, why has he been taken off? Word somehow gets around, Richardson has warned Constantine for short-pitched bowling and Grant has taken him off; Constantine, the home town hero removed from the game. The crowd calls for Constantine's return and barracks Richardson.[254]

Perhaps the returning Martindale can right the injustice. But the next wicket to fall isn't due to Martindale's pace but rather another mental error from England's batsmen. Hendren glides the ball into the slips and for reasons unclear sets off for a single. Constantine fielding at a wide slip pounces, Hendren is sent back as Constantine fizzes the ball to wicketkeeper Cyril Christiani, who drops it. In an ecstasy of fumbling, Christiani retrieves the spilt ball and breaks

---

254 *Cricket in the Sun*, Learie Constantine, page 73.

the wickets. Hendren is out of his ground. It is hard to take Learie Constantine out of a match and England who were set on saving the game have now lost two batsmen to run outs and another hit wicket. At seventy-nine for seven, a great ragged cheer surges from the stands and fills the blue bowl of the sky, surely the West Indies have them now? But whatever the merits of Wyatt reversing the batting order, it has ensured England have plenty of batting left. Maurice Leyland (test average forty-six) comes out to bat with Les Ames (test average 40.5). Errol Holmes who scored a slow eighty in the first innings is still to bat as is all-rounder Jack Iddon. The cheer is replaced by the raging silence of a tense cricket ground. Jack Grant brings on his brother Rolph to replace Martindale. Leyland and Ames block everything for four overs. Grant decides that, whatever the consequences, Leslie Hylton off, Learie Constantine back on. Now Constantine bowls a short ball to Leyland, it catches the edge and as a red flash heads towards Cyril Christiani – who drops it.

With three England wickets to fall, victory seems to be slipping away from the West Indies. The players though continue to press, scurrying to their fielding positions to get more overs in. Grant goes through all his bowling options replacing Constantine with Martindale and at the other end bowling Sealy for two overs and Jones and Da Costa for one each. With the clock ticking towards six and the close of play, Grant calls on Hylton. Trying everything he can think of, Hylton bowls a slow shoulder high full toss to Ames. Some felt Ames, unprepared for the angle of the delivery, "lost the ball", he prods uncertainly at it and spoons up a catch to

Achong – this time the ball is caught, and England are eight wickets down. Jack Iddon is the next England batsman and there are no slow full tosses for him, he survives his first two balls but the third catches the edge and Christiani catches the ball, two wickets in one over, one more needed to win, the match has turned again and it is Hylton, who many argued should be dropped from the team who has turned it.

The stands shake to the drumming of West Indian feet as Errol Holmes comes into bat, five minutes for the draw, one wicket for the win. Constantine returns and bowls a maiden. Leslie Hylton tries Leyland with another bouncer, this time he makes contact sending the ball soaring up and up into the Port of Spain sky; at fine leg Charles Jones waits. He shifts beneath the falling ball, reaches out, he drops it – Leyland down twice. The chance to win the match missed.

Time for one more over? Just one more. Constantine of Trinidad and the West Indies against Leyland of Yorkshire and England. As Constantine runs in, the spectators in the front rows stand, those behind them anxious not to miss a thing also stand, the whole ground is standing when Constantine delivers – Leyland blocks. Constantine rushes in again, the crowd rises, Leyland blocks, he blocks the third ball too; the fourth as well. Constantine switches to around the wicket. The fifth ball a disguised slower ball[255] hits Leyland on the pads, Constantine and the West Indian team appeals – 11,000 spectators appeal – the umpire, Victor Guillen, considers, and gives Leyland out. A West Indies victory – the crowd runs on to the field. Ancient

---

255 Page 42 of *Learie Constantine* (biography) by Peter Mason

Greeks pulled down their city walls when winners returned from the Olympic Games. Constantine is carried aloft from the field of play.

Christiani who had dropped Leyland in this game and had been involved in the run out of a set George Headley in the first, faints. He must have felt as if the weight of the West Indies had been on his shoulders.

But none of that matters, the West Indies have won. No matter Leyland always maintained the ball that got him out would have passed both over and wide of his leg stump.[256] no matter, no matter, the West Indies have won and levelled the series at one all with two tests left to play.

---

256 Constantine certainly thought it was pretty straight and the *Port of Spain Gazette* reported that Leyland stepped in front of a straight one.

Chapter 22

TRINIDAD AFTERMATH

If the first test of the 1935 series was one of the most bizarre ever played, the second, decided in the final minutes of the final day, was one of the most thrilling. Newspapers on both sides of the Atlantic covered not only the result of the match but the decision of umpire Arthur Richardson to stop Learie Constantine bowling bouncers. In a development that would horrify modern-day cricket administrators, Richardson was happy to explain the decision to a *Reuters*'s journalist:

> "Smith and Constantine at the beginning of the match bowled a few bodyline balls to which I took exception by quietly giving a hint in newspaper press articles that it should not be permitted. I noticed Smith thereafter refrained, especially after being told by Captain Wyatt to cease bowling short-pitched bumpers, but on the last day Constantine persisted in bowling three bouncers, one in the direction of Wyatt's head and two at Ames.

I immediately went to the West Indian captain and informed him that as the other side had discontinued such intimidating bowling the West Indies must act similarly, if not I intended to use my authority as an umpire under the new ruling of the MCC which is definitely against bodyline bowling and is applicable during the present tour. Grant replied that it would be all right and I noted Constantine was taken off next over."[257]

Richardson was acting at the very limits, if not actively exceeding, his powers. It is far from clear that the bodyline ruling he refers to applied in the West Indies in 1935, the revision to the LBW law which accompanied the bodyline rule certainly wasn't used in the series. In any event, Constantine was hardly adopting a systematic bodyline attack, Richardson only refers to three bouncers, there was no gaggle of leg-side catchers and no indication Constantine was bowling the ball at a batsman standing clear of the leg stump. Additionally the ball by ball analysis of the match suggests Richardson had intervened whilst standing at square leg when warnings about short-pitched bowling generally come from the umpire at the bowler's end.

There was also an issue of basic fairness. England in the bodyline tour had industrialised the former cottage industry of short-pitched bowling to win an ashes series. In India in 1933-1934 they hadn't used full bodyline but still bowled plenty of short-pitched stuff. Now they had come to the West Indies with only one fast bowler who was injured

---

257 Reproduced in the *Jamaican Gleaner*.

for this match and were up against a fine West Indies pace attack. And short-pitched bowling was suddenly banned. With his curious belief that the way to send a message to the team captains was in interviews to the press, Richardson was actively agitating for a change in the way that test match cricket was played, beyond the limited wording of the new bodyline rule. The result would be, like the ashes series of 1934, cricket without the bouncer.

Although Richardson had a somewhat sketchy understanding of the appropriate role of an umpire, it cannot be denied that he and his fellow bouncer pacifists had a point. The tragic death of Philip Hughes in 2014 demonstrated the dangers of short-pitched bowling. Cricket as envisaged by Richardson would have been a different game to the one we know; it may not have been sustainable as a mass spectator sport, but it would undoubtedly be a safer game.

Richardson was a former Australian test cricketer, who had coached extensively in the West Indies, and a white umpire stepping in to protect a white England team from a black fast bowler might suggest he was motivated by racism. But Learie Constantine in his account of the series doesn't make this accusation and the two men knew each other quite well. They played in the Lancashire leagues at the same time and almost exactly one year prior to the second test of 1935 they had been the umpires in an inter-colonial game between Barbados and British Guiana played in Port of Spain.

But although Constantine didn't accuse Richardson of racial bias, he wasn't prepared to allow the decision to take him out of the attack and Richardson's subsequent comments to pass unchallenged. Constantine was also quoted in the English press making a series of good points and signing off with patrician disdain: "I am able to say that it was in keeping with the policy pursued by the captain that I was relieved in the best interests of the side and not as a consequence of the lame accusation."

This brawl in English newspapers was eagerly picked up in the Caribbean and showed there was still no consensus on fast, short-pitched bowling; was it a legitimate tactic that could be used in the remainder of the series or was it, simply, not cricket? Some sections of the English press were quick to support Constantine. The *Daily Herald*, staunch bodyline advocate, included: "Nobody ever dreamed of accusing Constantine of play that was not in accordance with the spirit of the game until this week. He was said to have put a couple of balls over the head of Ames. I ask you. What is cricket coming to? Every fast bowler is under a cloud; if he does not wish to incur the wrath of our wonderful legislators the best thing he can do is to study hard to become a slow bowler."

The cricketing press wasn't only interested in bodyline. With such a close finish it was inevitable the game would be dissected and the captaincy of Bob Wyatt was identified as the cause of his team's demise. Wyatt didn't experience the odium Jack Grant had to endure after the first test but only because the Atlantic Ocean was between him and his critics. *Wisden*, generally reluctant to chastise amateur captains, referred to "the amazing and inexplicable course of almost completely reversing his batting order."

There is some justification in the criticism. In arranging the batting order the prime consideration is to minimise the lost contribution of the not out batsman, which is why the worst batsman goes in last. In batting Errol Holmes at eleven, Wyatt strayed from this clear principle and Holmes, the top scorer in the first innings only faced eight balls in the second. If he had gone up the order and lasted just two more deliveries than one of the promoted bowlers, England would have saved the match.

But although Wyatt's reversal of the batting order was culpable it was only a contributory cause to the eventual defeat. An England side, batting on a matting wicket that did not deteriorate, failed to last out two sessions of play, even though the West Indies helped them out by dropping four catches. Experienced batsmen Wally Hammond and Patsy Hendren were involved in run outs and George Paine kicked his own stumps over. If the team was not well led by the captain, the captain was not well served by his players. Such is the complicated psychology of cricket where failings of captaincy and playing standards are horribly intermingled. Incompetent performances panic a captain into desperate decisions to conceal the weaknesses of players he does not trust. Conversely a better captain than Wyatt might have created a clearer collective state of mind for his team. It is apparent from accounts of the 1935 tour that by the second test Wyatt was attempting to avoid defeat rather than win matches; what he communicated to his own team and his opponents was a fear of losing rather than a determination to win.[258]

---

258 Ken Farnes in his *Tours and Tests* echoes the impression of Constantine and Grant that Wyatt was playing for a draw.

With the series tied at 1-1, Wyatt didn't demand a more aggressive style of play. Now the summit of his ambitions was to return to England with the series drawn. The third test of 1935 was played in British Guiana and after rain had delayed the start of the match Wyatt, as in the second island match in Trinidad, led Jack Grant and the umpires on a tour of the ground pointing out all the damp patches that in his opinion made a start impossible. When play did get underway Wyatt opened the batting and treated the record crowd to an innings of twenty-one runs scored over 128 minutes. England crept to a total of 226 scored at just under two an over. The West Indies' reply of 184 was at an even slower rate but owed something to Wyatt's tactics. As in Australia in 1932-1933, the captain of an England side adopted a leg theory field. Wyatt was to go even further than Jardine having all nine fielders on the leg side. But this time the leg side field wasn't accompanied by bodyline bowling, instead Wyatt and left arm spinner George Paine arrowed the ball outside of the leg stump to keep the batsmen quiet. Wyatt and his team left British Guiana with the draw they had wanted and a good ticking off in the local press. "The exhibition by the MCC bowlers yesterday up to and for about an hour after lunch was not what was to be expected of teachers for the benefit of pupils."[259] Wyatt's tactics were described as "push, poke and hide" and James Neblett who played for the West Indies in the game said, "England is always playing for a draw and apart from the stodgy batting the bowling was often so negative that only a team of Headleys on top form could score freely off it."

---

259 In match report reproduced in the *Jamaican Gleaner*.

Wyatt responded that he didn't think people in British Guiana knew much about cricket, although he waited until he was back in Trinidad before he said it. Wyatt didn't often complain, he took the diplomatic side of his job seriously.

Diplomatic lapse aside, Wyatt responded to his difficult situation with the bravery and directness that characterised his cricket. The team had no opening batsmen and had to face a high quality pace attack – so in George Town, Wyatt opened the batting. The squad was short of good medium paced and quick bowling – Wyatt filled the gap with his medium pacers and finished on top of the tour bowling averages. In the first Jamaica tour game, William Farrimond was injured, leaving the MCC side without a wicketkeeper – Wyatt went behind the stumps. If the team bus had broken down he would probably have had a crack at trying to repair it.

But another part of Bob Wyatt as a cricketer was a certain grimness. The dour side of Wyatt doesn't seem to have been confined to his cricket – his biographer makes numerous references to his private, dry sense of humour – generally code that a person can also be hard work.

Wyatt wasn't of course the first or last England captain who sometimes rubbed people up the wrong way, Douglas Jardine could, like Wyatt, be uncommunicative and moody. But for all his distance, Jardine had the ability to understand the men who played for him. There is a story in Bill Bowes' biography about how in the early stages of the bodyline series he had asked Jardine for an extra fielder on the leg side. "No," said Jardine. "But you can have five." At this point Bowes didn't think much of his captain, and sent down a succession of long hops to make the point he didn't like the field he'd been set. After the day's play the two men walked back to the team hotel, unaccompanied. Bowes said he would do the same thing again if he didn't get the field he wanted. Jardine's response was, "Anybody who plays under me does as I say, or he goes home." "Right," said Bowes, "I go home." "You are prepared to go home on the next boat?" "Yes," said Bowes. "Well that's marvellous, Bill," said Jardine. "Shake hands, forget it and I'll do some talking." Jardine had realised Bowes couldn't be intimidated but would give everything for a captain who played to win, had the tactics to do so and who could explain those tactics to his bowlers. It was very different to the relationship between Jardine and Harold Larwood. Larwood seemed to be at his best when nursing a grievance, and Jardine ensured his star fast bowler always had one to hand. Larwood had made it clear he would like to sit out the final test of the 1932-1933 bodyline series. Jardine insisted he play and Larwood responded with 4 – 98 in the first innings. Just to turn the screw, in the England first innings Jardine sent Larwood in as night watchman. Larwood was furious and again took his anger at Jardine out on the Australians, scoring ninety-eight. Jardine was able to discern Bowes and Larwood had to be treated differently; it doesn't seem that Wyatt had that insight.

Perhaps a part of Wyatt's problem wasn't just his personality but that he was a transition captain for England. In one sense, his captaincy was a reversion from the iconoclastic, brilliant, but impossible captaincy of Jardine to a business as usual captain who was prepared to shoulder the diplomatic duties associated with the position. But Wyatt also marked a shift from the genuinely amateur captain towards a more "professional approach."

Although Wyatt was an amateur cricketer, he was employed as assistant secretary at Warwickshire. He generally played cricket both winter and summer and made some additional money from freelance journalism. In early 1934, Warwickshire had arranged for an annuity to be taken out that would pay Wyatt £1,000 in ten years' time.[260] Wyatt was very close to being a professional cricketer, just a rather poorly paid one even by the standards of the 1930s. His post as secretary was equivalent to a professional's salary for playing and the annuity the equivalent of a benefit season.

Wyatt was the first England captain since Archie MacLaren to be paid by a county cricket side, although MacLaren like Wyatt was, ostensibly, an amateur. Of the eighteen England captains between MacLaren and Wyatt all eighteen were educated at what would, using a broad definition, be a public school, with six of those coming from one of the seven Clarendon[261] public schools and thirteen of the eighteen going on to either Oxford or Cambridge. Wyatt was educated at King Henry viii school in Coventry that was (and is) a public school, but not one of the Clarendon public schools and he did not go to university.

Wyatt's family had connections, he was rich in social capital but lacking in the sort of capital accepted in shops. His father was a teacher who set up his own school, often a

---

260 Although it's not clear that Warwickshire ever actually paid him the money.
261 Harrow, Eton, Rugby, Charterhouse, Shrewsbury, Westminster and Winchester.

precursor to downwards mobility in inter-war Britain. Wyatt was a cousin of newspaper editor and chairman of the tote Woodrow Wyatt, but he left school with few qualifications and, prior to playing cricket for Warwickshire, worked in the repair shops of the Rover car company in Coventry, the first and very possibly last England captain to spend time on the factory floor.

Given his background, which was not at all dissimilar to Wally Hammond's, Wyatt could easily have become a professional cricketer. But by taking the amateur route he was able to captain Warwickshire and England. In the long run, holding out as an amateur may have also been financially beneficial for Wyatt. Initially he struggled to find a career outside of cricket, but he managed to parlay his position as England captain into a job at the insurance company, Sun Life of Canada. Wyatt established himself at the company and after World War II left Warwickshire for Worcester to become what he had always wanted to be, an amateur cricketer who fitted in matches around a well-paid job with an understanding employer. This contrasted with Charlie Barnett of Gloucester, another member of a downwardly mobile family but one who became a professional cricketer and played in the Lancashire Leagues after the war. After his career ended, Barnett was a cricket coach in a school and then ran a shop, both typical occupations for an ex-professional cricketer. It was as if Barnett's professionalism tainted the caste status Wyatt had so carefully preserved.

But although Wyatt valued his social status, he doesn't seem to have placed too great an emphasis on the distinctions between amateur and professional cricketers. When he started to work on the Rover production line his fellow workers believed he was taking a job from a working man. Tensions were heightened by Wyatt driving his motorbike, at high speed, through a picket line.[262] But from that very unpromising start Wyatt, according to his own account, began to appreciate the comradeship and friendliness of the production line and relations improved. It may have been that start in working life which led to Wyatt becoming good friends with professional cricketer and Warwickshire teammate, Billy Quaife. Quaife was one of the county's most prolific batsmen who had started his fast-class career in the nineteenth century and continued to score runs into the 1920s and he was a mentor as well as a friend to Wyatt.[263] Wyatt's generally good working relationships with professional cricketers continued throughout his career; Eric Hollies recalls that during away matches Wyatt would drop in at the professionals' hotel, buy a round of drinks and talk cricket, and that this level of interaction between professionals and amateur captains was unusual.

But ultimately, his amateur standing put a barrier between Wyatt and men like Wally Hammond and Les Ames who came from similar financial, if not social backgrounds and who were the senior professionals on the 1935 tour. Conversely, there was still a gap in terms of education and financial worth between Wyatt and Errol Holmes, vice-captain of the 1935 tour. Holmes had been educated at

---

262 From: *Three Straight Sticks* by Bob Wyatt.
263 Warwickshire's autocratic Chief Secretary, Rowland Ryder, felt such a friendship between amateur and professional was inappropriate and wrote to Wyatt's father.

Oxford, married in to the aristocratic Levenson-Gower family and "worked" in the "city".[264] This social isolation, being neither a traditional captain like Pelham Warner and Douglas Jardine with their colonial backgrounds nor one of the other ranks may have contributed to Wyatt's generally ineffective captaincy.

As Wyatt commenced the thousand-mile voyage from Trinidad to Jamaica, he had more immediate concerns than the status of amateur cricketers on his mind. With the series poised at one all there was the possibility that he would suffer the indignity of being the first England captain to lose a series to the West Indies – could he salvage his honour and hold on for a draw?

---

264 Although Wyatt and Holmes obviously got on, as Holmes wanted Wyatt to succeed him as captain of Surrey.

Chapter 23

JAMAICA

The MCC touring party arrived in Jamaica divided between amateurs and professionals; senior and junior players. Senior professional Patsy Hendren and his wife were scheduled to arrive first with the rest of the team travelling on behind by boat, except for amateur William Harbord, who would fly into Jamaica having taken a break in Miami. The Hendrens missed the boat they had planned to catch, leaving a welcome party from the Jamaican Cricket Board of Control waiting dockside for their expected visitors. Despite this embarrassment, the Jamaican cricket establishment still made an event of the touring party's arrival in Jamaica.

The official deputation was: Sir Arthur Jett, the Honourable SL Simpson (mayor of Kingston), the honourable SR Cargill, JGG Kieffer, Lieutenant CA Tod, CS Morrison, FR Martin (Jamaican cricketer who toured England in 1933), WEO Turrill, HA Evelyn, William Morrison (President of the Jamaican Cricket Board of

Control), Dr OB Robertson, JS Cesley, C Powell, WC Buie, WJ Palmer and Audley Morais. That was sixteen dignitaries to meet a party of thirteen cricketers, a manager and a scorer. And it wasn't only the official party on the quay side, the *Jamaican Gleaner* had a reporter on the scene and Reggie Matcham was, as ever, on hand.

Matcham "without whom no such gathering would be complete"[265] exemplified the spectator as one of the stars of West Indian cricket. He would attend all games played by Jamaica acting as an unofficial mascot and conducting a running commentary on the action. He was recognised as "one of the most fascinating, charming, intriguing, exhilarating and provocative cricket enthusiasts."[266] He seemed to have had particular fun simultaneously supporting and barracking RC Nunes, Jamaican captain and a dour opener of the English school. There were similar mascots in Trinidad and the anglophile Britannia Bill in Barbados. Although there is perhaps something slightly patronising in the *Gleaner's* reference to Matcham's ubiquity (Matcham is often referred to in the press as Reggie, in contrast to the official welcoming party with its forest of initials); his status as a semi-official figure acknowledged the role of black cricket supporters in taking an English summer game and making it into something of the West Indies. Matcham's involvement in West Indies Cricket wasn't merely decorative, he also helped in the setting up of the Matcham cup, a cricket competition for junior schools in Kingston – the rise

---

265 The *Jamaican Gleaner*.
266 http://westernmirror.com/index.php/mobile/permalink/5388.html

of cricket in the West Indies and elsewhere relied on unpaid and often unrecorded voluntary work.

Douglas Jardine believed spectators should be seen (though never behind the bowler's arm) and not heard. But from the earliest days of cricket tours to the West Indies, English players noted the involvement and noise of West Indian – largely black – crowds.[267] As cricket developed in the West Indies, the spectator remained as much a participant as the players and the cricket ground was a place for display, verbal intervention and self-expression. Players would be advised, chided and derided – it was perhaps as well that Douglas Jardine never toured the West Indies.

The 1935 test matches were watched by good sized crowds, a full ground in Barbados, record gates in British Guiana, an estimated crowd of 11,000 watching the final day of the Trinidad test and crowds of up to 10,000 at Sabina Park Jamaica. Not that many compared to the 30,000 or so in a full Lord's, but remarkable turn outs expressed as a proportion of the population of the islands[268] and considering the economic distress of the period. Access to the ground could be had for a shilling (four shillings to sit in the stands), so cricket was accessible to much of West Indian society. The *Jamaican Gleaner* carried a series of adverts listing discounts on rail travel from all over Jamaica to Kingston during the test match. You get an impression

---

267 For instance, page 103 of *The Development of West Indian Cricket*, Hilary Beccles.

268 Jamaica's population was 1.1 million in 1936, Trinidad's just over 400,000.

of what an event a test against England must have been, rippling out from Kingston to the parishes.

In both England and the West Indies, test cricket was an economic success in a period of depression. In a frank opinion piece, the *Jamaican Gleaner* recognised the growing financial importance of test match cricket. "There was a good deal of rather flowery talk about what is and what is not cricket, playing the game for the schoolboy, the evils of tests, etc., etc., but those who let themselves go along those lines… would do as well to bear in mind that cricket, like every other game today can only exist on gate money… Somebody has to pay for these tours and that somebody is not the school boy."

Adverts and editorials were only a small part of the totality of cricket coverage in the Jamaican press. Cricket's emergence as the dominant sport took longer and ebbed away faster in Jamaica than other West Indian islands but in the 1920s and 1930s it reigned supreme. For the *Gleaner*, the test match score was front page news and would be accompanied on the front page by a summary of the game and the opinions of the cricket correspondent.[269] Inside the paper there were match reports. There was no widespread radio service in Jamaica in 1935 and the *Gleaner's* reports were incredibly detailed, including a description of every over in the previous day (at least up to the tea interval). These were spread across the paper, a couple of columns on page four, two further columns on page thirteen, half of page fifteen and so on. During the Jamaica test the *Gleaner*

---

269 In contrast to the more sedate *Barbados Advocate* that kept cricket on the sport's pages.

was running these detailed reports not only for the ongoing test match but also for the closing stages of the third test played in British Guiana (the reports are taken verbatim from a Guiana paper that had presumably travelled on the same boat that brought the MCC party to Jamaica). Rather like playground cricket you have to concentrate, else it's easy to end up in the wrong game.

Hacking through over by over match reports provides glimpses of the character of West Indian cricket in the 1930s. In England, players' names were an important matter. Famously professionals were known by surnames alone, for amateurs the surname would generally be preceded by initials and in match reports these rules were generally observed. *The Times* cricket correspondent has a love for Wally Hammond so pure it would require poetry to do it justice, but he never lets slip a single Wally. In the West Indies things are rather more complicated. In the Jamaica vs MCC game that preceded the test, the Jamaican captain comes out to bat as Nethersole and proceeds to play himself in using the same name. However, as soon as a few scoring shots are played Nethersole has vanished and been replaced by someone called Crab.[270] Other players come in with a surname that is frequently if inconsistently replaced by the

---

270 Crab Nethersole is a fascinating cricketing character; Rhodes scholar "in days when these awards were just not normally given to men of a certain complexion" (/publication_jcarnagie.pdf) but as Jamaican cricket captain he is described as white (in photos he does look white). Subsequent to his career as a cricketer he was head of the West Indian Cricket Board of Control and was instrumental in George Headley being the first black West Indian appointed as test match captain in the 1948 series.

first name. The spinner Oscar Scott quickly becomes Tommy. George Headley is often just George and Learie Constantine is more often than not known as Leary. England players are generally surname only with the significant exception of Patsy Hendren who vies with Constantine in the battle for most frequently used first name.

Nor was the democratic spirit of West Indian cricket writing limited to using players' first and nicknames. Selection squabbles were pursued vigorously in both the letters and comment pages of the *Gleaner*. Tom Mudie who was to play in the Jamaica test match had a letter published including an attack on the Jamaican selectors for failing to pick Beckford for the second Jamaica against MCC game. "I view with much concern these distasteful blunders time and again," and, "The frequency of conduct of this nature from that privileged circle is destroying the structure of the future of the game." But the *Gleaner* also included articles and letters praising the Jamaica selectors for being identifiable and accountable in a way the WICBC was not.

In the West Indies, the meeting point of cricket and the newspapers provided room for debate, a place where strong opinions could be expressed and authority figures called to account. This was no small thing in an island of over a million people with an electorate of just 60,000 and where true power was in the hands of the British governor. But as well as providing a space for Jamaica's population to compete and express their opinions, cricket was a distraction that made it easier to disregard Jamaica's endemic poverty and race discrimination. Reading the *Gleaner*, 1930s Jamaica seems a rather quaint place where the emphasis is on cricket and the visit of the Duke and Duchess of Gloucester.[271] Yet on the 14th March 1935, the first day of the Jamaica test match, the representatives of the desperate Fyzabad hunger marchers including Buzz Butler were meeting with the governor of Trinidad and Captain Cipriani. And the situation was no better in Jamaica than it was in Trinidad. Jamaica's economy was dependent on exports: sugar, bananas and labour, and in the 1930s the market for all three dried up. Unemployment, in excess of 30% of the working population, was exacerbated by Jamaicans returning from Panama and Cuba. Many of those who could find work earned less than thirty shillings a week. But reading the island's newspapers there is no more than the occasional hint of the desperate situation confronting a swathe of the population. The *Gleaner* was, at heart, a business, it reported the news, things that were new. Cricket and the newspapers enabled people to look away from the grim business of life in Jamaica, for a few hours at least.

Looking past unpleasant issues extended to coverage of cricket. Some very sharp things were said about Jack Grant's captaincy in the *Gleaner* but the link is never made to the absence of a meritocratic approach in selecting the captain of the West Indian cricket side. We know from CLR James that in Trinidad in the 1920s the omission of certain players from representative teams was regarded as a snub to

---

271 The *Gleaner* and its editor HG De Lisser was not a simple tool of the white establishment but it was in keeping with its editor's politics generally conservative and against self-rule for Jamaica and the West Indies.

the black population as a whole.[272] Presumably there were similar suspicions of bias in the 1930s, but they were not openly expressed in the pages of the *Gleaner*.

Cricket's freedom of speech in the West Indies only went so far and if selection for West Indies home series was more liberal than for tours of England the games were played in a society where distinctions of class and race were enforced by a network of informal practices and customs. In Jamaica in 1935 Jack Iddon, the England all-rounder and Learie Constantine met over dinner. At the end of the meal Iddon said to Constantine he would see him at the dance that evening. But Constantine hadn't been invited to the dance, Constantine didn't even know there was a dance, the dance was a whites only affair.[273] There was a complicated hierarchy at work: professional English cricketers might not be invited to dinner by the governor, but they did get to go to the dance, black West Indian cricketers were excluded from both.

It is notable that Iddon and Constantine dined together, clearly their shared position as cricketers from Lancashire overcame the informal, but generally rigid, segregation of the British West Indies. It wasn't the only example of links between English cricketers and the black Caribbean population. Ken Farnes recalls Patsy Hendren and dressing room attendant "Old Shepherd" running "hypothetical short runs" in the dressing room in Barbados.

Such contacts, however, seemed to be the exception to the norm of the English tourists easily assimilating into

---

272 James himself thought most selection was free of racial bias, but that it wasn't perceived that way.

273 See page 63, *Learie Constantine* by Peter Mason.

a segregated society. New Years at the Marine Hotel was enjoyed "with the rest of the island's white population" [274]and the squad had membership rights at the exclusive Barbados yacht club. Farnes, in his detailed account of the tour, enjoys the little Britain of Barbados but becomes increasingly fractious as his surroundings become less familiar. There is the occasional glimpse of racism and Farnes shows every sign of enjoying a racist joke told to him by the Trinidadian Chief of Police. The amateur Farnes wasn't the only English tourist to enjoy a racist joke; Jack Hobbs identified Patsy Hendren as "Cricket's Prime Minister of Mirth"[275], and that racist jokes were Hendren's particular speciality. This isn't to say the England players were terrible people, but they, like most of us, tended to adapt to the society around them, a tendency particularly marked when they occupied a relatively privileged place within that society.

The racial divide in the British West Indies did not work in favour of the majority black population and, as on other islands, there were signs of the emergence of a different Jamaica. Particularly in Kingston there was support for the pan-African program of Jamaican born and resident Marcus Garvey. In outlying plantations and oil fields there were labour disputes and in May of 1935, soon after the MCC had left the island, police fired on striking workers on two separate occasions.[276] Labour disputes were to coalesce

---

274 *Tours and Tests* by Kenneth Farnes (Page 73)

275 Sport and the English, 1918–1939 by Mike Huggins and Jack Williams https://epdf.tips/sport-the-english-1918-1939-between-the-wars.html

276 http://www.socialisthistorysociety.co.uk/HART.HTM

in the Jamaican Labour rebellion of 1938 which was a watershed for Jamaican politics, marking the emergence of the Jamaican Labour Party and the People's National Party that dominated politics in the post-colonial era.

Cricket's permeability meant it was populated simultaneously by Jamaica's super-structure: The *Gleaner's* world of governors, legislative councils and visiting cruise ships; and also by black cricketers and cricket supporters. If a side with a majority of black players could match and defeat the MCC what did that say about British assumptions of racial superiority?

Chapter 24

GEORGE HEADLEY: ATLAS

The Jamaican test match was preceded by two games between MCC and a Jamaica xi. A sign of the strain on playing resources was that Trevor Arnott of Glamorgan who was in Jamaica on holiday was roped in to play for MCC in the second match replacing Wally Hammond. Even with Arnott in the team, the tourists had to borrow a substitute fielder from the Jamaican side.

As with the Trinidad test match, selection was straightforward for England: Eric Hollies, Ken Farnes and Wally Hammond missed the island games but were fit to play in the test, but injuries to Farrimond and Leyland meant there was no decision to make over who to leave out of the side. Leyland's injury, incurred when falling off a bar stool[277] must have been particularly dispiriting for Bob

---

277 Ken Farnes, *Tours and Tests*.

Wyatt. It would seem that some of those players who did make it out on the field were not completely fit. Ken Farnes commented, "With only a strained neck and ankle and a thrown-out arm, I was amongst the fitter members."

For the West Indies, selection was far more complicated, island sensibilities had to be assuaged and Jamaican commentators were aghast at the centralising tendency of the WICBC. An article in the *Jamaican Gleaner* began, "When one contrasts the painstaking methods we employ in selecting our side, with those of the so-called West Indies Cricket Board of Control the comparison is odious." The correspondent went on to point out the WICBC would not have any representatives in Jamaica prior to the test match, leaving selection in the hands of Jack Grant who arrived on the island in time to watch the two Jamaica vs MCC matches. The article ended with a stirring call to cricketing independence: "Have we not enough data before us to cut adrift from the West Indies Cricket Board of Control at home and abroad and manage our own affairs?"

The West Indies team selected for the third test in British Guiana had stoked the fire of Jamaican cricketing nationalism. In the first two tests of the series British Guiana had two representatives in the West Indies side, Christiani and Jones, but when the tour reached British Guiana this swelled to four players with James Neblett and Ken Wishart being included in the xi. The cricketing credentials of both men were suspect, the third test of 1935 was the only time either appeared in a test match; Wishart had a first-class average of twenty-three with Neblett averaging just nineteen. What particularly upset the *Gleaner* was the omission from the Guiana test of Oscar Da Costa, who had been sent to the eastern Caribbean to boost the number of Jamaicans in the team. British Guiana had nabbed all three of the "spare" slots in the test team whereas in Barbados and Trinidad the places had been shared out.

Now the feeling in Jamaican cricket was that the West Indies team should be turned in a Jamaican direction with a particular focus on the position of wicket keeper. As one of the eight permanent players,[278] Cyril Christiani arrived in Jamaica in advance of the test, but local opinion was he should be put back on the boat and returned to British Guiana, in the same way that Oscar Da Costa had been discarded. Ivan Barrow was the Jamaican wicketkeeper, had test match experience from the 1933 tour to England and, like Christiani, could open the batting. Barrow would be joined by the other seven core players, including Jamaicans George Headley and Leslie Hylton, leaving three other spots for local cricketers. If Jamaican opinion was united over Barrow, the sports pages and reader's letters sections of *The Gleaner* included a multiplicity of suggestions for the three additional positions.

Christiani was a fine keeper, one of the last to stand up to the stumps no matter how fast the bowling, he had stumped George Paine off the bowling of Constantine in the third test.[279] Constantine referred to him as a "Genius of a Keeper".[280] And in addition to the skills he brought

---

278 i.e. the seven who played in all four test matches plus Learie Constantine who appeared when available.

279 Although Constantine definitely bowled leg breaks in the fourth test, so perhaps wasn't bowling flat out at the time.

280 Letter to RH Mallett in MCC archives.

to the side, Christiani was the only player from British Guiana in the group of eight players at the core of the West Indies team in 1935. If Jamaica had six players in the team, British Guiana's representation would be eliminated. This would disgust all Guyanese cricket fans and one of those fans had particular influence. In his book, *Cricket Under the Sun*, Learie Constantine identifies George O'Dowd as a financial backer of the West Indies' 1928 and 1933 tours to England. O'Dowd's obituary in *Wisden* includes a statement that "Thanks largely to him, MCC teams visited West Indies in 1929 and 1935". MCC expected to make a loss from the 1934-1935 tour as they would pay the professional players on the tour and this outgoing would not be covered by match receipts.[281] But The MCC's travelling and accommodation expenses for the 1935 tour were underwritten by the West Indian cricketing authorities, with Jamaica and Trinidad each picking up one third of the costs and Barbados and British Guiana making up the remaining third between them. It's not clear whether O'Dowd put up the British Guiana share or if he was an additional source of funding entirely but, either way, Christiani of British Guiana played in the Jamaica test match, keeping wicket and opening the batting with his fellow wicketkeeper Ivan Barrow[282].

---

281 There is a reference in the *Jamaican Gleaner* to this effect. If this is correct, then these were more generous terms than were offered to either South Africa or India where the MCC's secretarial correspondence shows the home countries would be required to meet the costs of England's professionals.

282 Derek Sealy who also played in the fourth test kept wicket during the West Indies' 1939 tour to England.

Originally, the West Indies selectors named ten players for the fourth test match: Grant, Grant, Constantine, Sealy, Martindale, Christiani, Headley, Hylton, Barrow and Mudie. The last place was between Fuller, Scott and Beckford with the fast bowling all-rounder Fuller getting the nod.

The deciding fourth test match did not start well for the West Indies. The Jamaican, Ivan Barrow, was opening the batting with the man many believed he should have replaced in the team, Cyril Christiani. But Barrow went bowled by Farnes for three and the West Indies were 5 – 1 as George Headley came to the crease. Headley batted cautiously, first in a partnership of eighty-two with the much derided Christiani and then in a vital one of 202 with Sealy which went into the second day's play. Headley gave one chance when Ken Farnes dropped a sitter[283] at long leg off the bowling of George Paine when Headley was on eighty-two. He batted on to the end of the West Indian innings, completely in command and increasing the pace of his scoring.

In *A History of West Indies Cricket*, Michael Manley says of Headley's innings of 1935: "There are not many people still alive today who were there *(the book was first published in 1988)*, but everyone who has survived recalls it at some point at every test match played at Sabina Park."[284] Of course, those who were so lavish in their praise had the benefit of hindsight. The *Gleaner's* correspondent saw things

283 Farnes' own description from his book *Tours and Tests*.
284 One of those watching was Michael Manley – see *Jamaica at the Wicket*, as above.

rather differently, "They (*i.e. Headley and Sealy*) played some of the dreariest cricket between lunch and tea that has ever been played at Sabina Park ... That deadly two hours ... has just about lost us any chance of making anything but a draw of this game." But the sedate batting of Headley and Sealy on the first day allowed an acceleration on the second as Learie Constantine smashed thirty-four in thirty-two balls, including two sixes and four fours and Rolph Grant, playing in the Constantine manner, scored seventy-seven in a partnership with Headley of 147.

Jack Grant who had been blamed for declaring too early in the first test let the West Indian innings continue until after tea on the second day, giving his bowlers just over two days to bowl England out twice and win the series. Headley, with his highest test score of 270, had taken his side to a position where they could not lose[285] and had an excellent chance of winning.

Although Headley was only twenty-five years old, he had been batting the West Indies into winning positions and saving them from losing ones for the past five years. When the MCC had toured the West Indies in 1930 he had scored 176 on his test debut, in the third test of that series he became the first West Indian to score a hundred in each innings of a test match[286] to help West Indies level the series and in the final test with the West Indies facing defeat he scored 223 in the second innings and batted for over six hours. With the rain-affected "timeless" test having lasted

---

285 Unlike in 1930 the match was limited to four days.
286 https://en.wikipedia.org/wiki/George_Headley

nine days and the boat sailing for England, MCC accepted that both the match and the series would have to be declared a draw.

Headley then scored two test hundreds in the 1930-1931 West Indies tour of Australia, including one in the final test that ended in a West Indies win and the hundred in the second test of the 1933 tour of England that helped to secure the only draw in the series. He averaged more than sixty-six in first-class cricket in the English summer of 1933. In 1935 he had already scored ninety-three to set up victory in the Trinidad test. In addition to those big scores Headley had shown himself particularly adept at batting on rain-affected wickets, making an important thirty in the successful fifth test match in Australia in 1931 and a brilliant if unavailing forty-four out of 102 all out in the first test in 1935. Prior to World War II, Headley scored over 25%[287] of the West Indies' total runs; no other batsman has matched that percentage. It was CB Fry who first called Headley 'Atlas', because he carried West Indian cricket.

Like Douglas Jardine and Pelham Warner, Headley was not born in the islands he represented as a cricketer. Headley's father was from Barbados, his mother from Jamaica, but Headley was born in Panama where his father was working on the construction of the Canal. Although the West Indian diaspora in Panama played cricket[288] it doesn't seem that Headley participated in organised cricket whilst in Central America, although he did show an aptitude for

---

287 http://www.espncricinfo.com/magazine/content/story/459075.html
288 Pelham Warner played in Panama.

baseball. The course of cricket history was changed when work took Headley's father to Cuba and the young George was sent to live with an aunt in Jamaica. In Jamaica, Headley attended Calabar Elementary School.

Thomas Burchell Stephenson, an early headmaster of Calabar Elementary, was prominent in the Jamaican civil rights movement and a founder member of the Jamaican Union of Teachers.[289] He also played an important role in the development of Jamaican cricket, encouraging the playing of cricket at Calabar and organising an elementary school cricket competition that helped the spread of cricket to the non-white "artisan" classes. It was former pupils of Calabar Elementary who went on to form the Lucas cricket club that was to play against and beat the more established, white-dominated sides of Jamaica.[290]

There is an obvious comparison between Calabar Elementary and another great engine of West Indian cricketing progress, Combermere School in Barbados. Yet there were differences as well as parallels, Thomas Burchell Stephenson was a black man, a Baptist and a political progressive, there was no equivalent figure at Combermere prior to The Second World War. Cricket's genesis was similar but distinct across the islands of the British Caribbean.

Headley joined the cricket club at Calabar and having the best hands in the team kept wicket, bare-handed, as the school budget didn't run to gloves.[291] He also played

289 *Race, Sexuality and Identity in Britain and Jamaica: The Biography of Patrick Nelson*, by Gemma Romain.
290 *Jamaica at the Wicket*, Arnold Bertram, page 107.
291 From Bridgette Lawrence, *Masterclass: The Biography of George Headley*.

cricket in an array of more or less informal street games, often using improvised equipment. Cricket wasn't the only sport for Headley. Like the young Wally Hammond, he was a keen swimmer, often completing the three mile swim from Paradise Beach in Rae town, across Kingston Harbour and on to Pallisdoes.

Aged fifteen, Headley went to Kingston College,[292] he graduated two years later in 1928 and took up a temporary job in a magistrates' court allowing him to play for the Police team in Jamaican club cricket. Headley changed jobs to Keeling Lindo Estates, a supporter of cricket in Jamaica and the employer of West Indian bowler Tommy Scott. However, Headley only had a junior position at the firm and was considering a move to the USA and a career in dentistry when cricket history once again intervened, this time selecting Headley to play for Jamaica against Lord Tennyson's 1928 touring side. In the second game of the series Headley scored 211 and thoughts of dentistry were discarded. There was talk that Headley would tour England in the summer of that year and, although Headley was not selected, he was an ever present in the test series against England in 1930, the tour of Australia in 1930-1931 and the tour of England in 1933.

Prior to Headley, West Indian batsmen had generally disappointed in test matches and only George Challenor of Barbados had successfully adapted to English pitches. Even a talent such as Learie Constantine struggled as a test match batsman. But for the twenty-one-year-old Headley, success

---

292 As above.

was instantaneous, and he excelled in Australia and England as well as the West Indies. Part of the reason for Headley being so successful so early in his career was that he possessed a combination of physical abilities perfect for batting. First came an eye for a ball that was inhuman; Headley told CLR James that in his entire career there were only two deliveries he hadn't seen from the moment they left the bowler's hand. Allied to hand-to-eye coordination was fast and accurate footwork. In a *History of West Indies Cricket*, Michael Manley noted Headley's "sloping shoulders often associated with boxers who can punch". But what also jumps out from early photos of Headley, alongside the power, is his poise and proportion. In 1933 he was photographed in Liverpool, Headley, handsome, long limbed, narrow waisted, is carrying the tools of his trade, a bat and ball; dressed in immaculate cricket whites, with shirt cuffs buttoned at the wrist. The elegant figure was not an accident, he cared about clothes, matching his socks and ties and had an apparent liking for fedora hats; he is wearing one in this photo too. It should be incongruous with the cricket whites but it makes Headley look a little like Fred Astaire. Even in a photograph there is an air of fluidity about Headley. The *Morning Herald* described how: "This little fellow who shuffles so slowly to the crease nips about like a dancer once he has taken guard."

Although Headley was a supremely natural cricketer, that was only the foundation of his success. What allowed him to build a career was the work he put in – work memorably defined by Michael Manley as "A process that begins with analysis, proceeds to application and ends with the infinite capacity for repetition which alone develops virtuosity."

This ability to work not only hard but effectively was Headley's from an early age; CLR James describes how a seventeen-year-old Headley had watched Ernest Tydesley batting for a touring team led by the Honourable LH Tennyson. Headley had learnt "Everything he required to know about batting from watching Ernest Tydesley."[293] Presumably this watching was in part a conscious process where Headley looked for specific techniques he could adopt. But given how totally Headley had understood the requirements of top-level sport there may have been an underlying intuition, the workings of a subconscious intelligence.

The intuition was tested when Headley toured Australia with the West Indies side in 1930-1931. He arrived in Australia as an offside player, hitting the ball through the covers with an off drive played, according to Michael Manley, with the bat at an angle of between 45 and 90 degrees to the ground – it must have been more of a slash than a drive. Headley made a good start to the tour of Australia but by the test matches the Australian bowlers in general and Clarrie Grimmett in particular had begun to sort him out, bowling a leg stump line to limit his range of scoring strokes. Grimmett dismissed him in the first test at Adelaide for nought and eleven, he fell to medium pacers for fourteen and two in the second test and with the West Indies losing the first two tests of the series it was the first crisis of Headley's career.

---

293 CLR James, *Cricket: The Great Ones*, edited by John Arlott (1967) reproduced in *A majestic Innings*, page 190. James said Headley watched Tydesley score 300 but it looks rather like he would have seen him score three hundreds.

Pretty much every batsman goes through such a phase; bowlers pick up on young player's strengths and weaknesses, avoid the former and exploit the latter. What distinguished George Headley was how quickly he recovered. First he observed, watching how Australian batsmen Archie Jackson and Stan McCabe batted against Grimmett.[294] Then came adaptation, he put away once and for all the slash through the offside with an angled bat, it wasn't a business shot. He also changed his stance. CLR James believed Headley played every shot from the back foot; that is his first movement was back and across his stumps. Now he developed a front on stance enabling him to play the ball pitched on leg stump on the leg side. Cricket is supposed to be a side on game but the front on stance worked for Headley because his supreme footwork allowed him to get back into a side on position to play the ball on the offside. "Headley, although starting from his shuffling extremely square on, two eyed stance, could have been used as an instruction manual from the off."[295] There seem to be technical similarities with Shivnarine Chanderpaul.

The changes to his technique paid off for Headley. In 1934, *Wisden* made him one of its five cricketers of the year and commented; "The outstanding feature of his batting – the one by which he will be longest remembered – was his facility for going back to his right foot to drive to the on, and the manner in which he placed the ball almost exactly where he wanted." Out of Headley's onside weakness came strength.

---

294 CLR James in *The Great Ones*, as above.
295 Michael Manley, as above, page 43.

The unorthodox batting of Headley illustrates that a batsman needs a technique, a consistent approach that emphasises his strengths, but Technique as a body of received knowledge to be applied to all batsmen is a fallacy.

Once Headley had observed and adapted he practiced and repeated his new approach. "Those who toured with Headley during the Australian disaster recounted in loving detail how they were obliged to spend hour after hour in the nets bowling at him."[296] Headley's preparation wasn't confined to the nets, he would rarely get much sleep the night before he batted[297] as he ran and reran his innings of the next day. And when Headley batted, all his preparation had brought him to a point. "When I am walking down the pavilion steps, going in to bat, if I met my father I would not recognise him. And once I am at the wicket I am concerned with nothing else but seeing the ball from the bowler's hand."[298] [299] What is remarkable is not only the concentration coming down the pavilion steps but how Headley sustained that fixed purpose. He passed fifty fifteen times in his test career but two thirds of those innings ended up with a hundred. The only batsman with an equivalent conversion rate is, of course, Don Bradman who turned twenty-nine of forty-two fifties into hundreds.

---

296 Michael Manley, as above, page 43.

297 CLR James, as above.

298 From George Headley in *Race Today* reproduced in *A Majestic Innings*, as above, page 291.

299 It doesn't seem as if George Headley ever saw much of his father after he moved to Cuba.

Headley's responsibilities weren't only to his immediate team; like Learie Constantine he excelled at cricket, the sport of the British Empire, but the imperialist doctrine that sustained the Empire regarded black British subjects as less capable than white people. The success of Headley and Constantine demonstrated this was not the case in the even contest of cricket. Headley's success may have had even more resonance than Constantine's; in part because he was a batsman; excellent West Indian fast bowlers like Constantine could be accommodated within the social and racial structures of West Indian society, it was the African and Indian population of the Caribbean who did the heavy labour wherever it was found, why should cricket be any different? A batsman though was a different matter, by batting at first wicket down Headley was a black man in a white man's place.[300]

A, perhaps, more significant difference between Constantine and Headley was that Constantine was regarded as a thrilling cricketer of the moment, a force of nature, and that emphasis on Constantine's physicality could be accommodated in an expanded but still racial worldview. Headley, though, didn't play just in the moment, his batting had a past, a technique, it had been whittled down, shots discarded, his stance at the wicket altered. CLR James creeps around this, placing Headley in a pantheon of West Indian batsmen with the urge to dominate. But the facts don't

---

300 Although as Arnold Bertram points out there had been a tradition of black batsmen in Jamaican cricket prior to Headley, and Learie Constantine's father Lebrun was the first West Indian to score a hundred at Lord's.

bear this out; Headley was not a particularly quick scoring batsman, there are no instances of Headley shredding a test match attack in the way Don Bradman often did. It would not be fair to call Headley an accumulator, indeed he was clearly a batsman people would pay to watch. In its report on the first test at Lord's in 1933 *The Times* described Headley's batting as:

> "Persuading the onlooker that a test match can still provide the highest and most pleasant form of cricket."

But for all his style, Headley always had an eye on the match conditions and the needs of his fragile team. To have played an innings of the type Constantine played at Old Trafford in 1933, to respond to a situation where defence seemed to be called for, with an assault on the bowling, was not Headley's way. Gerry Gomez recalls Headley would often say of a teammate out to an impetuous shot, "Why him don't like to bat?" George Headley liked to bat; two double hundreds in test cricket and a highest score in first-class cricket of 344, he had the essential ability to grind out a big innings.

The contrast between Headley and Constantine is nicely summed up in the writing of Neville Cardus. For Cardus, Constantine was a jazz cricketer. Jazz was the music of black America; although Cardus liked jazz well enough, classical music was his true love. And when Cardus first saw Headley bat at Lord's in 1933 it was classical music he used for his analogy, "A chord struck by a Horwitz is enough, we need not hear him play the whole sonata through." George

Headley was undoubtedly a great batsman, as well as a great West Indian batsman.

And Headley's undisputed excellence seems, to an extent, to have transcended the racial divides of the British Caribbean. There doesn't seem to have been any opposition to Headley playing in a Jamaican or West Indian team as a batsman (that he should captain either side was a different matter) and it seems all West Indians could enjoy watching or hearing about George Headley's 270 runs against the MCC at Sabina Park in 1935.

There's a story told about George Headley as a child in Jamaica. Jamaican kids in the 1920s and 1930s played a cricket variant where all the players would field and the only way to become the batsman was to bowl or catch the incumbent. On one occasion George Headley took a catch on Tuesday and proceeded to bat till dark. He batted till dark on Wednesday and again on Thursday. On Friday he arrived bat in hand to find the game had been moved elsewhere.[301] Perhaps the real genius of George Headley was to retain that simple pitiless focus in test match cricket. As he batted through the second day at Sabina Park, breaking records, establishing a position, he was oblivious to all the outside pressures, social, political and financial. The world was reduced to George Headley and the ball, watched, of course; from the very instant it left the bowlers hand.

---

301 From *Jamaica at the Wicket*, it has the sound of a popular myth, one that I'm happy to propagate.

Chapter 25

"THIS WHAT MARTINDALE DO TO YOU"

As well as rain delays and slow play the test match in Georgetown, British Guiana, was distinguished by the attendance of Daddy Bell, one of the extrovert supporters come critics who were a notable feature of cricket in the British West Indies. Bell generally watched games from one of the trees overlooking the ground but at the start of the test match he descended from "his tree" next to the pavilion, crossed the boundary and entered the field of play determined, in the words of Ken Farnes, in his book *Tours and Tests*, "to cast obeah on our skipper." Walking up to Bob Wyatt, Bell thrust a small box into the hands of England's captain. The box was a modelled miniature coffin. Thinking it an odd sort of present Wyatt rolled back the wooden lid only to see "An accurate effigy of me to the last detail –

including a photograph cut from the papers to represent my face." "This what Martindale do to you,"[302] prophesised Daddy Bell.

Now on the second day of the final test, England had to bat for more than two days against Martindale and co if they were to save the match and draw the series. Before going out to bat, Wyatt had suggested to his vice-captain Errol Holmes that he, i.e. Wyatt, should move down from his opening position in the batting order, Holmes was firm in his belief that Wyatt should stay in place and blunt the West Indies pace attack.

The crowd is packed tight in the Sabina Park ground as Manny Martindale paces out his run up. The hum of chatter drops and rises to a roar as the long-legged, powerfully-built Martindale runs in to bowl. He leaps, the ball is too fast to be seen from the boundary's edge and the crowd gasps as it thuds into wicketkeeper Christiani's gloves. The second ball is just as fast, but Wyatt has things under control. He shuffles across his crease, nudges the ball into the leg side and takes a single. David Townsend takes the next two balls, running a bye on the fourth. Wyatt is back on strike and lets the fifth ball of the over pass outside off stump. Facing the last ball, he again shuffles towards off stump preparing to let the ball go. But this time the ball snakes back from the pitch and does not bounce quite so high, Wyatt has no time to react and is struck clean in

302 From *RES Wyatt: Fighting Cricketer*, Gerald Pawle

the face and with such force the crack can be heard "like a rifle shot"[303] in the England dressing room. He falls to the ground already unconscious and bloodied. With no team physios and no doctor, it is left to the onrushing players to help the England captain. Wyatt is carried from the field. There isn't even a stretcher. It takes five players, four West Indians and the other opening batsman, Townsend, to lift him up, Learie Constantine places his arm beneath Wyatt's damaged jaw, the England captain's arm hangs limp – he looks dead as they carry him off.

But Wyatt comes round in the dressing room. His jaw clearly smashed, spitting blood,[304] he uses sign language to ask for a pencil and, not for the first time in 1935, begins to rearrange the batting order.[305] That done, Wyatt is stretchered into an ambulance and, accompanied by William Harbord, taken to a Kingston hospital.

This was the not the first time that Martindale had injured Wyatt; he had broken a bone in Wyatt's foot with a full toss bowled during the MCC's 1929-1930 tour. Wyatt incurred a number of injuries during his career. In 1929 he suffered two broken ribs when hit by a ball from Harold Larwood. A bone in Wyatt's hand was broken when hit by Bill Bowes, he had his thumb broken by Ken Farnes, and rebroken by Australia's Tim Wall in the 1934 test series. And his arm was

---

303 Eric Hollies' account in *I'll Spin You a Tale* by Eric Hollies.
304 From Ken Farnes' *Tests and Tours*.
305 From *RES Wyatt: Fighting Cricketer*, page 146.

broken by a short-pitched delivery in the 1936-1937 tour of Australia. Wyatt may have wanted to go down the batting order at Sabina Park in 1935, but not because of a lack of physical courage or toughness, batsmen playing cricket in the first half of the 1930s had to be tough because their protective equipment was anything but. This quadruple fracture of the jaw was Wyatt's most serious injury. His jaw wasn't wired in the West Indies and during the long journey back to the UK by boat Wyatt developed sepsis, and could have died. But he fought off sepsis and, who knows, the curse of Daddy Bell, and incredibly was batting at the Oval for MCC against Surrey three weeks after his return to the UK.

Ken Farnes makes a specific reference to Martindale bowling "fairly" after Wyatt's sickening injury, so he was probably keeping the ball up to the bat reducing the chance of further casualties. But he was also bowling very fast, on a pitch described in a *Daily Herald* report as "like concrete." Wyatt reckoned Martindale was slower, but only slightly slower, than Larwood on the bodyline tour. Martindale had Townsend caught behind. George Paine, not for the first time in the series was promoted in the order to preserve the batsmen, including the now acting captain Errol Holmes (although presumably it was Wyatt's rewritten batting order that was adhered to). Paine was promptly LBW to Martindale for nought, which brought Holmes to the wicket with just a few overs left in the day – clean bowled middle stump by Martindale for nought to a ball that was "easily the fastest that has scorched the pitch at Sabina"[306] and England were 26 – 3

---

306 The *Gleaner*.

with the captain in hospital. As so often happens in cricket, as the England players were thinking they had at least got to the end of a terrible day, things took a lurch for the worse and Constantine had Hammond caught by Hylton "Out to a stroke a schoolboy might have been ashamed of."[307]

It was a miserable end to the series for England's best batsman. After an important twenty-nine not out to bring England a victory in the first test, he had been ineffective, averaging just twenty-five in the test matches. It was the West Indies fast bowlers that gave him problems, Hammond was dismissed by them six times in seven completed innings with one run out. Constantine dismissed Hammond on three occasions in 1935 as well as in England's only innings in the second test in 1933. So in 1933 and 1935 Constantine and Hammond came up against each other on seven occasions, with Constantine taking Hammond's wicket four times. Their long-running feud may have ended in 1933, but Constantine still had an edge over Hammond.

Holmes went to see Wyatt in hospital at the end of the day's play, passing on the news that the team were 27 – 4. Wyatt once again took up his paper and pencil and wrote "We must not lose."[308] He also wrote to Martindale to say it was a perfectly fair ball that had broken his jaw. Holmes made a similar statement at the end of the test and referred to Martindale as "One of the fairest fast bowlers playing cricket today".

---

307 The *Gleaner*, although the *Reuters* report states that he was yorked and Patsy Hendren told Ken Farnes the first ball he had faced from Constantine was like a bullet, so the *Gleaner* may be a bit harsh.
308 *RES Wyatt: Fighting Cricketer*, as before.

Already four wickets down and with their captain out for the match it might have been expected England would quickly succumb on the third morning but instead they responded with their best batting of the match. The most significant innings was played by Les Ames who scored 126.

Ames was supported by Patsy Hendren whose innings demonstrated resolve as well as skill. Hendren was forty-six years old when he went to face the bowling of Martindale, Constantine and Hylton on the morning of 16th March 1935. In 1931 he had been hit by a bouncer bowled by Harold Larwood, "the ball struck him just above the ear with a crack that could be heard where I was sitting, on top of the pavilion, towards the back. He went down with a thud, his legs jerking and twitching as though he had been shot."[309] Hendren was taken to hospital and missed three weeks of cricket. He returned with the three-peaked cap that was to make a re-appearance in the MCC vs West Indies match in 1933. Hendren's 1935 tour was in part a holiday and a chance to end his test career in the West Indies where he had played well and been a popular figure. His wife was with him on the tour, the couple travelling in advance of the touring party to allow Hendren to referee football games in Barbados. With his captain badly hurt and Hendren's own memories of being injured by fast bowling, it would have been understandable if he decided he was too old for test cricket and got out as quickly as he could. But Hendren had his pride and hooked and pulled the fast bowlers.

---

309 From *Patsy Hendren* by Ian Peebles.

Hendren was a good example of a cricketer who could draw different reactions from cricket watchers depending on their point of view. When CLR James wanted to compare Learie Constantine's verve with the solidity and conservatism of an English professional it was Hendren he choose as the archetypical English cricketer. It was this solidity and toughness that he demonstrated in facing Martindale and Constantine on a quick Jamaica pitch. But Neville Cardus emphasised the boy in Hendren, the way he ran his first run with his bat tightly secured in both hands as if he feared someone would take it away from him. And Hendren was particularly popular with West Indian crowds. During the 1929-1930 MCC tour when fielding on the leg side and with the bowler walking back to his mark, Hendren would mock surreptitiously inch himself closer to the batsman. The crowd would shout out from the stands, "Watch that man, watch that Patsy."[310] Once the batsman noticed, Hendren would round off his act with a show of petulance at the failure of his scheme. In West Indian press reports Hendren is often referred to as Patsy, although first names were normally only used for West Indian players. In Barbados, in the first test, he was cheered to the wicket.

What is notable about Patsy Hendren is how, like Learie Constantine, he brought the conflicting sides of his own personality to the field. He was the English professional, Irish practical joker,[311] nervous and vulnerable, triumphant.

---

310 From *Patsy Hendren*, Ian Pebbles as before.

311 The Hendren family name was originally O'Hanrahan but was probably changed on his parents' arrival in the UK, see Ian Pebbles, *Patsy Hendren*.

This was his final test match and he eventually retired at the end of the English 1937 season. In the 1935 test matches he averaged just under twenty-nine, compared to forty-eight in all test match cricket but still enough to top the MCC averages, and his partnership with Wally Hammond in the second innings of the first test had guided England to their only win in the series.

After Hendren was out for forty, Ames and Iddon dug in. At tea on the third day with the score at 222 – 5 England, down and defeated the night before, were beginning to make a game of it, West Indies needing to take thirteen more wickets (allowing for Wyatt's injury) in four more sessions. Constantine and Hylton both tried bowling spin, Ames got cramp and called for Farnes as a runner and then sent him back. Ames reached a hundred. Constantine, incredibly Constantine, dropped Iddon, was the match turning again?

Eventually it was George Mudie playing in his only test match who took the vital wicket of Ames assisted by a close in catch by Learie Constantine. In his book *Cricket in the Sun*, Constantine says he tricked Ames into thinking Constantine was fielding in the covers, although doesn't explain how this was done. Whatever the trickery involved, the catch, as described in the *Gleaner*, seems to have been quite something, "standing at silly mid-off about five yards from the batsman he took a full drive low down with one hand, travelling so fast he could not hold the ball but had to throw it up and catch it again."

Mudie got another important wicket having Iddon LBW for fifty-four with Constantine quickly mopping up the tail. All out for 271, after the West Indian embarrassment of The

Oval and Lord's in 1933 it was England who had to follow on. Even now the day had one slight but possibly vital twist, the doughty Iddon was sent in to open with Townsend and the two managed to reach the close of play at fourteen for nought.

The next day, Sunday, was a rest day and then England would have to bat out the Monday to save both the test match and the series. The *Jamaican Gleaner* cricket correspondent, generally given to pessimism, believed a draw was as good as certain unless Sunday rain affected the wicket. The Jamaican cricket board may have seen another possibility of winning the series; the MCC party was invited to the Silver Slipper in Kingston for a dinner and dance.

Rain did fall in Kingston Jamaica on Sunday 17th March 1935, but it was generally held it didn't affect the pitch.[312] The England team may have been a little frayed by Saturday night and Sunday morning at the Silver Slipper but most importantly of all the Sunday rest day had given the West Indies' pace attack a break, a big advantage to a side enforcing the follow on.

In the first over of the final day, a reenergised Constantine had Iddon LBW. In the second over, Martindale bowling tremendously fast and moving the ball in from the off, clean bowled Townsend. Hendren came in to join Hammond and the two managed to re-establish the England innings. The match lurched again in the moment the *Reuters* correspondent described as "The turning point of the game".

---

312 That was the view in West Indian newspapers, Ken Farnes thought, Patsy Hendren and Les Ames were out to "sticky wicket balls" in the second innings.

Jack Grant chasing a ball had to jump over spectators sitting at the boundary's edge. On landing he twisted his ankle and after a few overs had to leave the field.

"There was no player designated vice-captain. So I had to make the choice myself. I considered the matter and decided that Learie Constantine should have that honour. Once I had made up my mind I called my players together and said as simply and as quietly as I could that I had hurt my ankle, that unfortunately I could not remain on the field any longer and that I appointed Learie to act as captain in my place. Well do I remember the smile of approval given me by George Headley."[313]

It was Grant's last cricketing act, he walked off the ground and out of test cricket having played his final match at twenty-eight years of age. His brother Rolph was in the team when Grant left the field so it would have been possible to have handed the captaincy to another white man. As noted by Harry Pearson in his biography of Constantine, England also lost their captain to injury in this game and replaced him with Errol Holmes, the back-up amateur.

At 12.07pm the West Indies had victory in their grasp and their first black acting captain in command. But, as must have occurred to Constantine, victory hadn't yet been seized. If England were to slip away with a draw he would go down in history not only as a black captain, but a failed captain.

Constantine's first intervention after Grant's departure was a spectacular catch to dismiss Hendren off the bowling

---

313 *Jack Grant My Story*, as before, page 179.

of Mudie. Then he made the two strategic moves *Reuters* thought so important. Firstly, he brought himself on as a bowler at the opposite end of the ground and, bowling leg breaks, dismissed Ames, caught by Rolph Grant. Secondly, he brought Derek Sealy on to bowl for the first time in the match. Sealy in his second and final over dismissed Holmes. Captain Constantine went for the kill, bringing back Martindale. Bowling at great pace, Martindale pretty much clinched victory by clean bowling Hammond and then Smith, three wickets for Martindale – all bowled. With only the tail left, Martindale dismissed Farnes, this time, by way of variation, caught by Christiani, it was his final wicket of nineteen in the series for an average of 12.6.

The final wicket fittingly fell to Constantine who had Hollies caught by Martindale. England who at the start of the day had a chance to draw the match and series were bowled out for 103. A win for the West Indies. A test match win, bringing the West Indies their first series victory.

The series was a personal triumph for Constantine, fifteen wickets at thirteen, 169 violent runs at thirty-four, catches and captain. In the four test matches he played against England in 1933 and 1935 his record was won two drawn two, West Indies lost all three games when Constantine was unavailable. It has been said that Constantine's importance as a cricketer was as an entertainer, and a standard-bearer for the black, professional cricketer rather than a test match performer. His test match record, averaging just over thirty with the ball and nineteen with the bat was good, but not exceptional. But, it has to be borne in mind, Constantine played many of his eighteen test matches before he had fully emerged as a cricketer. In 1933-1935 he was in his prime and the rarest of cricketers – one who could turn a losing test match team into a winning one.

The West Indies left the field having won a test series against an England side picked by that bastion of the colonial establishment, the MCC. The next, and final, chapter looks at the implications of victory.

Chapter 26

THE DAWN OF
A NEW ERA?

The 1935 MCC tour ended in the first West Indies victory in a test match series. Taking a group of British colonial possessions in the Caribbean and making a cricketing nation had been an on-field success. The West Indies' 1935 victory was also the first series victory by one of the "nations" afforded test match status in the expansion of the ICC in 1926. There had been large crowds for all four test matches and extensive press coverage. The growth of test cricket as a multi-lateral activity after the Second World War owed much to the distinctive and intermittingly successful cricket played by West Indian teams in the 1930s.

In general, the English cricket establishment and press was generous in defeat. The MCC knew how to treat one of Kipling's twin impostors and was quick to telegraph the WICBC: "Marylebone offer you sincere congratulations on your victory."[314] *The Cricketer*, under its editor/proprietor Pelham Warner, acknowledged the success of the West Indies as "Certainly not a whit more than they deserved."

Some English commentators went further still, Trevor Wignall writing in the *Daily Express*, wrote "Snobs and others who like making excuses will loftily declare that the victory will do West Indies all the good in the world. That, however, is not how to regard this happening. The West Indians are just about as good as we are. Have we many better bats than Headley or finer bowlers than Constantine?"

Although Wignall was right about Headley and Constantine, he was rather optimistic about English cricket snobs, they existed but were not about to "declare that the victory will do West Indies all the good in the world."

The cricket correspondent of *The Times* couldn't resist: "Is there not a little too much of this so-called test match cricket." *Wisden* was not quite so churlish but its report on the 1935 tour is really just a long list of excuses for England's performance with very little said about the quality of West Indian play. At least *Wisden* was prepared to acknowledge the 1935 games as test matches, for a long time it downgraded the 1930 series in the West Indies to international matches as the MCC had sent touring parties simultaneously to both the West Indies and New Zealand. But the majority of English journalists happily acknowledged the West Indian achievement; sport in general and cricket in particular, normally if not invariably, shows the better side of human nature.

---

314 As reported in *The Times* 20th March

For the West Indies press a home victory provided perspective on the performances in England in 1933. The *Port of Spain Gazette* ended its report of the fourth test match by commenting that the series win "Confounds those undiscerning critics who were ready to say when the West Indies were beaten by an innings in England, "They're not up to test match standard.""

But there was little triumphalism in West Indian newspapers in 1935, if anything the papers fell over themselves trying to be fair to the English side. An instance from the *Jamaican Gleaner*, "Let us not omit to record the fact that no side which has hitherto toured these islands has ever met with the misfortune Wyatt's team has been called upon to face." West Indian victories placed members of the West Indian "establishment" in a difficult position, if a team with black players to the fore defeated England at cricket what did that say about the assumptions of imperialism? In the series, the West Indies won the second and fourth test matches but, in both games, the local paper predicted a draw before the final day. Indeed, the *Gleaner* had declared the fourth test would be a draw at the end of the first day. Perhaps a draw was the most comfortable result for the journalists concerned, it showed West Indian cricket teams could compete, but left the "Mother country" undefeated.

It doesn't seem the black population of the West Indies shared these reservations. The crowds who poured onto the outfields at Sabina Park and the Port of Spain Oval after victories seemed in no way inhibited. CLR James and Learie Constantine believed West Indian cricketing victory was the natural order, failure the aberration; due to the enervating impact of racism or the spirit of professionalism. Whilst the *Jamaican Gleaner* predicted a draw in the final match, Reggie Matcham, super fan, umbrella in hand, had declared, "We're going to win at the common canter."[315]

Although West Indian success in 1935 was a step in the steady forward march of test match cricket in the twentieth century, there were other aspects of the 1933 and 1935 series which hinted at future developments but where progress ebbed and flowed after the Second World War. My initial interest in the West Indian teams of the 1930s came from a report on the 1933 Old Trafford test match where Martindale and Constantine had bowled to bodyline fields. It seemed a clear predecessor to the cricket I had grown up with, England sides routed by explosive, highly-skilled West Indian teams. When Learie Constantine walked off the field at Sabina Park, the elements of that future West Indian dominance were in place. The (acting) captain was a black man, the team included four fast bowlers, one brilliant batsman in George Headley and more than one dashing stroke maker in support. West Indian talent and nationalism was seemingly ready to meld into a unique cricketing force. But West Indian cricket was far from dominant in the period immediately after the Second World War. With Weekes, Worrell and Walcott, the side was stronger than in the 1930s but not the best in the world. West Indian bowling was characterised by the spin pairing of Ramadhin and Valentine, not fast bowling.

---

315 Learie Constantine: *Cricket in the Sun.*

Indeed, rather than ushering in a period of West Indian fast bowling dominance, Kensington Oval 1935 was the final skirmish in the bodyline battle that had divided cricket in the first half of the 1930s. Arthur Richardson's intervention may have been resented by Learie Constantine and the *Daily Herald,* but it was Richardson's maximalist, Australian interpretation of the bodyline rules that gained general acceptance. The odd bouncer was bowled in county and international cricket after 1935 but any sign it was being used as a systematic tactic led to complaints and its discontinuance. It was only after the war when Don Bradman, captaining Ray Lindwall and Keith Miller, had a Damascene conversion that short-pitched bowling returned to test match cricket. And the full bodyline tactics seen in 1932-1933 had been banished for good.

Racial equality in cricket was another area where the direction seemingly established in the 1930s and immediately after World War II was not maintained. Herman Griffith being made captain of Barbados for one wartime match and the appointment of George Headley as captain in the 1948 test series against England seemed to have, finally, broken cricket's colour bar. But Headley only captained for one test in 1948 and with the cricketing great at the end of his career the reactionaries rallied, and a string of white West Indian captains followed. If, in the 1930s, cricket had been one cautious step ahead of a racially divided Caribbean, it now lagged behind politics where black men and to a lesser extent women were playing a central role in the progression to democracy and independence.

It was as if, in the 1930s, the dominant white community had been prepared to make concessions in sport, knowing they were invulnerable in politics and commerce. But after the Second World War that community felt beleaguered and hung on tightly to symbols of dominance, such as a white man as captain of the West Indian cricket team. A practical example of political success sublimating progressive developments in cricket is the career of Noel (Crab) Nethersole, Jamaican cricket captain of the pre-war period. From 1939-1955 Nethersole was a Jamaican representative to the WICBC[316] and prime mover in the captaincy being awarded to George Headley. Nethersole was also a prominent trade unionist and member of Norman Manley's People's National Party; his political responsibilities took him away from the central role he had played in cricket administration after the Second World War and he resigned from the WICBC when the PNP came to power. Another factor in the lack of progress towards meritocracy in West Indian cricket was the self-selecting tendency of the WICBC. In the 1930s this had insulated selection from island-based nationalism, but in the 1950s it allowed the board to stand out against more progressive administrators.

It took until 1960 for a black West Indian to be appointed permanent captain of the West Indies. Frank Worrell's elevation to the position owes something to the men included in this book. Derek Sealy was a schoolmaster and played with a young Worrell in the Combermere school team. CLR James, encouraged by Learie Constantine, returned to Trinidad in 1958 as editor of *The Nation* newspaper and used his position to start a public campaign for Worrell to be given the West Indian captaincy.

---

316 https://en.wikipedia.org/wiki/Noel_Newton_Nethersole

In England, as well as the West Indies, the reformist energy of the immediate post-war years seemed to dissipate as the 1950s wore on. In the 1930s bodyline and its aftermath coalesced general dissatisfaction with the amateur cricketing establishment and its Victorian outlook. During the 1935 series both the *Daily Herald* and *Daily Express* called for league cricket to be set up in the South of England which, presumably, would have swept away both the first-class counties and the amateur administrators who ran them. Jack Williams[317] is correct in emphasising cricket as a game which symbolised and developed continuity and ties between classes in inter-war Britain, but those ties were becoming increasingly stretched. The cricketing authorities made some significant moves towards a less snobbish approach immediately before and after the Second World War. Bob Wyatt was retained as captain for the 1935 home series against South Africa but when England lost the five match series 1 – 0, long-time professional Wally Hammond miraculously returned to the amateur state to captain the England team. In 1952 the selectors went the whole hog and appointed the professional Leonard Hutton to the captaincy. But the amateur order was re-established under, first, Peter May and then Colin Cowdrey. It was the second wave of the 1960s that swept away overt distinctions of race and class on both sides of the Atlantic. Frank Worrell was captain of the West Indies team for the famous 1960-1961 tour of Australia. In England the distinction between amateurs

---

317 Jack Williams, *Cricket and England: A Cultural and Social History of the Inter -war Years.*

and professionals went in 1962 and the death of Pelham Warner in January 1963 marked the end of an era. Cricket wasn't the only part of society to experience change in the 1960s; Jamaica and Trinidad became independent countries in 1962 followed by Barbados and Guyana in 1966.

That the pace and direction of change in cricket mirrored the communities it was played in is no surprise. Since the publication of *Beyond a Boundary*, it is understood that as cricket is played in society it must reflect wider social relations. But is it justifiable to see the causality going the other way? Could it be that changes in cricket changed society, were events such as Worrell's appointment as West Indian captain in 1960 or West Indian cricketing success in 1935 causes of the independence of the islands of the British Caribbean?

It is as well to be sceptical of such claims, to an extent sport is a simplified version of the society around it and a part of its appeal is it can feel important without having serious consequences. Additionally, in the Caribbean, cricket was always in part a game of the British colonial establishment and it can be viewed as a buttress to British ideas; an essentially conservative activity. Finally there must have been many West Indians, male and, perhaps, particularly female, who were not too fussed about cricket but who were keenly interested in political and social progress. If cricket contributed to West Indian nationalism it was only as part of a larger process.

But there are some reasons to believe cricket did play some part in the development of a democratic Caribbean. Most social and economic interactions are governed by ostensible laws and less well-defined rules of conduct. Both laws and social rules are complicated, and may reflect the balance of power in an interaction. But a game is a relatively simple activity with a defined outcome requiring rules that are clear and equal for both sides. The success of cricket teams with black players and captains under an equitable set of rules may have encouraged people to think of more prominent roles for other black leaders.

Commentators with first-hand experience of the West Indies and British Guiana in the period 1920-1960 often emphasise the role of sport as a blueprint for participation in political and economic power. We know from CLR James that in Trinidad in the 1920s and early 1930s, black West Indians regarded certain cricket teams as embodying their aspirations beyond the boundary. Certainly James felt his awareness of the forces of race, nationalism and economics in cricket preceded his consciousness of the same forces in society, "Cricket had plunged me into politics long before I was aware of it. When I did turn to politics I did not have much to learn." A similar story but from a different political perspective is told by Clem Seecharan in his excellent book *Muscular Learning*, which charts the intertwining of black West Indian involvement in cricket and politics in the period from emancipation to the end of the nineteenth century.

Ultimately at this time and distance it is impossible to judge the consequences of the test series between England and the West Indies in 1933 and 1935. But although we can't be certain that sport can change the world, we know, from personal experience, it can change the way we view the world.

It is 2.30pm on a hot, cloudy Jamaican afternoon. The players have left the field, replaced by the Sabina Park crowd who surge over the boundary's edge filling the ground's green grass and washing up against the pavilion where they are addressed by the players.

Grant and Holmes make short, nicely-judged speeches, but the crowd want to see their heroes. First Manny Martindale and then

"Making a somewhat belated appearance from the dressing room and urged on by the famous Reggie (Mr R Matcham) Messrs Constantine and Headley received a tremendous ovation.[318]"

Manny Martindale, Learie Constantine and George Headley stand on the pavilion's balcony as the rain, that an hour earlier would have saved England, begins to fall. How must they feel?

---

318 From *The Gleaner*

Image credits

Photos 1, 2, 3, 4, 7, 8, 10, 11 and 12: Copyright of Roger Mann

Photo 5: Copyright of Roger Martindale,

Photo 6 and Back Cover: Copyright of Getty Images / Pooperfoto

Photo 9 and Front Cover: Copyright The Gleaner, Kingston Jamaica.

Thanks to

Thanks to Roger Martindale for sharing his memories of his grandfather, Roger Mann for assisting with photos, Horace King for his hospitality and an afternoon spent talking about all sorts of things, cricket and the Empire Club included. Also Robert Curphey at the MCC archives and Margaret Broomes at the Cricket Research Centre of The University of the West Indies.

Bibliography

David Frith, *Bodyline Autopsy*, Aurum Press Limited 2002.

Duncan Hamilton, *Harold Larwood*, Quercus 2010.

Jack Williams, *Cricket and England A Cultural and Social History of the Interwar Years*, Frank Cass Publishers 1999.

Jack Williams, *Cricket and Race*, Berg 2001

Mike Huggins and Jack Williams, *Sport and The English: Between The Wars 1918 to 1939*, Routledge 2005

Jack Grant, *Jack Grant's Story*, Lutterworth Press 1980

Henderson Dalrymple, *Fifty Great West Indian Cricketers*, Hansib Publishing 1983

Bill Bowes, *Express Deliveries*, Stanley Paul and Co Limited

Simon Rae, *It's Just Not Cricket*, Faber and Faber 2001

Arnold Bertram, *Jamaica At The Wicket A Study of Jamaican Cricket and its Role in Shaping the Jamaican Society*, Research and Project Development Ltd 2009

Alan Hill, *Les Ames*, Christopher Helm Publishers 1990

CLR James, *Beyond a Boundary*, Yellow Jersey Press 2005

CLR James, *A Majestic Innings, edited by Anna Grimshaw*, Aurum Press Limited 2006

CLR James, *Cricket*, Edited by Anna Grimshaw, WH Allen and Co 1989

Learie Constantine, *Cricket and I*, Philip Allan, 1933

Learie Constantine, *Cricket in the Sun, Stanley Paul and Co*

Learie Constantine, *Cricketers Carnival*, Stanley Paul and Co

Harry Pearson, *Connie The Marvellous Life of Learie Constantine*, Little Brown 2017

Peter Mason, *Learie Constantine*, Signal Books Limited 2008

Keith A.P Sandiford, *Cricket Nurseries of Colonial Barbados, The Elite Schools 1865 – 1966*, The Press University of the West Indies 1998

Clem Seecharan, *Muscular Learning, Cricket and Education in the Making of the British West Indies at the End of the 19th Century*, Ian Randle Publishers 2005

Brian Stoddart, *Sport Culture and History, Region Nature and Globe*, Routledge 2008

Michael Manley, *A History of West Indies Cricket*, Andre Deutsch 1995

John Nauright, *Sport, Cultures and Identities in South Africa*, Leicester University Press, 1997

Gerald Howat, *Plum Warner*, Unwin Hyman Limited 1987

James Bradley, *The MCC, Society and Empire: A Portrait of Cricket's Ruling Body, 1860–1914*, In the International Journal of the History of Sport May 1990

Maurice St Pierre, *West Indian Cricket, a Socio – Historical appraisal*, In Carribean Quarterly June 1973

Hilary McD. Beckles, *The Development of West Indies Cricket, Vol 1 The Age of Nationalism*, The Press University of the West Indies.

Andre Odendaal, *Cricket and representations of beauty; Newlands Cricket Ground and the roots of apartheid in South African Cricket*, in the Cambridge Companion to Cricket, edited by Anthony Bateman and Jeffrey Hill, Cambridge University Press 2011.

Gerald Pawle, *R.E.S Wyatt fighting cricketer*, George Allen and Unwin 1985

RES Wyatt, *Three Straight Sticks,* Anchor Press Limited 1951

Christopher Douglas, *Douglas Jardine Spartan Cricketer*, Methuen 2003

Neville Cardus, *Good Days,* Rupert Hart Davies 1949

Bill Frindall, *Wisden Book of Test Cricket,* The Book Service Limited 1980

James C. Riley, *Poverty and Life Expectancy The Jamaica Paradox,* Cambridge University Press 2005

Bridgette Lawrence, *Masterclass, The Biography of George Headley,* Polar Publishing 2005

David Foot, *Wally Hammond The Reasons Why,* Robson Books Limited 1998

E.R.T Holmes, *Flannelled Foolishness,* Hollis and Carter 1957

Kenneth Farnes, *Tours and Tests,* Lutterworth Press 1940

Eric Hollies, *I'll Spin You a Tale,* Museum Press Limited 1955

Gemma Romain, *Race Sexuality and Identity in Britain and Jamaica, The Biography of Patrick Nelson,* Bloomsbury Academic 2017

Ian Pebbles, *"Patsy" Hendren, The Cricketer and His Times,* Macmillan 1969

Newspapers

The Times, Morning Post, The Argus, Melborne, Daily Express, Manchester Guardian, Daily Herald, Port of Spain Gazette, Daily Telegraph, The Sunday Leader, The Gleaner, Evening Standard, Barbados Advocate and Western Mirror

Periodicals

The Cricketer, Wisden

Other

Seventy Five Years – Anniversary Brochure, Empire Cricket Club MCC archives